Violent Transactions

To
Ronald Gaeta and Kenneth Post
for their guidance, encouragement and patience

Violent Transactions

The Limits of Personality

Edited by
Anne Campbell and
John J. Gibbs

Basil Blackwell

First published 1986

Basil Blackwell Ltd
108 Cowley Road, Oxford OX4 1JF, UK

Basil Blackwell Inc.
432 Park Avenue South, Suite 1503,
New York, NY 10016, USA

British Library Cataloguing in Publication Data

Violent transactions: the limits of personality.
1. Aggressiveness (Psychology)
I. Campbell, Anne, *1951–*   II. Gibbs, John J.
302.5′4   BF575.A3
ISBN 0–631–14633–4

Library of Congress Cataloging in Publication Data

Violent transactions.
Includes index.
1. Violence.   2. Aggressiveness (Psychology)
3. Personality and situation.   I. Campbell, Anne, 1951–   .   II. Gibbs, John J.
HM281.V517   1986   303.6′2   86–8228
ISBN 0–631–14633–4

Typeset by Freeman Graphic, Tonbridge, Kent
Printed in Great Britain by T.J. Press Ltd, Padstow, Cornwall

Contents

Acknowledgements

The Harry Frank Guggenheim Foundation through a grant to Anne Campbell did much to stimulate our interest and empirical work in the area of situational factors in aggression. Through the generosity of Rutgers University we were able to hold a two-day symposium on the topic in 1984, which made clear both the importance of the issue as well as the wide diversity of current approaches, both conceptual and methodological. Many of the chapters in this book were first discussed at that meeting. Chairing it and guiding our thinking were Don Peterson, Dean of the Graduate School of Applied and Professional Psychology at Rutgers, whose distinguished history in the field of personality research was of immense benefit, and Don Gottfredson, Dean of the School of Criminal Justice also at Rutgers, who, with his longstanding interest in the prediction of anti-social behavior, kept us mindful of the very real applications of research in aggression. Our thanks also go to all those whose published work has stimulated and goaded us into wanting a clearer picture of how people select, construct and respond to situations of aggression.

PART I

Understanding People in Aggressive Situations

1

Overview

Anne Campbell

Playing one round of golf does not make someone a golfer, but engaging in one apprehended act of violence can make someone a criminal. As Garfinkel (1956) pointed out, it is the business of degradation ceremonies – and the criminal court is surely the prime example – to take a single action and persuade us that it is an enduring characteristic of the actor. Even if never acted upon before, the audience must be persuaded that the tendency to aggression had been present and latent long before the overt behavior manifested itself, and indeed that, unless corrective action is taken, it will manifest itself again. The wrongdoer must be distanced from the audience and they must believe that they themselves are incapable of the evil action because they do not possess the potential to perform it. When a novice golfer walks into the clubhouse with an eagle, it is a fluke. When the same man smashes a bottle over another man's head, it is because he has an aggressive personality.

Although the tendency to ascribe enduring traits to others is a generalized aspect of human social perception (Nisbett and Ross, 1979), nowhere is it more evident than in the area of behavior we call "anti-social". So it is not surprising that the most evident approach to understanding and predicting aggressive behavior has come from analyses of individual actors. Sometimes it is done in aggregate by loading up multiple-regression programs with documented facts on the lives of violent men from their psychiatric history and test scores to their years of schooling. At other times it is done individually in treatment by psychoanalysts or in popular books about famous killers. Whichever way we go about it, the phrasing of the question remains essentially the same: what is it about these people that makes them different from us? This perspective on the problem places aggression firmly in that area of psychology called "personality" – the study of enduring dispositions as differences between individuals.

The crisis in the study of personality took shape and fluency in 1968 when Mischel published his now classic book *Personality and Assessment*, although the early rumblings have been traced back to Michel de Montaigne in 1580 (Bem, 1983). In the opening chapter of this volume, Pervin carefully outlines the growth of the debate through this century. The essence of the problem was this: the use of personality tests to understand and predict human behavior presupposes that, at least by adolescence, the traits which characterize a person are firmly established, and that these underlying dispositions guide direct visible action over time and over different situations. Closer analysis of these last two assumptions suggested that the evidence to support them was weak at best. People seem to show a great deal of variability in the way they react to different situations at different times. What could be causing this?

Psychoanalysts alleged that, since the relationship between underlying traits and overt behavior is not a linear one, there was no real problem. The traits (for example, masochism) continue to exist, but the overt expression of them depends upon various ego defences, which may alter from one situation to another (described in Endler, 1982). Others maintained that the problem was not a conceptual one at all. They alleged that the low correlations between behavior in different situations was a function of poor measurement (Epstein, 1979; Rushton, Brainerd and Pressley, 1983). The problem then was merely a technical one that could be corrected with better analysis (Epstein and O'Brien, 1985). In the other camp were those who took the crisis to be a meaningful one. Social-learning theorists thought the unexplained variance arose because of the failure to examine the reinforcing properties of the situations in which behavior occurred, and others pointed to the importance of self-regulating plans and strategies employed by individuals in responding to them (Mischel, 1973). Still others agreed that the answer lay in the situation, but wanted a greater stress laid upon the dynamic interaction between the social actor and his interpretation of the social setting (Pervin, 1977; Rausch, 1977). They wanted a model that included the reciprocity of actor and situation changing over time. They wanted something less mechanistic than the social-learning theorists.

There was agreement, however, that – as Endler put it – interactionism had come of age. The future lay in the study of how the biography, perceptions, abilities and strategies of the individual affected his or her response to an ever-changing social setting. While this recipe made sense, there was still a tendency to specialize in personology. Everyone acknowledged the importance of situations, but people were unsure about how to study them. This uncertainty still remains. Since we are now standing at the threshold of a new area of inquiry, perhaps, by looking at some of the discoveries made by personality theorists, we can avoid the conceptual traps that are waiting for us.

The unit of analysis for personality theorists is the individual, but the techniques that they employed to investigate the universal structure of personality traits were nomethetic. Ironically, the study of individual differences actually became the study of individual commonalities. This was not surprising, since science demands parsimony and predictive utility. What use is a statement that every individual is unique? People were grouped together in typologies as extraverts, psychopaths or neurotics so that the influence of that characteristic could be studied. Even when typologies were eschewed in favor of dimensions or continua, the end result was often much the same. A high correlation between anti-semitism and authoritarianism was interpreted to mean that those who possessed one characteristic also possessed the other. Personality proceeded in a piecemeal fashion, with each theorist favoring the overarching predictive utility of his own particular trait or set of traits. We associate Zuckerman with sensation-seeking (Zuckerman et al., 1964), Eysenck (1964) with extraversion, Witkin with field dependence (Witkin and Goodenough, 1981). Others favored a multi-trait or profile approach to personality, arguing that a single dimension could not capture the richness of individual differences. Hathaway and McKinley (1951) used ten scales of psychiatric adjustment on the Minnesota Multiphasic Personality Inventory, and Cattell (1979) favored 16 personality dimensions of the 16PF questionnaire. Whatever the test, norms were developed from aggregates of personal scores so that individuals could be classified in terms of their deviation from the norm, and a good deal of scientific energy was spent in mapping out the implication of these traits for a host of social behaviors and competencies.

There were those who disagreed with such an approach. George Kelly (1955), besides pioneering the importance of social perception, argued that the study of aggregated masses was a misleading approach to human personality. The statement of a correlation between one trait and another says nothing about the relationship between those traits for any given individual. They are statistical myths with no practical application for the prediction of a single person's behavior. He maintained that, rather than studying a few traits across thousands of subjects, we should be studying hundreds of traits as they are related within a single individual. Certainly, it might be that, as cases were accumulated, we should see a nomethetic pattern emerge, but the process must work up from the individual, not down to him. As researchers such as Forgas, and Marsh and Paton (chapters 4 and 5 below) begin to study the structure of situations, the unit or analysis problem remains with us. We could take a large number of universal, if vaguely labelled, situations, and with respect to a few dimensions examine how they are perceived or what behavior is evoked. We should end up with a taxonomy of situations compared and contrasted in terms of how they are interpreted on one or two dimensions by individuals. Almost certainly different researchers would select different dimensions of interest and spend a good deal of time justifying why their factors were more powerful than anyone else's. As with personality, we should have started with individual situations but ended with a classification scheme which sought to summarize their relationship to one another. Or we might go George Kelly's route. We could focus on a single situation and examine it in excruciating detail, looking at exactly how many dimensions are needed to capture its essence or distinguishing what perceptions are related to which differences in actual behavior or examining how perceptions of the situation change as a function of experience. The question is, do we want to look within situations or compare them? Do we want an aggregated description with little relevance for any single individual, or do we want a detailed knowledge of a few situations with fairly precise notions of how individuals differ in their reaction to them? Forgas's chapter on situational perception (chapter 4) moves somewhat in the latter direction by including demographic and personality differences in situational perception, while Marsh and Paton (chapter 5) concentrate on sex and social-class factors in the reading of aggressive situations.

Another question for early personality theorists centered upon establishing exactly which aspects of personality were the most central and organizing. The early empirical attempts to locate these central or key personality traits capitalized on the use of factor analysis to reduce a vast number of individual attribute adjectives to trait dimensions (Allport, 1937; Norman, 1963; Block, 1965). Recently Shweder and d'Andrade (1979) criticized these studies as artefacts of "systematic distortion". These researchers took the personality adjectives and interpersonal-behavior descriptors used by Norman (1963) and Bales (1970) respectively and asked subjects to rate the similarity of the *meaning* of the terms. In both cases, the resulting dimensions showed a high correlation with factors which had emerged in the original studies, where the terms had been used to rate people's attributes and behavior. The factors which resulted from ratings of others using these terms showed a considerably higher correlation with ratings of word-meaning than with the true behavior of the individuals rated. As Shweder (1982) concludes,

> One implication of the systematic distortion hypothesis is that one cannot trust evidence of personality syndromes derived from memory-based assessment procedures (inventories, rating forms, questionnaire interviews). And since most evidence in support of proposed personality syndromes is of this memory based type, a second implication is that the very idea that people have global traits consisting of covarying behaviors may be illusory, the product of a widespread human tendency to rely on similarity and conceptual proximity for estimating co-occurrence probability.

As we now begin studies aimed at uncovering the underlying dimensions of situations, we should do well to learn from these early errors. Language may take on a life of its own rather than acting as a convenient vehicle for the communication of perceptions.

If we avoid the confounding effects of language, we may face a very different kind of problem: that of situational specificity. A number of studies which have examined the principal dimensions of different kinds of situations, such as work, school, home and social events tend to uncover different central dimensions. Dimensions may not only turn out to be highly specific to the stimulus situations chosen, but also show low consensus in terms of the amount of variance that is accounted for. While we anticipate that the common expectations people have about behavior in differing situations will be reflected in the adjectives used to describe them (Cantor, 1981), we must also accept that the very business of individual differences or personality may lie in the fact that people differ in their reading of social settings.

At the heart of the personality crisis was, of course, the inability to find substantial consistency across people's behavior in differing situations. Mischel pointed to the magical number 0.30 as the average correlation and argued that the high discrimination which individuals show in differing situations is an adaptive strategy arising from situationally specific learning experiences. As both Pervin and Toch note (chapters 2 and 3 below), many early personality theorists, such as Allport, maintained from the beginning that situational differences were to be expected but that they would be constrained by the overarching effect of personality. Over time, the situational caveat was forgotten and the stress was increasingly placed upon the consistency of individual personality. It might be well to bear in mind the reciprocal truth of Allport's statements as we study situational factors. If situationalists are to avoid the same perils, they must make clear that, while situations are powerful, they do not expect that they will exert their effect uniformly across persons. Individual differences will exist, and it remains a challenge for situationalists to explain them. Some have maintained a trait solution to this problem: Bem and Allen (1974) suggested that we may be able to categorize persons in terms of high and low behavioral variability; Bem and Funder (1978) suggested the use of Q-sort descriptions of individuals as a function of how they respond to differing situations; Cantor (1981) examined the internal–external control dimension using the Snyder self-monitoring scale to investigate susceptibility to situational cues; and Endler (1975) studied the interaction between trait anxiety and stressful situational settings. Essentially these remain nomethic techniques. They represent a desire to classify people in order successfully to predict their reaction to differing situations. As such, these classifications can be seen as moderator variables (Paunonen and Jackson, 1985). In our haste to achieve better predictive power, we may be rushing past some important questions *en route*. For example, how does social perception vary over time within the same individual? How do situational perception and attribution affect the behavior which the individual selects. And, if situational perception varies over time and individual, why should we expect traits or moderator variables to remain constant?

In the debate over cross-situational consistency, personality theorists maintained that, if psychologists relied upon aggregated rather than single-item measures of behavior, they would achieve greater consistency, since measurement error would be reduced. Indeed, Epstein (1979) indicated that multiple measures of similar behaviors over time produce substantially higher correlations than the 0.30 which Mischel had suggested. Mischel and Peake (1982) replied with an elegant study in which they distinguished between measures aggregated over time and measures aggregated over situations. They found that aggregation increased temporal reliability to as high as 0.65, but that cross-situational consistency was raised non-significantly from 0.08 to 0.13. This indicates that people's behavior does not radically alter over time (at least, not over the rather modest time intervals which Mischel and Peake studied) but that individual behavior remains highly situationally specific (see also the reply to this study by Epstein and O'Brien, 1985). The debate over consistency has been lively in the area of aggression also, although the low base rate of occurrence of aggression has presented special problems. Olweus (1979), in a recent review paper, found respectably high consistency across time for aggressive behavior in longitudinal studies. But this leaves unaddressed the issues of cross-situtional specificity. Campbell et al. (1985) asked subjects to report their predicted reaction to 24 scenarios of social conflict. The resulting mean correlations of different forms of aggressive response over the situations was 0.19, pretty well in line with Mischel and Peake's findings for conscientiousness.

If aggregation is not the solution, perhaps greater attention to shared social perception is. In their thoughtful paper on consistency, Bem and Allen (1974) raised the issue of equivalence classes. When the experimenter examines the consistency issue, he or she sets up a range of situations in which it is believed a form of behavior (such as friendliness) may emerge. The experimenter also decides upon the set of items to be used as an index of friendliness. To achieve high consistency on a correlation, the subjects must maintain a near-perfect rank-order relation to one another in terms of the extent to which they manifest the various behaviors across the differing situations. The subjects must therefore agree that the behaviors and the settings form a graduated Guttman scale. But let us take two situations of potential aggression (a fight with one's spouse after a party and a fight with a co-worker about division of labor) and two forms of response (the use of abusive language and pushing the other person across the room). Subjects may disagree about which of the two situations is the more aggression-producing and about which response is the more aggressive. If they disagree then the correlation will be low. But they may disagree with one another and yet show perfect behavioral stability with respect to themselves, depending upon their own, idiosyncratic equivalence classes. People are likely to respond consistently to the extent that two situations are characterized as similar and to the extent that their rank-ordering of aggressive responses remains identical. This suggests that we must take seriously the way in which people assign situations to classes or prototypes.

This kind of work has already been started by Cantor and Mischel (1979) with respect to how we form impressions of other people. Drawing upon the work of Tversky (1977), they are examining how individuals search for key features or family resemblances that unite disparate instances of behavior and permit economical coding of information. The original impetus to this work was the desire to explain why people believe that others are consistent in spite of the manifest discontinuity of behavior across settings. Situationalists here have one advantage: while personality theorists need to account for the illusion of consistency, which has misled psychologists as well as lay people, situationalists have no such problem. Situations take on their human significance precisely through the way that they are understood and responded to. They do not mislead us because they take their effect through human perception and not independently of it. We can learn another important lesson from this kind of work. Not only can descriptive dimensions of situations not be obtained by experimenter-provided scales (which cue the subject to the dimensions of interest), but it is equally false to believe that we walk about the world with a set of descriptor scales in our heads. It is far more likely that situations present us with a number of possible ways of interpreting them and that the scales we select are chosen for their ability to discriminate the situation from others like it, as well as to unite it with other similar situations. Thus the perception of social situations arises out of the situations themselves as we construct a set of properties which uniquely define them and yet indicate their class membership. When we ask ourselves to think of situations of aggression, we scan our memories for certain key features – raised voices, physical aggression, a door slamming shut – and retrieve memories which fit into this class. But the boundaries are fuzzy rather than precise, for we are dealing with prototypes not hard sets.

The following chapters have been written by researchers who have struggled with these problems and many others in their own studies. All agree that the study of situations cannot be divorced from the individuals who select to enter, interpret and respond to them. Lawrence Pervin (chapter 2) describes even-handedly the crucial features of the personality-by-situation debate, but, with his characteristic sense of historical and epistemological context, gives a salutary warning that our current concerns are not new but have been voiced from the beginning by many of the major figures in trait psychology. His extensive research has directly addressed the reciprocal effects of individuals and social settings in the real world, moving toward an affective goal-oriented approach to the individual's interaction with his environment (Pervin, 1983). Thus situations achieve their effect through the individual's interpretation of their relevance to the goals the individual seeks to achieve.

Hans Toch (chapter 3) was a committed interactionist before that term became a buzz word in psychology tests. His classic text on violent men (1969) takes as a starting-point the view that violent behavior, while characterizing some individuals better than others, is realized within particular social settings. The understanding of these settings can only be achieved by comparing and contrasting the common properties of the psychological situation. His notion of contingent consistency stresses that only some elements of a situation are relevant for the behavioral realization of a disposition. The discovery of the matrix of person- and situation-variable combinations that produce aggression must be made at an individual level. As a clinician, he focuses also on the applied value of such insights for his subjects themselves. The common elements that trigger aggression may not always be consciously or readily available, but, if individuals can be encouraged to synthesize them from reconstructions of their experiences, they may be able to avert the same outcomes in the future.

Joseph Forgas (chapter 4) has pioneered the use of multidimensional scaling analysis as a means of representing the typical schema or dimensions which individuals use in the interpretation of situational factors. He has analysed countless social settings, using housewives, rugby teams and even other academics (see Forgas, 1979). In the chapter he has contributed to this book, he discusses the advantages of such an approach and makes the case that perception of real-life aggressive episodes is far from unidimensional. Cognitive schema or prototypes not only assist recall, but also render the social world more predictable (Forgas, 1982). In concert with the goals of the participants, cognitive schema assist the social actor in tailoring his behavior to the appropriate script for goal realization.

Marsh's use of multidimensional techniques moves us directly into the issue of situational behavior as opposed to perception. In his previous work he has pioneered the position that aggression, far from being anomic or chaotic, is in fact constrained by the presence of social rules. These rules operate to limit extensive injury in routine conflict situations while at the same time allowing participants to demonstrate courage and integrity – important components of self-concept among working-class adolescent males. His and Renée Paton's contribution to this volume (chapter 5) moves on to examine empirically the nature of these social rules and the similarity of their structure among middle-class teenagers and among girls.

In his provocative chapter (6), Leonard Berkowitz takes issue with impression-management and rule-following views of aggressive behavior. In his opinion, these approaches overstress the role of social cognition and normative behavior. Aggression, he argues, results from frustration, which drives the individual to attack either the source of the frustration or a similar but less punitive target. Through interviews with convicted violent men, he draws attention to the impulsive nature of the act and to the clearly expressed desire to hurt or injure. Berkowitz has shown a willingness to move beyond the laboratory situation and to enter the world of re-created life situations. However, using self-report data has its own hazards if we are to believe, as Nisbett and Wilson (1977) argue, that people often tell more than they can know about the causes of their own actions.

The crucial question for all the writers revolves around the relationship between the social situation and the behavior which it evokes. For Berkowitz the mediation may include drive states and prior learning experiences. For Toch, psychological needs for selfhood that must be met. For Forgas the selection of scripts and, for Marsh, the identification of the social rules that are operative in the situation. Most researchers are now committed to the belief that the subjectively perceived situation is likely to be more closely related to action than is the "objective" or external situation. But how are we to approach this internal understanding? Answers to this question range from the categorizing of consistent behavior across situations, through the use of adjective rating scales to introspective verbal report. They range from single case studies built up by inductive eliminative analysis to broadly sampled demographic populations. In the chapters which follow, a selection of the alternatives open to researchers helps us to focus these issues more clearly.

REFERENCES

Allport, G. W. 1937: *Personality: a psychological interpretation.* New York: Henry Holt.

Argyle, M. 1981: The experimental study of the basic features of situations. In D. Magnusson (ed.), *Toward a Psychology of Situations,* Hillsdale, NJ: Lawrence Erlbaum Associates.

Bales, R. F. 1970: *Personality and Interpersonal Behavior.* New York: Henry Holt.

Bem, D. J. 1983: Toward a response study theory of persons in situations. In M. Page (ed.), *Personality–Current Theory and Research* (Nebraska Symposium on Motivation, 1982), Lincoln, Nebr.: University of Nebraska Press.

Bem, D. J. and Allen, A. 1974: On predicting some of the people some of the time: the search for cross-situational consistencies in behavior. *Psychological Review,* 81, 506–20.

Bem, D. J. and Funder, D. C. 1978: Predicting more of the people more of the time: assessing the personality of situations. *Psychological Review,* 85, 485–501.

Block, J. 1965: *The Challenge of Response Sets.* New York: Appleton.

Campbell, A., Bibel, D. and Muncer, S. 1985: Predicting our own aggression: person, subculture or situation? *British Journal of Social Psychology,* 24, 169–80.

Cantor, N. 1981: Perceptions of situations: situation prototypes and person–situation prototypes. In D. Magnusson (ed.) *Toward a Psychology of Situations,* Hillsdale, NJ: Lawrence Erlbaum Associates.

Cantor, N. and Mischel, W. 1979: Prototypes in person perception. In L. Berkowitz (ed.), *Advances in Experimental Social Psychology,* New York: Academic Press.

Cattell, R. B. 1979: *Personality and Learning Theory: the structure of personality in its environment*, vol. I. New York: Springer.

Endler, N. S. 1975: A person–situation interaction model of anxiety. In C. D. Spielberger and I. G. Sarason (eds), *Stress and Anxiety*, vol. I, Washington DC: Hemisphere.

—— 1982: Interactionism comes of age. In M. P. Zanna, E. T. Higgins and C. P. Herman (eds), *Consistency in Social Behavior, The Ontario Symposium*, vol. II, Hillsdale, NJ: Lawrence Erlbaum Associates.

Epstein, S. 1979: The stability of behavior, I: on predicting most of the people much of the time. *Journal of Personality and Social Psychology*, 37, 1097–126.

Epstein, S. and O'Brien, E. 1985: The person–situation debate in historical and current perspective. *Psychological Bulletin*, 98, 513–37.

Eysenck, H. J. 1964: *Crime and Personality*. London: Routledge and Kegan Paul.

Forgas, J. 1979: *Social Episodes: the study of interaction routines*. New York: Academic Press.

—— 1982: Episode cognition: internal representations of interaction routines. In L. Berkowitz (ed.), *Advances in Experimental Social Psychology*, vol. XV. New York: Academic Press.

Garfinkel, H. 1956: Conditions of successful degradation ceremonies. *American Journal of Sociology*, 61, 420–4.

Hathaway, S. R. and McKinley, J. C. 1951: *The Minnesota Multiphasic Personality Inventory*, rev. edn. New York: Psychological Corporation.

Kelly, G. A. 1955: *The Psychology of Personal Constructs*. New York: Norton.

Mischel, W. 1968: *Personality and Assessment*. New York: Wiley.

—— 1973: Toward a cognitive social learning theory reconceptualization of personality. *Psychological Review*, 80, 252–83.

Mischel, W. and Peake, P. K. 1982: In search of consistency: measure for measure. In M. P. Zanna, E. T. Higgins and C. P. Herman (eds), *Consistency in Social Behavior: The Ontario Symposium*, vol. II, Hillsdale, NJ: Lawrence Erlbaum Associates.

Nisbett, R. E. and Ross, L. D. 1979: *Human Inference: strategies and shortcomings of informal judgement*. Englewood Cliffs, NJ: Prentice Hall.

Nisbett, R. E. and Wilson, T. D. 1977: Telling more than we can know: verbal reports on mental processes. *Psychological Review*, 84, 231–59.

Norman, W. 1963: Toward an adequate taxonomy of personality attribute: replicated factor structure in peer nomination personality ratings. *Journal of Abnormal and Social Psychology*, 66, 574–83.

Olweus, D. 1979: Stability of aggressive reaction patterns in males: a review. *Psychological Bulletin*, 86, 852–75.

Paunonen, S. and Jackson, D. 1985: Idiographic measurement strategies for personality and prediction: some unredeemed promissory notes. *Psychological Review*, 92, 486–511.

Pervin, L. A. 1977: The representative design of person–situation research. In D. Magnusson and N. S. Endler (eds), *Personality at the Crossroads: current issues in interactional psychology*, Hillsdale, NJ: Lawrence Erlbaum Associates.

—— 1983: The stasis and flow of behavior: toward a theory of goals. In M. Page (ed.), *Personality: current theory and research* (Nebraska Symposium on Motivation, 1982), Lincoln, Nebr.: University of Nebraska Press.

Rausch, H. L. 1977: Paradox, levels and junctures in person–situation systems. In D. Magnusson and N. S. Endler (eds), *Personality at the Crossroads: current issues in interactional psychology*, Hillsdale, NJ: Lawrence Erlbaum Associates.

Rushton, J. B., Brainerd, C. and Pressley, M. 1983: Behavioral development and construct validity: the principle of aggregation. *Psychological Bulletin*, 94, 582–9.

Shweder, R. A. 1982: Fact and artifact in trait perception: the systematic distortion hypothesis. In B. and W. Maher (eds), *Progress in Experimental Personality Research*, vol. XI, New York: Academic Press.

Shweder, R. A. and D'Andrade, R. G. 1979: Accurate reflection or systematic distortion? A reply to Block, Weiss and Thorne. *Journal of Personality and Social Psychology*, 37, 1075–84.

Toch, H. 1969: *Violent Men: an inquiry into the psychology of violence*. Chicago: Aldine.

Tversky, A. 1977: Features of similarity. *Psychological Review*, 84, 327–52.

Witken, H. A. and Goodenough, D. R. 1981: *Cognitive Styles: essence and origins*. New York: International Universities Press.

Zuckerman, M., Kolin, E. A., Price, L. and Zoob, I. 1964: Development of a sensation seeking scale. *Journal of Consulting Psychology*, 26, 250–60.

2

Persons, Situations, Interactions: Perspectives on a Recurrent Issue

Lawrence Pervin

INTRODUCTION

Some time ago, an article concerning aggression appeared in the *New York Times*. Entitled "When Parents Kill", the article detailed the beating to death of a three-year-old boy by his parents. Whatever the social, economic and political aspects of what occurred, individuals and a personal story were involved. In particular, we learn of a young woman, overwhelmed with a situation, who felt that her son reminded her of herself when she was small – of the life she hated. While not an ideal mother to her other children, none of them suffered the combination of neglect and brutal beatings that this child did. In the words of the article, the mother "scorned him even as she identified with him, re-enacting with him the rejection she had felt as a child" (*New York Times*, 2 December 1983, p. B4). Undoubtedly the situation, if one chooses to call it that, has much in common with those of many of the 5,000 other children each year who are killed by a parent. It is also clear, however that the phenomenon cuts across socio-economic classes, races and cultures and involves person variables that are as important as situation variables.

At about the same time as I read this story I learned of two other situations concerning aggression which struck me as particularly interesting. The first involved members of the French Foreign Legion. Despite the past record of anti-social behavior and violence for most Legionnaires, reportedly discipline is a relatively minor problem in the Legion itself. The second situation related to a juvenile detention center and a drug-treatment therapeutic community with which I am familiar. In both, most of the residents have a history of anti-social behavior and physical violence, yet within the institutions relatively little physical aggression occurs. While we do not understand all of the critical factors involved, it is clear that aspects of the institutional setting serve to curb and limit the expression of physical violence. And, while I do not know of data that bear upon this, I should not be surprised if it were demonstrated that in such settings not only are offenders generally less prone to physical violence than they used to be, but also many (though by no means all) of the previously most violent individuals are no longer a problem – in more technical terms, not only has there been a decline in the general level, but the rank order has also changed.

Now, what do these stories have to do with the issues before us? Other than involving aggression, they bring us to the issue of person and situation determinants of aggression. Are there personality characteristics common to those who abuse children? What is the significance of the fact that one child rather than another is abused? Are there situational characteristics associated with violence? What is the significance of a shift in rank-ordering of violence between settings? Most psychologists believe that both person and situation factors are important in aggression, but my reading of the literature suggests that a person–situation issue remains. I shall return to this issue in relation to aggression, but first I should like to review some of the history in relation to psychology generally and personality in particular.

SOME HISTORY RELEVANT TO THE PERSON–SITUATION ISSUE

The current phase of the person–situation issue dates back to Mischel's 1968 book on personality assessment. However, the underlying issue of the role of internal and external variables in psychological functioning dates back long before that. Indeed, it probably has always been with us. Gordon Allport (1955) asked whether behavior is governed from within or from without, whether it is active or merely reactive. He found this to be the principal issue dividing psychologists and attributed the differences to commitment to either the Lockean or the Leibnitzian tradition. According to Allport, the Lockean view is that of a passive organism reactive to external stimuli. It is found in such Anglo-American approaches to psychology as environmentalism, associationism, behaviorism and stimulus-response psychology. In contrast to this tradition, the Leibnitzian tradition emphasizes the active, purposive qualities of the organism and is expressed in European schools of psychology such as Gestalt psychology and Freud's psychoanalysis. For Allport, the key difference between the two approaches is the emphasis on what is *external* to the organism as opposed to what is *internal* to it. For Lockeans, "cause" remains external to the organism, but for the Leibnitzian it is internal to the organism.

Historically, we can see shifts in the relative emphasis given to the internal and the external, with periodic calls for a redress of the imbalance. Thus, while in 1971 Carlson could ask, "Where is the person in personality research?", some 30 years earlier Ichheiser (1943) had spoken out against the tendency to overestimate the unity of personality and underestimate the importance of situational factors. In fact, Ichheiser went so far as to say that "the persisting pattern which permeates everyday life of interpreting individual behavior in the light of personal factors must be considered one of the fundamental sources of misunderstanding personality in our time. It is both the cause and the symptom of the crisis in our society" (p. 152).

Going back slightly before this, the views of Floyd Allport and Henry Murray are noteworthy. F. H. Allport (1937) referred to the "generalist–specifist" quarrel, or that between those who point to consistencies in individuals and emphasize traits, and those who point to the dependencies of behavior on the specific situation. His own suggested solution was to emphasize teleonomic trends or characteristic behavior patterns that reflected what the organism typically tried to do. Finally, at about the same time, Murray (1938) drew a distinction between peripheralists and centralists, similar to the one later drawn by Gordon Allport, and emphasized the importance of both person and situation factors in behavior. There is much wisdom in Murray's discussion of the issue, including an emphasis on the organization of behavior, of different behaviors expressing the same personality characteristics or needs, and of situations varying in their press for specific behaviors. Also noteworthy is his rejection of the trait concept: "According to my prejudice, trait psychology is over-concerned with recurrences, with consistency, with what is clearly manifested (the surface of personality), with what is conscious, ordered and rational" (p. 715). Emphasizing a dynamic approach, Murray attempted to understand patterns as well as recurrences, inconsistencies as well as consistencies, the "out of character" as well as the "in character".

While not a necessary linkage, a relationship between conceptual emphasis and methodological approach can be found. Thus, for example, Cronbach (1957) in his important paper "The Two Disciplines of Scientific Psychology", contrasted two historic streams of method, thought and affiliation present in psychology – experimental psychology and correlational psychology. In the former the goal is to produce consistent variation in behavior as a result of certain treatments or manipulations of independent variables. Conditions are changed to observe consequences that are uniform for all subjects. In the correlational approach, existing individual differences are emphasized and treatment or situational factors are minimized or regarded as sources of annoyance. In sum, in the experimental approach the interest is in consistent sources of situational variance, with individual differences considered sources of annoyance – the very effects that are of prime interest in the correlational approach. Similar distinctions were drawn earlier by Dashiell (1939), who contrasted the experimental attitude with the clinical attitude, and by Bindra and Scheier (1954), who contrasted the experimental and psychometric approaches. While Dashiell saw evidence, in 1939, of a coming-together of those who emphasized situational determinants of behavior (experimental) and those who emphasized personality factors as leading to consistency over situation and time (clinical), Cronbach in 1957 and again in 1975 had to sound a plea for an emphasis on complex person–situation interactions. Undoubtedly, the same plea might still be sounded today.

In sum, Mischel's attack (1968) upon traditional personality theory as exaggerating the consistency of individual behavior across situations, and as neglecting the importance of situational variables, did not represent the development of a new issue. Two additional points are noteworthy. First, Mischel's book was not the only publication at the time to raise serious questions concerning the direction of personality theory. For example, Peterson (1968) also called attention to the error of an imbalanced emphasis on person determinants of behavior. Second, Mischel greatly exaggerated the extent to which traditional personality theorists neglected the importance of situational variables. For example, Gordon Allport, a trait theorist, specifically recognized the importance of situations in behavior and suggested that traits could not be regarded as fixed and stable, operating mechanically to the same degree on all occasions (1961, pp. 180–1). Similarly, Cattell, another trait theorist, emphasized the importance of situations in his specification equation and also suggested that moods, states and roles operate to create behavioral diversity within the person. Finally, the dynamic emphasis of psychoanalysis not only accepts the possibility of varying behavior in different situations but also calls attention to the regularities that may underlie phenotypic diversity or irregularity.

Regardless of the points just made, Mischel's book did serve to focus attention on the relations of persons and situations to behavior. It represented an excellent marshalling of evidence supporting the importance of situational variability, and presented an alternative model, social-learning theory, which at the time emphasized the importance of evoking and maintaining conditions of the environment. Some major critical issues were hinted at. How are we to understand the patterns of stability and change that characterize human behavior? What are the processes relevant to understanding organism–environment transactions? What units of the person and situation are most usefully employed in our analyses? However, these were not in the main the issues that were addressed. Controversy focused on *which* was more important, persons or situations, and then on *how much* each contributed to the variance. In a peculiar way, there was a replay of the nature–nurture controversy: first, arguments about which is more important, followed by arguments about how much each contributes, and finally the question of *how* the two interact to produce the observed phenomenon. Just as there always is nature and nurture, so there is always person and situation. Genes and environments, persons and situations, are always interacting with one another. The relative importance of each depends on the phenomenon observed. For any particular behavior or group of behaviors, the role of persons or situations may be greater. Everyone was now happy to be an interactionist

(Magnusson and Endler, 1977). The only problem was that there was not complete agreement about what interactionism meant or how it should be investigated.

RECENT STATUS OF THE PERSON–SITUATION CONTROVERSY: THE ISSUE OF CONSISTENCY

One would have hoped that at this point research would have focused on *how* person and situation variables interact to produce behavior (Pervin, 1977, 1978). Instead, much of the relevant research has focused on two challenges to the trait position. The first, most clearly articulated by Shweder (1982), suggests that traits represent systematic distortions based on conceptual and semantic notions of "what goes with what", rather than actual behavioral co-occurrences. The issue is an important one, particularly in so far as personality research is based on questionnaire data. In other words, there is good reason to suspect that, in answering questions concerning our own behavior and that of others, we smooth out irregularities and are biased in terms of our own implicit theory of personality. Three things, however, are worth noting. First, the same arguments could be made in relation to ratings and descriptions of situational influences on behavior: that is, we also have implicit and explicit views concerning which situations are linked and which are similar in the behaviors they elicit or help to structure. To extend this issue a bit, it would seem clear that there is as much reason to be concerned about situational-attribution error as there is about person-attribution error, though attribution theorists have tended to focus on the latter and ignore the former. Second, while there may be systematic distortions, presumably our notions of "what goes with what" are based on some reality. Thus, even Mischel recognized that "structure exists neither 'all in the head' of the organism nor 'all in the person' perceived; it is instead a function of an interaction between the beliefs of observers and the characteristics of the 'observed'" (Cantor and Mischel, 1979, pp. 45–6). Finally, Shweder's systematic-distortion hypothesis may enlighten us concerning certain cognitive processes and trait-ascription data, but it does not enlighten us concerning the process of person–situation interaction itself.

The second challenge to trait theory concerns evidence of personality consistency, and it is this issue which has virtually dominated discussion and research over the past five years. The position argued by Mischel, based on his review of the literature in his original presentation and most recently on his own research (Mischel and Peake, 1982, 1983), is that there is evidence of considerable diversity or variability of behavior across situations. Furthermore, similarities in reinforcing conditions in situations contribute to some cross-situational stability. Individual difference and person factors are not denied, but broad dispositional traits are. The response of trait theorists has taken varied forms, including the following.

1 *Poor research.* Studies that fail to find evidence of consistency are poorly conducted. When such research is properly conducted, more supportive evidence can be found (Block, 1977; Olweus, 1977, 1981).

2 *Repeated measures – multiple occasions.* The trait argument here is that one cannot consider single acts or single-occasion measures as adequate reflections of the presence of a trait. The prime proponent of this point of view has been Epstein (1979, 1980, 1982, 1983), though the position has been taken by others as well. The suggestion is that there is too much error involved in the measurement of single acts or single occasions and that reliability and consistency increase as multiple measures are obtained. In this sense individual acts are like individual test items and generally one would not want to base a performance or personality score on the basis of a single test item. This emphasis has led to the principle of aggregation, which is being accepted with enthusiasm – probably too much enthusiasm – by many psychologists.

3 *Phenotype–genotype.* Trait psychologists suggest that the multiple acts expressive of a trait may be different topographically–phenotypically while genotypically expressive of the same trait (Buss and Craik, 1983). In other words, one is less interested in literal consistency or behavioral sameness than in predictability and psychological coherence (Loevinger and Knoll, 1983).

4 *Some people more than others.* The argument has been made in defense of trait theory that some people are more consistent than others (Bem and Allen, 1974; Funder, 1983). One will only find evidence of consistency, then, if one studies people who are consistent on that trait.

5 *Some situations more than others.* The argument is made that people will be more consistent in some situations than in others, since situations vary in constraint and in the degree to which they may be perceived as similar by the person (Bem and Funder, 1978; Lord, 1982). One may add here another historical note. Woodworth in 1937 asked: How consistent is the individual in his personality traits? What is consistency? He suggested that no individual shows perfect consistency in behavior, since behavior depends on the situation as much as on the individual. He concluded that "consistency should mean like behavior in like situations. And, we have to ask, what are like situations to a given individual? . . . We have to ask how he sees the situation and what he is trying to do or get out of the situation" (p. 104). One may note here that laboratory situations generally are high in constraint and thereby minimize individual differences and the potential for cross-situational consistency.

6 *Real world versus the laboratory*. Given the constraints in laboratory situations, trait psychologists argue that data from life allow for consistency in a way that is not possible in laboratory research. In particular, whereas in the real world one selects situations, this is not possible in most experimental settings. This point, made by Gordon Allport some time ago, has become a major area of research (Snyder, 1981).

This is not the place to discuss these as well as other arguments made in support of the trait position, or the counter-arguments made by those who continue to be critical of such a view. These are reviewed in Pervin (1985). A few points, however, are worth noting. First, there appears to be some agreement, at least between Mischel and Epstein, that there is evidence for both consistency *and* variability of behavior across situations. There is disagreement about *how much* consistency and what to make of it: that is, is there sufficient consistency to warrant a trait position? Second, it again must be pointed out that the debate concerning consistency tells us nothing about units of personality and situations or processes involved. One need not be a trait theorist to argue for personality consistency, and trait theorists differ among themselves concerning which traits exist and how they are to be discovered. One need only consider the very different views held by Allport, Cattell, Eysenck and Epstein – all trait theorists!

My own criticism of the trait concept is similar to that made by Henry Murray in 1938: it is too static and too tied to behavior at the overt level. I believe that Mischel makes a telling point in arguing against some forms of aggregation – that it cancels out some of the most interesting data about a person (Mischel and Peake, 1982, 1983). The person, it seems to me, is best defined by a pattern of stability and change in relation to various situations (Pervin, 1983). To argue for stability or change, consistency or variability, is to miss the point that both exist and contribute to defining the individual's personality. Beyond this, an emphasis on similarities among behaviors may lead to the neglect of underlying structures and conflicts within these structures. My own research has focused on goal structures within individuals. Goals are seen as being associated with affect and with plans or behaviors designed to implement them. The same plan or behavior can be associated with many different goals, and the same goal can be implemented through many different behaviors – plans. In other words, it is important to keep in mind concepts such as equipotentiality, equifinality, multiple determination, and probabilistic relationships (Rorer and Widiger, 1983). Organization exists at the goal–motivational level rather than at the plan–behavioral level (Carbonell, 1981; Schank and Abelson, 1977; Wilensky, 1978). Generally the person in a situation is behaving in terms of multiple goals, with the particular goals involved and relations among them shifting from time to time and situation to situation. The challenge presented to us, then, is in understanding the organization and plasticity of the goal system and its relation to situations created by, as well as imposed upon, the person.

PERSONS, SITUATIONS, INTERACTIONS AND AGGRESSION

Now, how does all of this relate to the area of aggression and to a book on situational determinants of aggression? I hope that in reviewing the history of the person–situation controversy I have drawn attention to certain pitfalls to be avoided. Parenthetically let me note that the focus of this collection itself raises difficult questions. Not only are we without agreement concerning a definition of violence and aggression, but how to define and assess situations is a problem that continues to bedevil psychologists (Pervin, 1978). Whether by "situation" we mean the actual, objective situation or the perceived situation is the issue that has gained the most attention, but beyond this there is the question, as in personality, of the units to use in analysing and assessing situations. If we are struggling with a psychology of personality, it is no less true that we are struggling with a psychology of situations (Magnusson, 1981).

My own reading of the aggression literature suggests that the person–situation, internal–external issue is very much with us. A chapter on aggression in my book *Current Controversies and Issues in Personality* (Pervin, 1978, 1984) bears upon and takes its cue from, the sub-title "Does the Finger Pull the Trigger or Does the Trigger Pull the Finger?" The reference is to Berkowitz's research on weapons as aggression-eliciting stimuli (Berkowitz and Lepage, 1967), which, in contrast to instinctual and ethological theories of aggression, places emphasis on cues in the situation that elicit aggressive behavior: "The finger pulls the trigger, but the trigger may also be pulling the finger" (Berkowitz, 1968, p. 22). The chapter on aggression in the best-selling social-psychology text by Baron and Byrne (1981) treats situational and personality determinants separately, but by classifying affect or emotion as a situational factor they clash with those who would argue that it should be considered in relation to personality. Many situations contribute to aggressive behavior, but even most social psychologists suggest that the effect of a situation is mediated by how it is perceived and by the attributions made by the person. Our response is different if we attribute intention to another person's behavior than if we attribute it to mood or accidental factors (Dyck and Rule, 1978). How situational cues and personal dispositions relate to such attributions is, of course, also of some import. Berkowitz (1982, 1983) emphasizes the role of aversive or unpleasant events in aggression: that is, the interpretation of these events rather than the objective events themselves. The emphasis is on conditions in the immediate situation though, again, people undoubtedly differ in their dispositions toward various attributions. An illustration of an interactional relationship is the work of Eron (1972) on television-viewing and aggression. Eron describes a bidirectional relationship in which viewing violence increases aggressive behavior and violent programs are more likely to be watched by aggressive children.

Finally, let us note that the issue of consistency has arisen in relation to aggression. Olweus (1979, 1980) has reviewed the literature relevant to longitudinal and cross-situational consistency of aggressive behavior and concludes that "the influential conclusions with regard to [lack of] consistency drawn by Mischel are not supported by existing empirical evidence in the field of aggression" (1980, p. 377). Olweus's own work on "bullies" and "whipping-boys" in the Swedish school system suggests a pattern that is repetitive and stable over a three-year period. At the same time, Olweus does not dismiss the role of situational factors. Thus, he cautions that "knowledge of the strength of an individual's habitual aggressive tendencies cannot in general lead to very accurate predictions of the behavior of that individual in a particular, concrete situation" (1978, p. 137). Whether a bully becomes aggressive at a particular time, whether a whipping-boy is attacked on a particular occasion, or whether a boy either joins in mobbing a victim, or himself becomes the object of such an attack, very much depend on situational factors. Group pressures can operate to strengthen or weaken aggressive tendencies in the individuals present. And, just as an animal in a heightened state of aggressive arousal may choose a less appropriate object if the desired object of attack is not available, so someone who is not a whipping-boy may become the object of attack if a whipping-boy is not present.

SUMMARY

In sum, the complexity of human social behavior demands complex explanations. Different acts of aggression may have diverse causes, and any single act of aggression or sequence of aggressive acts may depend on multiple internal and external factors. Genetic and experiential factors lead some animals and some people to be generally more aggressive than others. Such animals and people may initiate more acts of aggression or may respond more aggressively to activating situations in the environment. On the other hand, clearly some situations are more likely to lead to aggression than are others, and the activating or inhibiting potential of any single situation may vary for the individuals involved. In sum, the internal state of the organism may influence the quality and intensity of the response to cues in the environment, while the quality of the cues in the environment and the general surrounding context may in turn influence the internal state of the organism. An interactional perspective suggests that both internal (person) and external (situation) factors are always operating in social behavior and must be taken into account in any systematic conceptualization of such behavior. A truly interactional perspective requires us to go beyond questions of which set of variables is more important, or how much each contributes to the total variance, to questions concerning the processes involved. It is also clear, however, that adopting the term "interaction" will not in itself preclude controversy concerning such questions or tell us the units and processes to consider. In other words, if it is true that we all are now interactionists the task before us remains that of defining the relevant person and situation units and processes of interaction that are involved in all social behavior.

REFERENCES

Allport, F. H. 1937: Teleonomic description in the study of personality. *Character and Personality*, 6, 202–14.

Allport, G. W. 1955: *Becoming: basic considerations for a psychology of personality*. New Haven, Conn.: Yale University Press.

—— 1961: *Pattern and Growth in Personality*. New York: Holt, Rinehart and Winston.

Baron, R. A. and Byrne, D. 1981: *Social Psychology: understanding human interaction*. Boston, Mass.: Allyn and Bacon.

Bem, D. J. and Allen, A. 1974: On predicting some of the people some of the time: the search for cross-situational consistencies in behavior. *Psychological Review*, 81, 506–20.

Bem, D. J. and Funder, D. C. 1978: Predicting more of the people more of the time: assessing the personality of situations. *Psychological Review*, 85, 485–501.

Berkowitz, L. 1968: Impulse, aggression, and the gun. *Psychology Today*, September, 18–22.

—— 1982: Aversive conditions as stimuli to aggression. *Advances in Experimental Social Psychology*, 15, 249–88.

—— 1983: Aversively stimulated aggression. *American Psychologist*, 38, 1135–44.

Berkowitz, L. and Lepage, A. 1967: Weapons as aggression eliciting stimuli. *Journal of Personality and Social Psychology*, 7, 202–7.

Bindra, D. and Scheier, I. H. 1954: The relation between psychometric and experimental research in psychology. *American Psychologist*, 9, 69–71.

Block, J. 1977: Advancing the psychology of personality: paradigmatic shift or improving the quality of research. In D. Magnusson and N. S. Endler (eds), *Personality at the Crossroads: current issues in interactional psychology*, Hillsdale, NJ: Lawrence Erlbaum Associates.

Buss, D. M. and Craik, K. H. 1983: The act frequency approach to personality. *Psychological Review*, 90, 105–26.

Cantor, N. and Mischel, W. 1979: Prototypes in person perception. *Advances in Experimental Social Psychology*, 12, 3–52.

Carlson, R. 1971: Where is the person in personality research? *Psychological Bulletin*, 75, 203–19.

Carbonell, J. G. 1981: Politics: an experiment in subjective understanding and integrated meaning. In R. C. Schank and C. K. Riesbeck (eds), *Inside computer understanding: five programs plus miniatures*, Hillsdale, NJ: Lawrence Erlbaum Associates.

Cronbach, L. J. 1957: The two disciplines of scientific psychology. *American Psychologist*, 12, 671–84.
Dyck, R. and Rule, B. G. 1978: The effects of causal attributions concerning attack on retaliation. *Journal of Personality and Social Psychology*, 36, 521–9.
Dashiell, J. F. 1939: Some rapprochements in contemporary psychology. *Psychological Bulletin*, 36, 1–24.
Epstein, S. 1979: The stability of behavior: I. On predicting most of the people much of the time. *Journal of Personality and Social Psychology*, 37, 1097–126.
—— 1980: The stability of behavior: II. Implications for psychological research. *American Psychologist*, 35, 790–806.
—— 1982: The stability of behavior across time and situations. In A. I. Rabin, J. Aronoff, A. M. Barclay and R. Zucker (eds), *Further Explorations in Personality*. New York: Wiley.
—— 1983: Aggregation and beyond: some basic issues on the prediction of behavior. *Journal of Personality*, 51, 360–92.
Eron, L. D. 1972: Parent–child interaction, television violence, and aggression of children. *American Psychologist*, 37, 197–211.
Funder, D. C. 1983: Three issues in predicting more of the people: a reply to Mischel and Peake. *Psychological Review*, 90, 283–9.
Ichheiser, G. 1943: Misinterpretation of personality in everyday life and the psychologist's frame of reference. *Character and Personality*, 12, 145–52.
Loevinger, J. and Knoll, E. 1983: Personality: stages, traits, and the self. *Annual Review of Psychology*, 34, 195–222.
Lord, C. G. 1982: Predicting behavioral consistency from an individual's perception of situational similarities. *Journal of Personality and Social Psychology*, 42, 1076–88.
Magnusson, D. (ed.) 1981: *Toward a Psychology of Situations: an interactional perspective*. Hillsdale, NJ: Lawrence Erlbaum Associates.
Magnusson, D. and Endler, N. S. (eds) 1977: *Personality at the Crossroads: current issues in interactional psychology*. Hillsdale, NJ: Lawrence Erlbaum Associates.
Mischel, W. 1968: *Personality and Assessment*. New York: Wiley.
Mischel, W. and Peake, P. K. 1982: Beyond déjà vu in the search for cross-situational consistency. *Psychological Review*, 89, 730–55.
—— 1983: Analyzing the construction of consistency in personality. In M. M. Pge (ed.), *Personality: current theory and research*, Lincoln, Nebr.: University of Nebraska Press.
Murray, H. A. 1938: *Explorations in Personality*. New York: Oxford University Press.
Olweus, D. 1977: A critical analysis of the "modern" interactionist position. In D. Magnusson and N. S. Endler (eds), *Personality at the Crossroads: current issues in interactional psychology*, Hillsdale, NJ: Lawrence Erlbaum Associates.
—— 1978: *Aggression in the Schools*. Washington, DC: Hemisphere.
—— 1979: Stability of aggressive reaction patterns in males: a review. *Psychological Bulletin*, 86, 852–75.
—— 1980: The consistency issue in personality psychology revisited with special reference to aggression. *British Journal of Social and Clinical Psychology*, 19, 377–90.
—— 1981: Continuity in aggressive and withdrawn, inhibited behavior patterns. *Psychiatry and Social Science*, 1, 141–59.

Pervin, L. A. 1977: The representative design of person–situation research. In D. Magnusson and N. S. Endler (eds), *Personality at the Crossroads: current issues in interactional psychology*, Hillsdale, NJ: Lawrence Erlbaum Associates.

—— 1978: 2nd edn 1984: *Current Controversies and Issues in Personality*. New York: Wiley.

—— 1983: The stasis and flow of behavior: toward a theory of goals. In M. M. Page (ed.), *Personality: current theory and research*, Lincoln, Nebr.: University of Nebraska Press.

—— 1985: Personality: current controversies, issues, and directions. *Annual Review of Psychology*, 36, 83–114.

Peterson, D. R. 1968: *The Clinical Study of Social Behavior*. New York: Appleton-Century-Crofts.

Rorer, L. G. and Widiger, T. A. 1983: Personality structure and assessment. *Annual Review of Psychology*, 34, 431–63.

Schank, R. C. and Abelson, R. P. 1977: *Scripts, Plans, Goals, and Understanding*. Hillsdale, NJ: Lawrence Erlbaum Associates.

Shweder, R. A. 1982: Fact and artifact in trait perception: the systematic distortion hypothesis. *Progress in Experimental Personality Research*, 11, 65–100.

Snyder, M. 1981: On the influence of individuals on situations. In N. Cantor and J. F. Kihlstrom (eds), *Personality, Cognition and Social Interaction*. Hillsdale, NJ: Lawrence Erlbaum Associates.

Wilensky, R. 1978: Why John married Mary: understanding stories involving recurring goals. *Cognitive Science*, 2, 235–66.

Woodworth, R. S. 1937: *Psychology*. New York: Holt.

3

True to You, Darling, in My Fashion: The Notion of Contingent Consistency

Hans Toch

G. W. Allport points out that "the situational theorist is right when he claims that psychological theory looks too much inside the skin. But it is likewise true that the situationist looks too much outside the skin" (1961, p. 178). One way of looking too much inside or outside the skin is to look at the two sides of skin separately, ignoring the fact that "if there is no personality apart from the situation, it is equally true that there is no situation apart from personality" (p. 181). As an example, it should be obvious that "most people do a good deal to *create* the situation to which they respond" (p. 178).

Another way of accentuating the role of personality or the impact of situation is to oversell or to undersell the consistency of situational responses. Allport himself believed that "dispositions are never wholly consistent. What a bore it would be if they were – and what chaos if they were not at all consistent" (p. 362). The conceptual problem for us as for Allport is to find ways of crediting people with the consistencies they manifest, to accommodate specificities where they exist, and to recognize that individual personalities and the situations people encounter are not wholly divisible. The last aim is furthered by adopting a situation-centered term, "disposition", which Allport defines as a personality component "with the capacity to render many stimuli functionally equivalent, and to initiate consistent (equivalent) forms of stylistic and adaptive behavior" (p. 373).

The next order of business is to find dispositions that matter, which is different from predefining as a "disposition" a personality attribute that happens to be of interest to us. Bem and Allen point out that "when we are asked to characterize a friend, we do not invoke some a priori set of fixed dimensions which we apply to everyone. Rather, we permit ourselves to select a small subset of traits which strike us as pertinent and to discard as irrelevant the other 17,993 trait terms in the lexicon" (1974, p. 510). Any population of interest – such as that of recurrently violent persons – must contain a sub-group of persons who have dispositions that are relevant to a given range of situations, such as those in which violence can be perpetrated. Such dispositions can be described and their effects can be specified, but we can do no more. As Bem and Allen point out, "one simply cannot, in principle, ever do any better than predicting some of the people some of the time. It is an idiographic fact of life" (p. 512). There must also be persons for whom reactivity is somehow a way of life, and they also make up a sub-group. Bem and Allen note that "if some of the people can be predicted some of the time from personality traits, then some of the people can be predicted some of the time from situational variables" (p. 517).

The combination of the two approaches yields what I shall call a picture of "contingent consistency". Where this concept applies, *and only where it applies*, we should be able to assert that a given confluence of person and situtions is likely to yield a given outcome, such as violence. Some such outcomes will be proactively produced (they will be provoked by dispositions the person brings to the situations); others will be reactively induced (they will be fruits of seduction by the situation). In both cases, though, the prediction is that, if the individual finds himself in a given situation, a certain outcome (such as violence) is likely.

Norval Morris speaks of contingent predictions and calls them "anamnestic predictions", which suggests a lingering disposition that can only be inferred from behavior. Morris prescribes the obvious strategy of extrapolating from past patterned behavior. He writes, "an anamnestic prediction is: the young man behaved in a criminal fashion in a similar situation in the recent past; he has often done so; he is now entering the situation again; he is not unlikely to be involved in crime in the near future" (1974, p. 32). Monahan differentiates the same process further. He suggests that we

> rate the kinds of environment in which the person has been violent in the past. Thus, if the individual had four previous assaults, and two of them were against males and two against females, one would rate an item "victims tend to be females" as neither characteristic nor uncharacteristic of the environments in which violence has occurred. If all four victims were females, the item would be rated highly characteristic, and if all four were males, the item would be rated highly uncharacteristic.
>
> After one has obtained a profile of the kinds of situations in which the individual is expected to be (or, better yet, has in the past been) violent, it remains to categorize the environments in which he or she will likely be functioning during the period for which one is predicting. (1981, p. 139)

Neither Morris nor Monahan is concerned with understanding the process of person–situation links, nor do they address (as do Bem and Allen) the criteria we must use to circumscribe candidacy to those for whom the "shoe fits". The latter fact is understandable because experience with actuarial prediction (which lurks in the backdrop of sophisticated writings about violence prediction) suggests that it is always safe and sensible to extrapolate from chronicity. In actuarial prediction the issue is the probability of future predations, given an established record of past predations. But contingent consistency not only means that "he (or she) will do it again, given half a chance", but also implies a process that describes and explains repeat performances. In the remainder of this paper I shall address this process, especially as it bears on consistencies in violence chronicity.

To start with, consider Monahan's item "all four victims were female", which appears to describe a specialized sex offender or a chronic spouse-abuser. Both specializations are noxious, but they differ as regards the process of victimization. While the sex offender stages predatory *incidents*, the wife-abuser creates a predatory *relationship* (Dobash and Dobash, 1979), which his incidents of violence exemplify. The consistency of incidents tend to reflect a consistent approach to male–female relations or interpersonal relations in which vitims are placed under increasing pressure until an explosion is inevitable.

One example of specialization is reviewed in *Violent Men* (Toch, 1969), a study of violence chronicity. A group of social scientists and of offenders dissected and summarized this case, and they reported – among other things – that

> what seems to unify the entire set of incidents is that this man has a habit of placing other people into the most awkward situations without appearing to realize what he's doing – without anticipating the obvious reactions to his tactless opening moves. He isn't aware, for instance, that when you cohabit with a woman you just can't come in one evening and simply announce your imminent departure, and then expect to spend a congenial evening with her. Now, when the other person reacts – the person who is going to be abandoned or who has just been insulted – then we have a second stage in which our friend sees himself as attacked out of the clear blue sky. He can then be quite brutal while viewing all of it blandly as an act of self-defense. . . . So he has this pattern of provoking people in a rather selfish way, not seeing the consequences. There is a complete blindness to the other person's point of view. Then, if possible, fear and whining if aggression is not possible. And a kind of general demonstration of his weakness and his lack of ability to get along in the situations that he himself engineers. (pp. 31–2)

Another person who proved dangerous to women and whose case is considered in the same study defined each of his spouses as flirtatious and irresistible to any man within range, and (as a corollary) he worked himself into paroxysms of jealousy whenever his current wife was temporarily inaccessible to physical supervision. Ensuing tragedies and prison terms did not deter this redundant offender from selecting new spouses using the same fateful criteria of attractiveness and conviviality.

Not atypically, the consistency of domestic violence includes the husband frequently coming home drunk, which he and his wife define as a necessary but not sufficient precondition of violence (Gelles, 1972). The wife's assigned role may be that of a recriminator who centers on her husband's unregenerate drinking-career and/or deficiencies as breadwinner. An alternative scenario may involve unreasonable demands by the drunken husband for an early-morning supper, or unacceptable invitations to amorous interludes.

Examples of this kind can be multiplied, but the point is obvious: the statement "all four victims were females" is at best a *clue* to situational consistency – it is a clue to what may be personally relevant to the offender in recurrent situations or what may be situationally relevant to the person that helps us explain the violent outcome of incidents. Where consistency exists – and it *need* not exist just because all victims are female – we must describe and review scenarios to dissect out of them the dispositions that script them. The first of our random examples, the "unilateral abrogation of terms of relationship", shows that the offender's disposition is shameless egocentricity combined with blindness to the needs of other parties in a relationship. The second scenario, "drunken request for spousal services", reflects the very same combination of disposition and trait.

The issue of alcohol involvement alerts us to a problem which is dealt with elsewhere in this volume: that of normatively defined violent scenarios. The taxonomy of perpetrators presented in *Violent Men* includes one type, the "rep defender", whose predations seemed situationally constrained. The following paragraph is quoted from one of the case summaries:

> The man appears to be defending his status as a gang leader, which in turn is expressed in his defense through violence of the integrity of his gang (which is his racial group of friends). There is no effort, as in many other situations of this kind, to try to justify violent acts in terms of some kind of code of justice. In other words, he does not argue that people are taking advantage of his friends, therefore, he fights. Rather it is that they are his friends, and he needs them, therefore, he fights. He is undoubtedly seen as a source of strength and support and is willing to help create and keep this image as a tower of physical strength for the group. It does appear, though, that he's not just a strong-arm-member of the group, but is actually a leader, and this leadership is maintained through his ability to use force to help the boys – to help protect his boys. (Toch, 1969, p. 157)

The passage contains the clue to the source of consistency, that of the offender's "status as a gang leader". The role assigned to this status ("fights for his group") is a precondition of violence. It provides the disposition which can be invoked by pressing the relevant button. The group presses the button by informing the offender that his services are required. Whenever the group does this, a situation exists in which violence is likely to result. When the group does not draft the offender, no violent situation exists.

For a group to invoke norms is different from an offender invoking norms, or invoking what he claims are norms. There exist offenders who "do not require others to come to them for help or advice (no one does); they do not need anyone to nominate them as champions or to recognize them as spokesmen for their people (no one does); they are convinced that the job needs to be done and that they must do it" (p. 168). Such men rank high on participation in bar-room violence; they become involved not simply because bars are scenarios of normative violence but primarily because bars furnish arenas for self-generated interventions.

Bars also provide arenas for the manifestation of other dispositions. One very prevalent enterprise is what the same study calls "self-image promoting". The following quotation describes a person who manifests this disposition:

> We have two images we can invoke for this man. First, there is an element of the wild and woolly west about him. There is some swaggering and drawing. Secondly, somewhat inconsistent with the first, we have the image of a young man who is trying to keep his head above water. What happens specifically is the following: Our man has the image of people here and there in the world around him who are likely to pick on him and who are not fair. In the face of such people, he feels it incumbent upon him to rise to the challenge and to provide a good show. Now, admittedly, the people whom he fights don't appear to be particularly vicious, nor do the issues appear very monumental. These are really not Main Street duels but side street duels. The most prominent of the fighting issues is cheating at dominoes. Typically, we have a situation where our man spots the evil one in the shape of another person cheating and he promptly calls the man's attention to what is happening. Then he decides that he isn't going to let it pass. His feelings are hurt, and you have a kind of spiral in which he stages a fight. A small fight will do, and when it has taken place he walks away reasonably satisfied because he has made his point . . . the point of the fight is to demonstrate to our man's own satisfaction that he cannot be crowded, monkeyed with, challenged, cheated, unfairly treated, pushed. When he feels that someone is thus playing unfair, he feels that he must take a stand, that he must fight in order to show himself that he is no one's fool. There is no need to hurt, draw blood, do damage, destroy. A gesture suffices.
>
> The duels are small time – they have a "spitball or marshmallow at thirty paces" flavor. But then, the issues are small. And this is the case, because our man lives in a world of minor detail. Where the world of others includes momentous battle grounds for matters of valor, power, prestige, or love, our man plays dominoes. He plays dominoes full time – and it matters to him that no one should pull anything sneaky on him in this serious, important game. If someone does, he draws attention to it testily, and makes sure that the other understands that the gauntlet has been thrown. We call him the "Domino Kid". (pp. 142–3)

I have quoted this vignette at length because it helps me make several points. The first is that a part of most redundantly violence-prone dispositions is a perceptual set which enhances the salience of violence-relevant situational features. In the case of the "Domino Kid" (and others who are similarly disposed) one such salient feature is "people . . . who are likely to pick on him", and it may matter to the point where innocent remarks or innocuous gestures are interpreted as aspersions. Where such a condition obtains, situational consistency can involve a violence-promotive response to situations *perceived* as challenging or affronting by the offender and by no one else. Since the stimulus that makes for consistency is not (or may not be) available to observers, an "objective" description of successive situations may reveal no consistency, even where (as with those we call "self-image defenders") consistency is very strikingly present. For such persons, the consistency lies in the fact that wherever they are involved in violence they react to perceived affronts and aspersions, though the context in which such perceptions arise may vary.

Self-image promoters select their proving-grounds (rather than reacting to affronts where they perceive them) and may select them in such a way as to make criteria discernible. In the case of the "Domino Kid", the assertion "violence recurrently arises in domino games" is both informative and uninformative. The uninformativeness could be ascertained by following the strategy prescribed by Morris (1974) of making abstention from dominoes a condition of parole, a proscription which would require the subject to find other areas of imperfection to monitor so as to demonstrate his toughness and integrity.

The second point illustrated above is that of the role assigned to spectators. Some violence is consistently public; other violence consistently seeks gloomy alleys or prefers dark bedrooms. Public violence is violence that makes a point for consumption, or seeks to do so. The point is something like, "Look how tough I am", or "You can see, nobody fools with me", or "Guess who is in charge around here?" Where violence is the medium for such messages, spectators are a requisite; where there is no audience the show closes. When it does, challenges or irritants and insults lose their sting.

For some (such as predatory sex offenders), the victim is the audience. Targets are selected for their impressionability, or because they belong to a group (such as women) who ordinarily are unimpressed with the offender. In extreme cases, victims are selected as easy marks. Defenselessness guarantees impact.

Domestic violence is private violence, and it may be deferred violence where the grievances that spark it are publicly experienced. Where this happens – as in fights after embarrassing social occasions – the "situation" is hard to define because the stimulus is separated in time from the response. The delay matters in terms of dynamics, because time provides the opportunity for resentment and rage to escalate. In retrospect we often see "unprovoked violence" where provocation, as defined by the offender, is history. The offender's history can also create susceptibilities which make innocuous stimuli provocatory in a way no one anticipates.

I know of no "unprovoked violence" in the sense that the behavior is *unmotivated,* but there is a great deal of violence that shows a disjuncture between what most of us think *ought to be* motives for violence and what actually motivates the offender. Situational explanations often founder because the offender's motives are too idiosyncratic to be inferred. Where this happens over time we may conclude that the offender explodes crazily, for no reason, "all over the place". Allport has pointed out that "we usually find that contradiction diminishes if we spot correctly the deepest (most propriate) disposition that is operating. . . . Descriptions in terms of 'here and now' are *phenotypical.* Explanatory accounts, seeking deeper dispositions, are *genotypical*" (1961, pp. 363–4).

The distinction, which Allport adapted from Lewin, is not easily applied. Extremely idiosyncratic ("crazy") violence requires genotypic explanation, but most violence combines long-term and short-term motives. The "here and now" gains potency from the baggage the offender brings to it. Most of us do not react violently to situations that some of us react to violently time after time.

Violent men have dispositions to react violently, and these dispositions are triggered by a limited range of situations, in the sense that only some situations are disposition-relevant. Where the relevance of situations to dispositions seems obvious we talk about "phenotypic" motivation, but we can be wrong, and we often are. Dominoes and female victims may be consistent but incidental features in games with consistent motives that have nothing to do with dominoes or women. Full explanations must encompass both phenotypic consistency and genotypic consistency, where they exist. We cannot afford to wait until the props are removed and the predatory show goes on, as with rapists who become prison bullies.

Most phenotypic motivation has a touch of the genotypic. We can only be true (or untrue) to those to whom we are true (or untrue) "in our fashion", because we must react to situations as we perceive and interpret them in line with the dispositions we bring to them. Where phenotypic explanations looks adequate to us, it is because we assume standard interpretations and dispositions. The most conventional dispositions are those we suspect respond to norms. Allport has noted that "situational determinants are most important where duties and roles, where tasks and functions, are heavily prescribed. Personality determinants are most important where the task is more free and open and unstructured" (1961, p. 179). Marital norms are presumed to inspire marital fidelity. Infidelity is usually ascribed to "personality determinants" (to an unseemly need for promiscuity), but it may be governed by group norms that prescribe rakishness, the use of sex to relieve boredom, or faddish libertarianism.[1] This latter sort of (conventional) deviance is what we call "sub-cultural behavior". Some students of the phenomenon speak of sub-culturally motivated *violent* behavior. The offender who is deemed to be so motivated is presumed to rape, assault or kill people because he has internalized violence-permissive norms (Wolfgang and Ferracuti, 1967).

Sub-cultural portraits are phenotypic portraits. The sub-cultural model assumes that, when a rape is reliably a group event, and/or when it occurs in a neighborhood where violence is prevalent, the offender's personal dispositions are of limited interest (Amir, 1971). A conceptual distinction predefines the slum rapist as a product of norms – as a man who is phenotypically motivated – but may see the middle-class rapist as a product of pathology – a man who is genotypically motivated.

Sub-cultural explanations are incomplete explanations. Where the offender engages in gang rapes, the gang he belongs to is obviously relevant to his disposition to rape. But does the gang "motivate" behavior? No one forces the youth to join a group which rapes, and the group does not impel him to rape. What the group *may* be doing to the youth is to goad and excite him, to help him depersonalize the victim, to redefine his sleaziness as "manliness", to appease the residues of his conscience, to compensate (through force of numbers) for his inadequacy, and so forth. The group, in other words, may be the medium through which the man's personal motives are shaped, manifested and expressed.

Violence is often not just individual personal behavior. Much repeated violence is interpersonal, in the sense that dispositions of the victim and the offender must intersect for violence to occur. Contingent consistency in such cases means that one person provides the other's contingency, and *vice versa*. Person *A* may require contact with a sub-set of others (*B*, *C*, *D*) for violence to occur. No violence occurs when *A* encounters non-members of his sub-set (*E*, *F*, *G*). Similarly, any of *A*'s opponents (*B*, for instance) may react with violence when he encounters a sub-set of people which includes persons like *A*. If this is so, when *A* meets *B* violence becomes virtually inevitable.

In studies of police–citizen violence it has been found that some officers are repeatedly involved in violence, and that many such officers overreact when they think citizens are displaying "disrespect", which they perceive as reprehensible (Chevigny, 1969; Westley, 1970). Such officers often generate their own "disrespect" by challenging and harassing people of whom they disapprove. Many citizens, of course, object to being challenged; some object more vociferously than others; and some object with gusto and profanity. This select group includes persons all of whose contacts with authority figures are sensitive and tinged with resentment. For such persons, police incursions are violence contingencies. Conversely, for officers in search of malefactors, those citizens who have anti-authoritarian dispositions (who "flunk the attitude test") invite further invocations of power which virtually guarantee that the citizen will become a violence contingency for the officer (Toch, 1969).

The stage is typically set with a dialogue such as

O (*swaggering*):	You, there! Let's see some identification.
Z (*sullenly*):	I don't have to (profanity) show you nuttin'.
O:	Unless I see some identification, you're under arrest, punk!
Z:	I ain't done (profanity) nuttin', and you (profanity) pigs have no right to (profanity) pick on me! and I ain't showin' you no identification.

Violence generally erupts during the next stage of the game, when the officer tries to arrest the citizen and the citizen predictably "resists". I have called explosive encounters of this kind "violence transactions". The term is borrowed from Dewey and Bentley (1949) and it underlines the *trans-* (as opposed to *inter*actional) view, which "sees man-in-action not as something radically set over against an environing world, nor yet as merely action 'in' a world, but as action of and by the world in which the man belongs as an integral constituent" (p. 228). A transaction denotes a unique confluence of buyer and seller. Our aggressive officer and resistant suspect may be characterizable as "violence-prone", but neither produces an incident without the other, nor does a "violence situation" reach fruition until the two have irritated each other sufficiently. For both the officer and suspect, "consistency" is a complicated relationship. It is a combination of tendencies, which includes selectivity in

1 seeking out or being sought out;
2 perceiving an occasion as calling for intervention;
3 perceiving an intervention as calling for an escalating response;
4–*n* escalation to taste, culminating in physical aggression.

What philosophers have called "action *of* and *by* the world in which the man belongs" refers to a definition of the violent incident which comprises the sum of moves by the actors in the incident. For our officer and suspect, contingent consistency denotes recurrent involvement in analogous scenarios to similar effect. What is consistent is not just the identity of the opponent but also the way the offender and the opponent react to each other, and the process whereby they manage to generate violence through their encounter.

The psychological dispositions that are at issue are those that govern perception of the other party, reactions to these assessments, and responses to the behavior generated by these reactions. Such dispositions are not necessarily dispositions to behave violently, but, rather, dispositions to behave so as to enhance the probability that violence will result from an encounter. As I have noted elsewhere,

> Goals such as the need to demonstrate manhood, propensities such as callous manipulativeness, perspectives such as readiness to take instant offense are preludes to confrontations given negligible provocations. However, there are attributes which are not violence-prone but may evoke violence-proneness.

> Flirtatiousness or disputatiousness, authoritarianism or rebelliousness, hyperactivity or hypoactivity, loquaciousness or withdrawal, silliness or moodiness are traits that can intersect – sometimes fatally – with inhospitable dispositions. Where a rebellious offspring or a flirtatious adult encounters an impatient parent or a suspicious mate, emerging violence-prone states (punitiveness or jealousy) may evolve in the encounter; such states may escalate over time, reaching violence-prone levels. (Toch, 1985)

The concept of disposition is one that covers propensities to interpret situations and react to them in a characteristic way. The applicable definition is "the tendency of something to act in a characteristic manner under given circumstances" (*Webster's Dictionary*). This definition is a transactional definition because it presumes that "circumstances" must occur before a "disposition" is manifest, and implies that when we "act in a certain manner" we do this because Dewey and Bentley's "buyer" (circumstances) and "seller" (tendencies) have met. "Tendencies" must remain stillborn if no relevant "circumstances" arise; "circumstances" bore us if they do not arouse "tendencies". The probability of consistency in dispositions hinges on the range of circumstances they cover. On the one hand, if a buyer's specifications for an acceptable acquisition are very particular, he will discover little to buy and there will be less room for noting consistency than with a more voracious buyer. On the other hand, indiscriminate acquisitions reduce consistency, because by their very range they become unclassifiable. All one can say of the career shopper is that he is an avid consumer.

Indiscriminate exploders show little contingent consistency; once-in-a-lifetime murderers show none. A repeat offender who over time shows comparable reactions (say, a tendency to loudly challenge or to cast aspersions) under similar circumstances (convivial surroundings) to similar people (physically unimpressive) is a candidate for classification. Any descriptive commonalities we find among the incidents in which the offender is involved become codable cues to hypothesized consistencies of disposition (in this case, possibly a need to stage cheap demonstrations of toughness).

Once we think we have diagnosed a disposition, we can further hypothesize that the disposition may manifest itself non-violently as well as violently. For instance, between pugilistic encounters a bar-room bully may lord it over his subordinates or abuse his progeny. On the other hand, dispositions may change or decay. Rewarded violence may be perpetuted; dispositions that boomerang may be abandoned (Bandura, 1973). Where dispositions to change over time, contingent predictions can be disconfirmed, but diagnoses may stand as historically valid.

Where the offender's problem is patterned violence, it may be wasteful to define his problem – and to have the offender define it – as a "propensity to violence". As an analogue, suppose you have an infection, a culture is taken, and a virulent micro-organism obligingly shows up under the microscope.

Your physician would at least regard it as not cost-effective to continue to treat your condition with broad-spectrum antibiotics. Nor would he think of desensitizing an allergy of yours by administering every conceivable allergen (feathers, eggs, pollen, dust and so forth) if you report that you *only* react (with hives, labored breathing and intemperate language) whenever a cat appears on the premises.

To think in terms of specific patterns has practical value, in part because such thinking can be shared. Morris has commended to parole boards his emphasis on patterned violence and noted that the "relationship [of contingent predictions] to [the offender's] past behavioral history can and should be made apparent to him" (1974, p. 43). The point of such information-sharing is to explain to the offender why some situations that have impelled him to violence must remain "off limits" as long as he stays on parole. Most parole terms end sometime, however, and no one can be continuously watched while on parole. The hope must be that the intelligent offender will see a relationship between his history and the rationale for the constraints imposed on him, and so further regulate his own behavior to avoid foreseeable trouble.

Even this aim is conceptually narrow, though, because it assumes that offenders have no temptation resistance and no ability to modulate reactions to provocation. It assumes that any catalytic situation the offender encounters must be constraining. For some addictive offenders this assumption may hold, but for most offenders (and the rest of humanity) it does not. We are creatures, not prisoners, of habits. Some of us can invent new responses to familiar stimuli when we are (1) genuinely convinced of the need to change, (2) motivated to change by experiences such as demonstrated failure, (3) conscious of habits that require change, (4) familiar with other options or alternative means of reaching goals, and (5) sufficiently unconstrained to afford change and to be capable of change. Persons who have been punished for crimes generally have the incentive provided by their demonstrated failure to achieve goals. An offender with a patterned offense history – particularly if it conforms to phenotypic patterns (for instance, fights in barrooms), but also if genotypic patterns that are credible and plausible (goals pursued through fights) – can, by reviewing his past, acquire easy-to-understand, assimilable self-knowledge that may define and facilitate change.

The interviews conducted during the research for *Violent Men* included exchanges such as the following:

I: . . . You say you don't like people pushing you around or that you hit this guy because he was pushing you around. You feel the same way about officers?

S: Yeah.

I: Did you feel the same way about these three guys that came along and hollered at you while you were walking with your girl?

S: Yeah. I felt the same.
I: Have you felt the same way in other fights you've had? That people were pushing you around and you got in a fight with them because you want to stop them pushing you?
S: Yeah.

(Toch, 1969, p. 121)

The offender may not really gain "insight" into his pattern – not deep down inside where it counts – but, if he does, this may be the prelude to reform. Though dispositions that are known are not necessarily dispositions that are abandoned, the mapping of dispositions defines target areas for intervention, pending the day when the offender may be ready, willing and able to change.[2] I myself suspect that there are more offenders who have reached that day than we are ready to acknowledge and to support through shared knowledge.

NOTES

1 Norms govern specified ranges of situations, just as dispositions do. Some norms, for instance, apply to play situations, and some to work situations. Infidelity norms may take benevolent (or even supportive) views of promiscuity whenever the offender is "out of town" (say, at a business meeting or a scientific convention), or may prescribe alcohol involvement so to excuse the behavior as drink-induced. Wolfgang and Ferracuti have suggested that "sub-culture of violence" theory is applicable if violence is envisaged as an option in "a variety of situations" (1967, p. 159), but not in all situations.

2 Contingent consistency implies that the offender's pattern of violence – rather than violence generally – must be the object of treatment. This does not mean simply to draw an offender's attention to what he is doing and to point out to him that there are more civilized options available. Only the most phenotypically motivated violence (such as some types of police violence) can be addressed by attending exclusively to behavior patterns, as do peer review panels in police departments (Toch, Grant and Galvin, 1975). Where personal dispositions combined phenotypic and genotypic motives (as do most violence-related dispositions), change strategies must become correspondingly multi-targeted. This means that one may have to challenge the offender's "basic" assumptions (as through rational–emotive therapy) or modify his interpersonal approaches (as through transactional analysis) or modulate his control of anger (as through stress inoculation) or change his responses to reinforcements or self-reinforcements (through modelling and rehearsal or structural interventions). No matter which approach is used, however, the aim of the game is to change a disposition to react to situations in destructive ways, rather than to achieve general self-improvement or to gain "mental health".

REFERENCES

Allport, G. W. 1961: *Pattern and Growth in Personality*. New York: Holt, Rinehart and Winston.

Amir, M. 1971: *Patterns in Forcible Rape*. Chicago: University of Chicago Press.

Bandura, A. 1973: *Aggression: a social learning analysis*. Englewood Cliffs: Prentice-Hall.

Bem, D. J. and Allen, A. 1974: On predicting some of the people some of the time. The search for cross-situational consistencies in behavior. *Psychological Review*, 81, 506–20.

Chevigny, P. 1969: *Police Power: police abuses in New York City*. New York: Pantheon.

Dewey, J. and Bentley, A. F. 1949: *Knowing and the Known*. Boston: Beacon Press.

Dobash, R. E. and R. 1979: *Violence against Wives: a case against the patriarchy*. New York: Free Press.

Gelles, R. J. 1972: *The Violent Home: a study of physical aggression between husbands and wives*. Beverly Hills: Sage.

Monahan, J. 1981: *Predicting Violent Behavior: an assessment of clinical techniques*. Beverly Hills: Sage.

Morris, N. 1974: *The Future of Imprisonment*. Chicago: University of Chicago Press.

Toch, H. 1969: *Violent Men: an inquiry into the psychology of violence*. Chicago: Aldine. (New edn Cambridge, Mass.: Schenkman, 1984.)

—— 1985: The catalytic situation in the violence equation. *Journal of Applied Social Psychology*, 15, 105–23.

Toch, H., Grant, J. D. and Galvin, R. T. 1975: *Agents of Change: a study in police reform*. Cambridge, Mass.: Schenkman.

Westley, W. A. 1970: *Violence and the Police: a sociological study of law, custom and morality*. Cambridge, Mass.: MIT Press.

Wolfgang, M. E. and Ferracuti, F. 1967: *The Subculture of Violence: towards an integrated theory of criminology*. London: Tavistock.

4

Cognitive Representations of Aggressive Situations

Joseph P. Forgas

INTRODUCTION

Although aggression and violence are probably essential features of the human condition (Fox, 1982; Freud, 1917/1952; Koestler, 1978; Lorenz, 1966), public perceptions of aggression typically focus on the abnormal, deviant and threatening aspects of everyday aggressive incidents. Aggression and violence are often portrayed as a dangerous social problem facing modern liberal democracies, while the adaptive, functional aspects of aggression are largely ignored (cf. Marsh et al., 1978). Clearly an understanding of how everyday aggressive situations are perceived and cognitively represented by people is of paramount importance in coming to terms with this issue. Fortunately, there are now techniques available which are subtle and sensitive enough to chart how people subjectively represent and differentiate between common types of aggression. This chapter presents a general review of research on cognitive representations of social situations in general and aggressive situations in particular, followed by an empirical illustration of research on the implicit representations people have of everyday examples of aggression.

Recent trends in psychological research on aggression are increasingly consistent with the present approach in placing major emphasis on the internal, cognitive processes which influence the perception and evaluation of aggressive incidents. Psychological definitions of aggression have shifted from emphasizing objective, behavioral criteria to paying more attention to the processes of interpretation, evaluation and judgment involved in classifying aggression (Tedeschi et al., 1974; Tedeschi, 1984; Mummendey, 1981, 1982; Mummendey et al., 1984). Traditional objective definitions emphasized such criteria as intentionality, harmfulness, other-directedness and norm violation as essential features of aggression. Such objective definitions leave something to be desired in that they usually do not fully coincide with what is perceived as aggressive in everyday life. Our implicit perceptions of what are aggressive situations seem to be far more subtle and elaborate, incorporating a far greater number of subjective criteria than objective definitions are able to deal with.

Yet it is implicit perceptions of aggression which really matter when dealing with aggression as a "social problem". Despite the voluminous literature on violence and aggression, little is known about the kinds of distinctions people naturally make between aggressive incidents as they are experienced in real life. A clearer understanding of the attribute dimensions underlying the perception of aggressive episodes would be of obvious practical, as well as heuristic, interest. The problem of classifying aggressive incidents lies at the heart of the criminal-justice system, which ultimately must reflect the way different kinds of aggressive acts are perceived by the population at large (Mulvihill and Tumin, 1969). There is another sense in which implicit perceptions of aggression and the objective codification of aggression as manifested in the legal system are related: the legal system is ultimately the tangible embodiment of the integrative mores and values of a given society, and serves to symbolize and reinforce the acceptable range of conduct within a defined culture (Durkheim, 1964). Public and private perceptions of aggressive situations are thus closely interdependent. Much of the existing research shows that perceptions of aggression are not based on any absolute criteria. Rather, implicit representations of the surrounding social situation play a major role in determining how people define and react to everyday instances of aggression. Studies of how people perceive and form cognitive representations of common social situations may thus help indicate how best to study implicit representations of aggression, as we shall see in the next section.

SOCIAL EPISODES AND THE PERCEPTION OF AGGRESSION

Aggressive encounters, just like most other forms of human interaction, usually occur in a highly predictable, even ritualized, form. In studying perceptions of aggressive situations, research on how people deal with other kinds of encounters can be of considerable relevance. Everyday interactions between people largely take place within the framework of routine, well-defined interaction episodes. Most of our daily social encounters can be conveniently categorized into a surprisingly manageable number of repetitive routines (Pervin, 1976; Forgas, 1979, 1982). In a society, it is our knowledge about such interaction episodes which gives structure and predictability to social life, and which strangers to our milieu find most difficult to learn and imitate (Goffman, 1974; Triandis, 1972).

Despite considerable historical interest in studying such recurring event sequences both in psychology (Barker, 1968; Brunswik, 1956; Murray, 1951;

Lewin, 1951) and in sociology (Goffman, 1974; Mead, 1934; Schutz, 1970; Thomas, 1928/1966; Wolff, 1964), the empirical study of interaction episodes is a relatively recent development in social psychology. The emergence of a new sociol-cognitive paradigm (Carroll and Payne, 1976; Forgas, 1981; Hilgard, 1980) has resulted in the recognition that one of the most pertinent cognitive domains relevant to social behavior is the implicit cognitive representations people have of their daily interactions. Such implicit representations are studied under various labels, such as "scripts" (Abelson, 1976; Bower et al., 1979), "situations" (Mischel, 1979; Pervin, 1976), "action plans" (Miller et al., 1960), "event schemata" (Lichtenstein and Brewer, 1980) and "social episodes" (Forgas, 1979, 1982).

For present purposes, we may define social episodes as

> cognitive representations about stereotypical interaction sequences, which are representative of a given cultural environment. Such interaction sequences constitute natural units in the stream of behaviour, distinguishable on the basis of symbolic, temporal and often physical boundaries. More importantly, however, there is a shared, consensual representation in the given culture about what constitutes an episode, and which are the norms, rules and expectations that apply. (Forgas, 1979, p. 15)

The concept of social episodes should be of considerable usefulness when approaching the problem of how everyday aggressive incidents are perceived and cognitively represented. We have already seen that definitions of aggression, and reactions to particular aggressive episodes, are largely subjective and situational. Just as most social encounters are manifestations of typical, shared episode scripts, most aggressive incidents also appear to have a similar consensual cognitive structure. Intensive ethnographic studies of football fans, delinquent girls and rowdy schoolchildren (Marsh et al., 1978; Campbell, 1981) certainly suggest the existence of clear-cut and shared scripts of aggressive situations in the behavior repertoire of these people. The concept of social episodes to analyse deviant behavior has already been employed with some profit to study such specific issues as the perception of drinking-episodes in Finnish culture (Simpura, 1983). Numerous other studies of episode perception have looked at such issues as the features of episodes in a university milieu (Battistich and Thompson, 1980) and the links between social skills (Forgas, 1983) and cultural background (Forgas and Bond, 1985) in episode representations. Studies of implicit representations of aggressive episodes may be a most suitable strategy to shed light on the situational features of reactions to aggression, and the hidden characteristics people use to discriminate between classes of aggressive incidents. One such illustrative study is discussed later in this chapter. First, however, we shall briefly consider the collective influences which play a role in shaping public perceptions of aggressive situations.

AGGRESSIVE SITUATIONS AND THE PUBLIC VIEW

Violent and aggressive behaviour has been part of the adaptive repertoire of our species, and most others, since the dawn of evolution. However, it seems that it is only since the emergence of industrialized large-scale societies that aggression has taken on the character of a dangerous social problem. Fox suggested that "in a paradoxical sense, it is because we are cut off from the roots of violence – from the roots of reproductive struggle – that we make these things into problems" (1982, p. 9). It is perhaps not mere coincidence that the Western ideology of liberated individualism heralded by the French Revolution and most perfectly embodied in the US Constitution has resulted in what is commonly seen as a dangerous increase in anti-social, as distinct from functional, kinds of aggression.

It is precisely in societies where individual liberty (including the liberty to deviate) is most treasured that the increase in aggression is viewed with the greatest public alarm. There appears to be a clear link between the growth of individual liberty and the potential for abusing that liberty. The controlled, functional and often ritualistic character of aggression in most small-scale societies has apparently changed to what is now commonly perceived as an uncontrolled, threatening aggressive repertoire in societies where individual liberty is a central value. Aggression and violence thus seem to be particularly emotional issues in open societies, not necessarily because of any increase in intrinsic revulsion against violence, but because of people's subjective perception of the growing personal threat that contemporary forms of aggression entail. The filtering and interpreting function of the media, which in such societies tend to be pluralistic and commercially motivated, is an important contributor to the shaping of such perceptions.

It is thus of great political as well as practical importance to understand the dynamics underlying people's subjective representations of various forms of aggression and violence. Typically, it is assumed that, for public consumption at least, the many-faceted characteristics of aggressive acts can be condensed into a single dimension of social danger or severity. There is strong evidence suggesting, however, that the consensually perceived severity of aggressive incidents is not static over time (Coombs, 1967) or consistently related to the legally prescribed punishments (Mayer, 1972; Rose and Prell, 1955–6; Sherman and Dowdle, 1974). Perceptions of aggressive situations are likely to be partly rooted in the political and economic conditions of particular cultures, representing the specific (and often shifting) views of given groups or milieux.

The strongly situational character of public interpretations of aggression is nicely illustrated by recent controversies surrounding such aggressive incidents as the shooting of muggers on the New York subway by a self-declared vigilante, or the widespread concern about "football hooligans" in Britain. The situation-contingent nature of these public representations of aggression is glaringly obvious, yet rarely addressed in any explicit form. The New Yorker who shot the black muggers who threatened him on the subway was initially treated as a folk hero by major sections of the media and the population at large. The situation was collectively defined as one involving legitimate self-defense and even justifiable revenge. Somewhat later, a different situation definition was imposed on the same sequence of events: through the emphasis of some features (for instance, the fact that one of the attackers was shot in the back and certain words the vigilante was alleged to have uttered) and subtle de-emphasis of others, the situation now seemed more consistent with the premeditated-murder scenario. This incident provides a striking illustration indeed of the way perceptions and definitions of violence are largely dependent on consensually accepted and activated situational scripts. The case of British football hooligans is another fascinating example of situation-contingent perceptions of aggression, treated in considerable detail elsewhere (cf. Marsh et al., 1978).

The point is that people view aggressive situations with a subtle and refined classificatory system in mind, about which we still know relatively little. Not all displays of aggression are threatening, and those which are judged to be threatening are only threatening in certain situations. The study of implicit perceptions of aggressive situations is thus of considerable importance in understanding the causes of public concern with aggression, and could ultimately play an important role in the way the criminal justice system is constructed.

The present chapter is thus based on the assumption that people have enduring and sophisticated cognitive strategies for the interpretation of everyday occurrences and situations. Recent psychological research (Battistich and Thompson, 1980; Forgas, 1982; Pervin, 1976) certainly indicates that cognitive representations of situations and episodes are based on some quite surprising connotative characteristics, which can be reliably studied using empirical procedures such as multidimensional scaling (MDS). Similar implicit cognitive models about aggressive incidents no doubt play a role in regulating everyday reactions to aggression. Such implicit situation models have recently been shown to play a crucial role in the way racial prejudice shapes social interactions (van Dijk, 1985), and no doubt also play a very important part in the way aggressive incidents are perceived and categorized. There is likely to be a very wide gap indeed between the simplified public representations of aggression, and the implicit cognitive models people use to interpret familiar aggressive scenarios.

IMPLICIT MODELS OF AGGRESSIVE SITUATIONS

Existing taxonomies of aggression are often speculative, usually based on criteria rooted in intuition or deductively derived from theories. For example, psychologists may differentiate between aggressive acts in terms of whether the cause of aggression is identified in instincts, emotional arousal, frustration, pain, imitation or a variety of situational influences such as the presence of weapons (Berkowitz, 1962, 1969; Toch, 1969). In contrast, sociological views of aggression emphasize social strain, anomie, labeling, lack of social controls or culture conflict as the predominant causes of aggressive behavior (Downes, 1982; Merton, 1968; Wolfgang et al., 1962).

In everyday life, implicit perceptions of what constitutes aggression are highly dependent on subjective and contextual factors (Berkowitz, 1973). The general features of situations and episodes in which aggression occurs play an overwhelming role in influencing how a given incident will be perceived, evaluated and cognitively represented. The essentially situational quality of what constitutes aggression is of course also reflected in the many unsatisfactory attempts to arrive at a comprehensive psychological definition of this construct. Intentionality, injury and other-directedness are the most common criteria suggested, though by no means universally accepted. None of these criteria deals adequately with the way common and consensual cognitive representations about recurring social situations interact with the specific features of an observed incident in generating a classification as "aggressive" or "non-aggressive".

Research on perceptions of aggressive situations has taken a variety of forms. An early attempt at an empirical study of implicit representations of aggression (in this case, criminal offences) was performed by Thurstone (1928), as a demonstration of his method for scaling subjective magnitudes. A follow-up investigation was performed 40 years later by Coombs (1967), who found that perceptions of the offences studied by Thurstone became more diffuse over time, with sexual and property offences being seen as less, and offences against the person as relatively more, serious. In 1933, Durea also used Thurstone's method to establish severity ratings for 14 offences related to juvenile delinquency, and found this distribution "to compare favourably with the distribution found by Thurstone for crime" (p. 534). In a more exhaustive study, Rose and Prell (1955–6) looked at the relationship between the severity of 13 crimes, the punishments actually imposed and the punishments thought to be appropriate by their respondents. A significant difference between popular and legal estimates of the seriousness of these crimes was found, which Rose and Prell attributed to a "cultural lag" in the incorporation of changing popular perceptions into the legal system.

Some more recent studies have relied on sophisticated statistical techniques, such as multidimensional scaling (MDS) to represent implicit perceptions of aggression and crime. I shall have more to say about the suitability of this method later. Sherman and Dowdle (1974) used MDS to analyse the perceptions of crime and punishments in a university sample. Results showed that perceived seriousness was only moderately related to punishments prescribed by law. It was also found that judges' implicit perceptions of the 34 crimes studied could not be readily described in terms of the ubiquitous "seriousness" dimensions. Instead, a far more subtle and differentiated four-dimensional perceptual space had to be constructed, defined by (1) the willingness and loss of the victim, (2) the degree of premeditation by the perpetrator, (3) the type of citim (persons *versus* institutions) and (4) the extent of the publicly reported harm to the victim.

These studies suffer from some common shortcomings. The arbitrary selection of the stimulus domain is a major problem. Crimes as classified by the legal system do not necessarily constitute meaningful units of perception for individuals. Since these crime labels describe episodes which were not personally experienced by most judges, their reactions may well reflect the semantic, rather than the experiential, features subsumed under categories such as "arson", "assault" and "fraud". If a realistic representation of implicit perceptions of aggression is to be achieved, it is essential that commonly experienced aggressive incidents be used as stimuli, something that was attempted in the investigations described below. A related problem is that studies of crime perception are not necessarily relevant to the more universal question of implicit representations of aggression. The category of "crimes" includes both aggressive (robbery, murder) and non-aggressive (fraud) offences. In turn, many everyday kinds of aggression are not classed as criminal (a parent hitting a child, arguments with a shop assistant, and the like). Again, the use of naturally occurring aggressive episodes as stimuli is one way of overcoming this limitation. A further problem with most studies of perceptions of aggression and crime is that preselected judgmental dimensions – most typically, seriousness – are used to obtain ratings. This makes it impossible to study the implicit distinctions people naturally make between varieties of aggression. The study of Sherman and Dowdle (1974) is a noteworthy exception, and, as we have seen, they found implicit perceptual dimensions which are very different from those commonly employed by researchers. I shall next discuss some of the alternative methodological approaches which may be employed in studying perceptions of aggression. In particular, a recent illustrative study using advanced statistical techniques to identify the implicit cognitive representations people have of commonly experienced aggressive episodes will be outlined.

EMPIRICAL RESEARCH ON IMPLICIT PERCEPTIONS OF AGGRESSIVE EPISODES

To overcome some of the problems described above, the studies that I and my colleagues have undertaken of aggressive situations have focused on everyday, commonly experienced examples of aggression, using non-biasing statistical techniques such as MDS to analyse people's perceptions of such incidents. Before describing the results of one such illustrative study, a few words may be in order about the appropriateness of the MDS procedure used.

Carroll and Chang's Individual Differences Multidimensional Scaling (Indscal) program (1970) was used in most of our studies of perceptions of episodes (Forgas, 1982). This model assumes that people cognitively represent the stimulus field to be studied within a shared implicit multidimensional space. This consensual stimulus space is empirically derived from the (dis)similarity judgments of a number of individuals. It is further assumed by the Indscal model that individual differences between judges are reflected in the different weights they assign to the cognitive dimensions defining the stimulus space, including the possibility of zero weighting (not using a particular dimension at all). In addition to the stimulus space representing the perception of the stimuli by a hypothetical "average" subject, a subject space is thus also constructed, where individual judges are located within the same co-ordinate axes as the stimuli in terms of their relative weighting of each stimulus dimension.

Indscal has the further advantage that, since stimulus dimensions are unique in expressing the "consensus" of a group of judges, these axes normally "correspond to meaningful psychological dimensions in a very strong sense" (Carroll and Chang, 1970, p. 265) and need not be further rotated. The Indscal procedure has been used with considerable success over recent years to analyse cognitive representations of a wide range of elusive social stimuli, such as jargon terms (Friendly and Glucksberg, 1970), social episodes (Battistich and Thompson, 1980; Forgas,s 1979, 1982), political stimuli (Forgas, 1980b) and interpersonal relationships (Forgas and Dobosz, 1980; Rands and Levinger, 1979).

On the basis of such Indscal analyses of aggressive situations it is also possible to establish empirical links between how a person perceives aggression, and his/her other individual characteristics. Since each judge's specific view of aggression can be empirically expressed in terms of subject dimension weights, empirical measures of that person's demographic, personality, attitudinal and political characteristics may be linked to perceptual styles. This was an important subsidiary aim of the research described below.

Selection of naturalistic aggressive situations

It was essential for the purposes of this study that familiar and naturally occurring aggressive incidents should be used as stimuli, instead of the *ad hoc* and often unfamiliar kinds of aggression commonly studied. In order to achieve this, over 100 subjects were used in a preliminary study designed to elicit personally experienced aggressive incidents. Subjects were given a diary form, and asked to list as many personally experienced aggressive incidents as they could recall, irrespective of when, where and to whom each incident happened. For each episode, they were also asked to record the behavior setting, the persons involved, and sanctions or punishments, who was thought to be responsible, as well as two descriptive adjectives best characterizing the incident. Surprisingly, most subjects could only think of one or two such aggressive incidents, as against the seven or eight kinds of "general" episodes commonly reported by subjects in studies of episode perception (Battistich and Thompson, 1980; Forgas, 1976, 1982; Pervin, 1976). Of the over 140 individual examples of aggression thus elicited, the 22 listed below were selected, on the basis of their overall frequency of occurrence and typicality. Individual descriptions were paraphrased to produce generally comprehensible episode vignettes.

1 A brief punch-up between two players on the football field during a game.
2 A husband, after accusing his wife of infidelity, to which she reacts by making fun of him, hits her.
3 A man gets slightly pushed by a stranger in a pub, spilling his beer; he calls the stranger to task, leading to a fight.
4 Bob Hawke responds aggressively to David Frost's questioning on a TV show.
5 Two males are heckled, and later physically attacked, by a group of bikies late Saturday night at King's Cross.
6 Two schoolboys fight in a school playground at lunchtime.
7 Foundation Day flour-bombs hit a non-participant bystander.
8 Police use violence to break up a demonstration.
9 Two adolescent boys fight over the alleged insult of one's girlfriend by the other.
10 After a minor accident, the motorists get out of their cars, and after abusing each other, a physical fight ensues.
11 A girl is attacked on the street at night by a group of drunken males after pub closing-time.
12 A mother angrily hits her 5 year old child on the bus, after he has been irritating her for some time.
13 A father slaps his adolescent daughter for not helping around the house.

14 A 4 year old boy throws a stone at his elder sister who wouldn't give him a toy he wants.
15 A knife-fight in a pub between two "heavies" after an alleged insult.
16 A husband attempts to strangle his wife, after she torments him about his inefficiency and lack of achievement.
17 While stopping at a traffic light, a man is punched on the nose by the driver of the next car, who is irritated by his cutting in front of him.
18 A brawl at a party between a group of gatecrashers, and the host and his friends who are all slightly drunk.
19 An angry argument during a lecture, between a student and the lecturer, about an assignment submission.
20 A publican physically ejects an aggressive, and drunk, customer.
21 Fights break out in the crowd after a football match.
22 A large group of bikies demolishing parked cars at the Bathurst bike races, until arrested by police.

The perceptual space for aggressive situations

Judgments of these 22 aggressive episodes were obtained in the form of bipolar scale ratings (cf. Forgas, 1979), which were converted to dissimilarity matrices and used as input to Indscal. The bipolar scales themselves were constructed on the basis of subjects' own lists of descriptive adjectives, to ensure that the judgmental dimensions were relevant and meaningful to subjects. In addition to rating the aggressive episodes, each subject also completed a series of personality and attitude measures during a separate session.

The results of the Indscal analysis showed that four dimensions were both sufficient and necessary adequately to represent the perceived differences between aggressive episodes (see figure 1). The interpretation of the four defining dimensions was based on their empirical correlation with the known bipolar scales on which the episodes were rated. The first dimension was found to separate common, everyday kinds of aggression which did not involve alcohol (for instance, mother hitting child, flour-bombs on Foundation Day from more violent, rare and esoteric kinds of aggression which involved alcohol (street attack on girl, motorcycle-gang attack). This was called a *probability of occurrence* dimension. The second perceived dimension describing aggressive episodes was marked by such bipolar scales as fair/unfair, sympathetic/unsympathetic to aggressor, and justifiable/unjustifiable. This second, *justifiability* dimension separated fairly violent situations which were seen as unjustifiable (for instance, street attack on girl) from similarly violent, but justifiable incidents (publican ejecting a drunk). The third dimension, labelled *provocation*, separated aggressive episodes which were the result of emotional reactions following provocation (for instance, husband

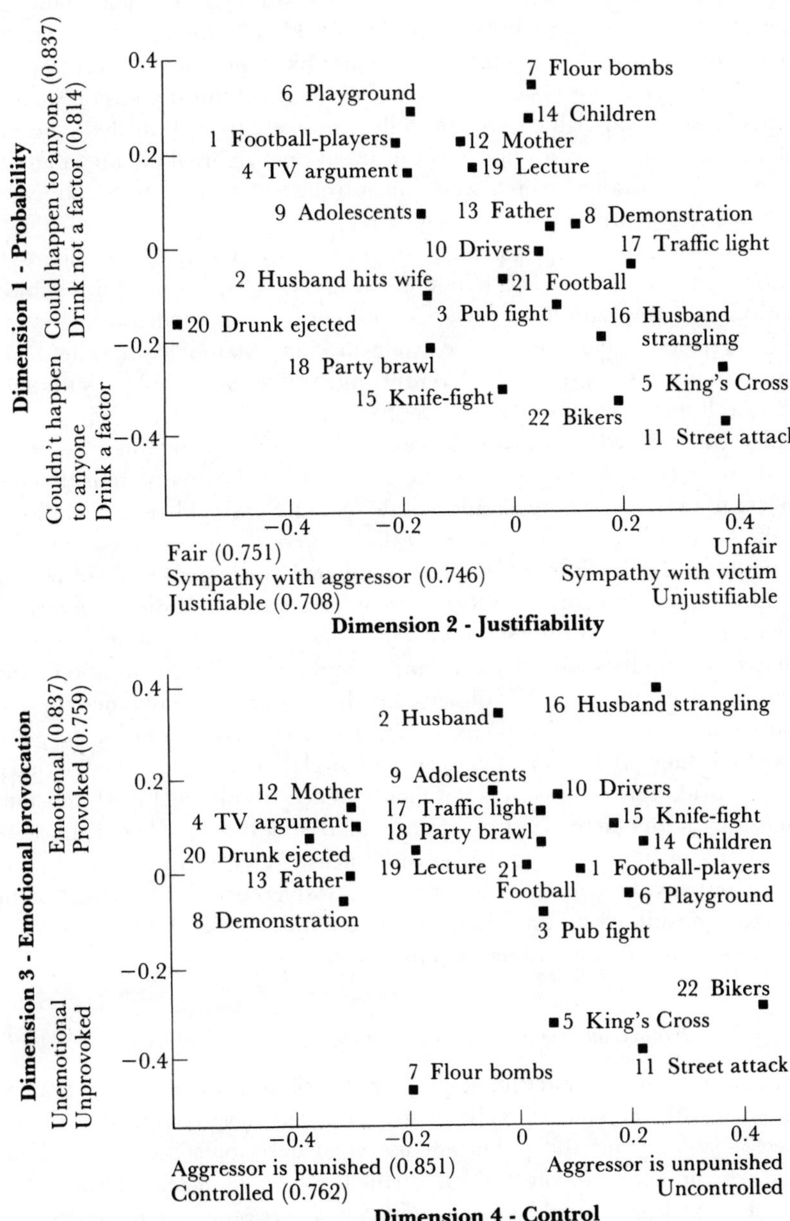

Figure 1 The four-dimensional representation of how the 22 aggressive episodes were cognitively represented by subjects, with each of the four axes empirically labeled in terms of their correlations with bipolar scales

against wife) from incidents which were non-provoked and non-emotional (premeditated or random kinds of aggression). Finally, the fourth perceptual dimension reflected the amount of *control* and likely *punishment* characteristic of different sorts of aggression. At the two extremes of this dimension we find aggressive situations which are controlled, unlikely to be punished and are generally sanctioned by authority (for instance, police breaking up a demonstration), and episodes which were uncontrolled and likely to be punished (husband attacks wife, street attack on girl).

The resulting four-dimensional "cognitive map" for episodes (figure 1) may be regarded as the way a hypothetical "average" member of this subject group viewed this sample of incidents. Of course, this model of aggressive incidents is both culture- and episode-specific. Members of other subcultures may view aggression differently, and a different sample of situations might well have resulted in different cognitive dimensions being used. Despite these restrictions, this space for aggressive incidents does offer several insights not found in earlier studies. Perhaps the first point is that our subjects used a very complex and subtle four-dimensional representational scheme to differentiate between naturally occurring aggressive episodes, as distinct from the much more simple, usually one-dimensional categorization schemes commonly assumed. Of the very few descriptive studies of perceived dimensions of aggression, Sherman and Dowdle's investigation (1974) is perhaps the one most directly relevant to ours. Their "premeditation" and "willingness of the victim" dimensions bear some resemblance to our "emotional provocation" dimension. As in their study, none of our four perceptual dimensions were significantly correlated with perceived seriousness. Instead, seriousness was implicitly reflected in several of the four dimensions found here. It thus appears that seriousness when applied to perceptions of aggression is not a unidimensional concept as commonly assumed. Instead, several facets of an aggressive encounter seemed to be implicitly considered by this group of judges, and none of these facets could by itself be reduced to a seriousness dimension.

Implicit and explicit categorizations of aggressive situations

The implicit cognitive space for aggressive situations described above may be contrasted with the kind of explicit categorizations most commonly used by the legal system and the public media when describing aggression. This latter scheme often involves such distinctions as domestic *versus* public violence; illegal *versus* legal kinds of aggression; aggression which does or does not involve a sexual component; and alcohol-related *versus* alcohol-unrelated types of aggression. We were interested to determine whether these explicit *a priori* distinctions between different classes of aggressive acts were significantly reflected in subjects' implicit representations. Using the co-ordinates of each aggressive episode within the four-dimensional perceptual space, it is possible to test the hypothesis that the locations of different clusters of aggressive episodes are significantly different from each other. Using the four kinds of explicit category distinctions listed above (domestic/public, legal/illegal, sexual/non-sexual and alcohol-related/non-alcohol-related), four multiple-discriminant analyses were carried out to determine whether these explicit, *a priori* divisions were also reflected in subjects' implicit judgments.

Results showed that subjects in fact made a significant distinction in their implicit representations between, respectively, public and domestic, legal and illegal, and alcohol-related and non-alcohol-related kinds of aggressive situations. Sexuality, however, was not a significant differentiating factor in judgments. The multiple-discriminant analysis also allows us to determine which of the four implicit perceptual dimensions were most important in differentiating between various types of aggression. Domestic/public aggression was mainly seen as different along the emotional-provocation dimension, a finding which is not only intuitively meaningful but also supported by criminological evidence. Legal and illegal kinds of aggression were, in turn, significantly separated from each other in terms of the three other dimensions: probability of occurrence, justifiability and control. It is perhaps the legal/illegal distinction which is most commonly associated with "seriousness" of aggression, which corresponds to at least three different implicit dimensions used by subjects acording to our results. The last explicit category, alcohol-related/non-alcohol-related aggression, was most differentiated along the "probability of occurrence" perceptual dimension, with drunken violence seen as infrequent and less likely to occur. This finding no doubt reflects the particular middle-class social milieu from which our subjects came; it is likely that different perceptual styles may be found in other sub-cultures.

Generally, these findings suggest that implicit representations of aggression also incorporate most of the commonly used explicit category schemes, but go well beyond such schemes in subtlety and complexity. Also, implicit representations are of course more likely to reflect the particular values and attitudes of the group making the judgments. The question arises: is it possible to demonstrate empirical links between the perception of aggressive situations and the characteristics of individual judges? We shall turn to this question next.

Individual differences in the cognitive representation of aggression

In addition to judging the aggressive vignettes, subjects also provided demographic data and completed four instruments measuring conservatism, New Left ideology, machiavellianism and alienation. An empirical comparison was made between males and females, younger and older subjects, and subjects rating at the two extremes of each of the four instruments in terms of their styles of perceiving aggression, again using multiple-discriminant analyses.

Males and females had significantly different implicit representations of aggression. Males relied on the "probability of occurrence" dimension more heavily than did females, while for females the "control" dimension, differentiating between sanctioned and non-sanctioned kinds of aggression, was more important. Age also made a difference: older subjects found the "probability of occurrence" dimension more salient than did younger judges, who in turn relied more on the "emotional provocation" dimension. Of the four attitude and personality measures, only scores on the machiavellianism scale were related to perceptions of aggression. High scorers weighted the "emotional provocation" dimension relatively more heavily, while low scorers saw aggressive episodes more in terms of the "justifiability" and "control" dimensions. It is perhaps not surprising that these two dimensions, which are most directly relevant to judging the moral character of aggression, were not particularly important to those with high scores for machiavellianism.

The absence of a link between conservatism, New Left ideology or alienation, on the one hand, and perceptions of aggression, on the other, was somewhat unexpected. Other studies (for instance, Sherman and Dowdle, 1974) found a link between such individual characteristics as authoritarianism, external/internal control and aggression. Given the controversy surrounding some of the personality scales in general, and these measures in particular, it is perhaps to be expected that the relationship between personality measures and judgments of aggression will fluctuate over time and across situations.

CONCLUSIONS

This chapter has sought to present an argument for the serious study of implicit representations of aggressive situations as a necessary prerequisite to understanding everyday reactions to aggression. The argument has been supported by an illustrative study showing that aggressive episodes are perceived by people in a complex multidimensional psychological domain. Contrary to popular belief as well as implicit legal assumptions, perceived severity is not the most important attribute of aggressive encounters. Our judges certainly relied on a much more sophisticated and elaborate cognitive framework in their judgments of aggression. Probability of occurrence, emotional provocation, justifiability and control were the four implicit dimensions used. It was also found that this complex four-dimensional representation of naturally occurring aggressive incidents incorporated such commonly made *a priori* distinctions as whether the incident was domestic or public, whether legal or illegal, and whether or not alcohol-related. Finally, the methods described here also allowed us to demonstrate some important empirical links between demographic and personality variables and perceptual styles.

The approach outlined here has several important implications. It paves the way for a better understanding of the cognitive processes involved in the definition and interpretation of everyday instances of aggression. Such interpretations reflect consensually shared cognitive scripts about prototypical examples of aggressive episodes, and the methods described here represent one way of empirically describing this implicit cognitive domain. The study of the information-processing strategies used in perceiving aggression would offer a complementary avenue to socio-cognitive research on aggression. The links between the empirically established location of an aggressive episode within our cognitive map of aggression, and the way details of that episode are processed, remembered and interpreted are the focus of some of the more recent research on this topic in which I and my colleagues have engaged (cf. Forgas, 1982).

The study of implicit representations of aggression is also important for a much more practical reason. Since individuals engaged in law enforcement and the legal system usually have a considerable degree of latitude in interpreting and labeling observed incidents as "aggressive" or "criminal", the perceptual dimensions used by them are of particular importance. In other investigations (cf. Forgas, 1980a) we have found that perceptions of crimes show a similar subtlety to the perception of aggressive situations found here. The evidence shows that both aggression and crimes are always perceived and interpreted within the context of familiar social-situation scripts. The situation–perception strategies and representational schemes that people use in identifying aggression are one of the more important topics that cognitive social psychologists have to address.

REFERENCES

Abelson, R. P. 1976: Script processing in attitude formation and decision making. In J. Carroll and J. Payne (eds), *Cognitive and Social Behavior,* Hillsdale, NJ: Lawrence Erlbaum Associates.

Battistich, V. A. and Thompson, E. G. 1980: Students' perception of the college milieu. *Personality and Social Psychology Bulletin,* 6, 74–82.

Barker, R. G. 1968: *Ecological Psychology.* Stanford, Calif.: Stanford University Press.

Berkowitz, L. 1962: *Aggression: a social–psychological analysis.* New York: Atherton Press.

—— 1969: *Roots of Aggression.* New York: Atherton Press.

—— 1973: Words and symbols as stimuli to aggressive responses. In J. F. Knutson (ed.), *Control of Aggression: implications from basic research,* Chicago: Aldine–Atherton.

Bower, G. H., Black, J. B. and Turner, T. J. 1979: Scripts in memory for text. *Cognitive Psychology,* 11, 177–220.

Brunswik, E. 1956: *Perception and the Representative Design of Psychological Experiments*. Berkeley, Calif.: University of California Press.

Campbell, A. 1981: *Girl Delinquents*. Oxford: Basil Blackwell.

Carroll, J. D. and Chang, J. J. 1970: Analysis of individual differences in multidimensional scaling via an N-way generalization of "Eckart-Young" decomposition. *Psychometrika*, 35, 283–319.

Carroll, J. S. and Payne, J. W. (eds) 1976: *Cognitive and Social Behavior*. Hillsdale, NJ: Lawrence Erlbaum Associates.

Coombs, C. H. 1967: Thornstone's measurement of social values revisited 40 years later. *Journal of Personality and Social Psychology*, 6, 85–91.

Downes, D. 1982: The language of violence. In P. Marsh and A. Campbell (eds), *Aggression and Violence*, Oxford: Basil Blackwell.

Durea, M. A. 1933: An experimental study of attitudes toward juvenile delinquency. *Journal of Applied Psychology*, 17, 522–34.

Durkheim, E. 1964: *The Division of Labor in Society*. New York: Free Press.

Forgas, J. P. 1976: The perception of social episodes: categorical and dimensional representations in two different social milieus. *Journal of Personality and Social Psychology*, 33, 199–209.

—— 1979: Multidimensional scaling: a discovery method in social psychology. In G. P. Ginsburg (ed.), *Emerging Strategies in Social Psychology*, London: Academic Press.

—— 1980a: Images of crime: a multidimensional analysis of individual differences in crime perception. *International Journal of Psychology*, 15, 287–99.

—— 1980b: Implicit representations of political leaders: multidimensional scaling analysis. *Journal of Applied Social Psychology*, 10, 295–310.

—— 1982: Reactions to life dilemmas: risk taking, success and responsibility attribution. *Australian Journal of Psychology*, 34, 25–35.

—— 1983: Social skills and the perception of interaction episodes. *British Journal of Clinical Psychology*, 22, 195–205.

—— (ed.) 1981: *Social Cognition: perspectives on everyday understanding*. London: Academic Press.

Forgas, J. P. and Bond, M. 1985: Cultural influences on the perception of interaction episodes. *Personality and Social Psychology Bulletin*, 11, 75–88.

Forgas, J. P. and Dobosz, B. 1980: Dimensions of romantic involvement: towards a taxonomy of heterosexual relationships. *Social Psychology Quarterly*, 43, 290–300.

Fox, R. 1982: The violent imagination. In P. Marsh and A. Campbell (eds), *Aggression and Violence*, Oxford: Basil Blackwell.

Freud, S. 1952: *A General Introduction to Psychoanalysis* [1917], tr. J. Rivière. New York: Washington Square Press.

Friendly, M. L. and Glucksberg, S. 1970: On the description of subcultural lexicons: a multidimensional approach. *Journal of Personality and Social Psychology*, 14, 55–6.

Goffman, E. 1974: *Frame Analysis*. Harmondsworth: Penguin.

Hilgard, E. R. 1980: The trilogy of mind: cognition, affection and conation. *Journal of the History of the Behavioural Sciences*, 16, 107–17.

Koestler, A. 1978: *Janus: a summing up*. Melbourne: Hutchinson.

Lewin, K. 1951: *Field Theory in Social Science: selected theoretical papers*. New York: Harper.

Lichtenstein, E. H. and Brewer, W. F. 1980: Memory for goal-directed events. *Cognitive Psychology*, 12, 412–45.

Lorenz, K. 1966: *On Aggression*. New York: Harcourt Brace Jovanovich.

Marsh, P., Rosser, E. and Harre, R. 1978: *The Rules of Disorder*. London: Routledge and Kegan Paul.

Mayer, S. E. 1972: Does the punishment fit the crime? A replication after 18 years, plus a study of present day race differences. Paper presented to the Midwestern Psychological Association Convention, Cleveland, Ohio.

Mead, G. H. 1934: *Mind, Self and Society*. Chicago: University of Chicago Press.

Merton, R. 1968: *Social Theory and Social Structure*. New York: Free Press.

Miller, G. A., Galanter, E. and Pribram, K. H. 1960: *Plans and the Structure of Behavior*. New York: Holt.

Mischel, W. 1979: On the interface of cognition and personality. *American Psychologist*, 34, 740–54.

Mulvihill, D. J. and Tumin, M. M. (eds) 1969: *Crimes of violence*, vol. II: *Staff Report to the National Commission on the Causes and Prevention of Violence*. Washington, DC: US Government Printing Office.

Mummendey, A. 1981: Der Stand der psychologischen Diskussion um das Konzept aggressiven Verhaltens'. In W. Michaelis (ed.), *Bericht über den 32. Kongress der Deutschen Gesellschaft für Psychologie in Zürich 1980*, Göttingen: Verlag für Psychologie, Dr C. J. Hogrefe.

—— 1982: Zum Nutzen des Aggressionsbegriffs für die psychologische Aggressionsforschung. In R. Hilke and W. Kempf (eds), *Naturwissenschaftliche und kulturwissenschatliche Perspektiven der Aggressionsforschung*, Bern: Huber.

Mummendey, A., Loschper, G., Linneweber, V. and Bornewasser, M. 1984: Social–consensual conceptions concerning the progress of aggressive interactions. *European Journal of Social Psychology*, 14, 379–89.

Murray, H. A. 1951: Toward a classification of interaction. In T. Parsons and E. A. Shils (eds), *Towards a General Theory of Action*, Cambridge, Mass.: Harvard University Press.

Pervin, L. A. 1976: A free response description approach to the study of person–situation interaction. *Journal of Personality and Social Psychology*, 34, 465–74.

Rands, M. and Levinger, G. 1979: Implicit theories of relationship: an intergenerational study. *Journal of Personality and Social Psychology*, 37, 645–61.

Rose, A. M. and Prell, A. E. 1955–6: Does the punishment fit the crime? A study in social evaluation. *American Journal of Sociology*, 61, 247–59.

Schutz, A. 1970: *On Phenomenology and Social Relations*. Chicago: University of Chicago Press.

Sherman, R. C. and Dowdle, M. D. 1974: The perception of crime and punishment: a multidimensional scaling analysis. *Social Science Research*, 3, 109–29.

Simpura, J. 1983: *Drinking Contexts and Social Meanings of Drinking. A study with Finnish drinking occasions*. Helsinki: Finnish Foundation for Alcohol Studies.

Tedeschi, J. T. 1984: A social psychological interpretation of human aggression. In A. Mummendey (ed.), *Social Psychology of Aggression: from individual behavior to social interaction*, New York: Springer.

Tedeschi, J. T., Smith, R. B. and Brown, R. C. 1974: A reinterpretation of research on aggression. *Psychological Bulletin*, 81, 540–62.

Thomas, W. I. 1966: Situational analysis: the behavior pattern and the situation [1928]. In M. Janowitz (ed.), *W. I. Thomas on social organization and social personality*, Chicago: Chicago University Press, 1966.

Thurstone, L. L. 1928: The method of paired comparisons for social values. *Journal of Abnormal and Social Psychology*, 21, 384–406.

Toch, H. 1969: *Violent Men: an inquiry into the psychology of violence*. Chicago: Aldine.

Triandis, H. C. 1972: *The Analysis of Subjective Culture*. New York: Wiley.

Van Dijk, T. A. 1985: Cognitive situation models in discourse production: the expression of ethnic situations in prejudiced discourse. In J. P. Forgas (ed.), *Language and Social Situations*. New York: Springer.

Wolff, K. H. 1964: Definition of the situation. In J. Gould and W. K. Kolb (eds), *A Dictionary of the Social Sciences*, New York: Free Press.

Wolfgang, M. E., Savitz, L. and Johnston, N. 1962: *The Sociology of Crime and Delinquency*. New York: Academic Press.

5

Gender, Social Class and Conceptual Schemas of Aggression

Peter Marsh and Renée Paton

It is an often-voiced complaint that too little research is directed towards an understanding of female youth. This is true in the sociology of youth cultures and is particularly evident in the social psychology of aggression. One notes the work of Anne Campbell (1984, 1986) and that of Angela McRobbie and her colleagues (1976) as rare examples in an otherwise fairly barren or poorly conducted field of inquiry. In many cases the complaint becomes a focus of attention in itself, effectively precluding collection of worthwhile research material. Even McRobbie and Garber (1976), for example, conclude an article on girls and sub-cultures by saying "girl culture . . . is so well insulated as to operate to effectively exclude not only other 'undesirable' girls – but also boys, adults, teachers and researchers". The sentiment is somewhat defeatist.

Experimental studies, conducted largely in the United States, seem to many of us to lack that essential relevance to everyday life which we take to be a requisite of a salient social science. At the other extreme, some "field" research focusing on female youth aggression and conflict is too reliant on anecdotal evidence and unsystematic research procedures.

The net effect of these lacunae has been to render serious examination of gender differences in aggression extremely difficult, since a genuine basis for comparability is largely absent. In addition, we shall argue, many of the gender comparisons that have been made have failed to control for effects due to socio-economic class. We shall propose later that class differences strongly interact with those attributable to gender and that an understanding of the nature of the interaction between the two variables is required for a full appreciation of variation in the expression and social management of aggression.

Our work on female aggression, and on gender and class differences in the

We should like to acknowledge the invaluable assistance given to the research by Janet Gallagher, Amanda Brookes and Ann Allen. The research reported here was supported by the Social Science Research Council (HR 8379) and the ESRC (GOO230113).

social management and expression of aggression, followed on from extensive research with male informants (Marsh, 1978, 1982). This relies heavily on a theoretical framework developed by Harré and others (Harré and Secord, 1972; Harré, 1977, 1979; Marsh, Rosser and Harré, 1978) which is usually referred to as ethogenic social psychology. This is not the place to attempt a full summary of the philosophical and methodological implications of this approach. Note, however, can be made of some of the central features.

It is assumed that individuals are capable of rendering meaningful their own social behavior and the recurring situations in which they find themselves. Thus, the first stage of any research procedure involves the collection of *accounts*. Informants are asked to explain and offer justifications for their own behavior and for that of others with whom they have contact. Contained within such accounts will be indications of the tacit social rules which might be seen as directing or governing social action within a variety of contexts and of the meanings attributed to situations, events and behavior.

The notion of social rules is quite central to the ethogenic approach, which insists that even apparently random or gratuitous patterns of behavior (particularly those involving aggression and violence) can be shown to be *orderly* given a full insight into the insider's perspective.

In many cases, evidence of social rules and the orderly nature of social behavior can be retrieved directly from accounts. Take, for example, this account offered by a soccer fan from Chesterfield, England concerning events at football games.

> There's an organized pattern of events. I mean you know what's going to happen. Bringing a knife, probably by your own supporters, it's looked down on as being a form of, you know, cowardice. There's not many people who will carry knives about. There's not many who set out to harm someone.

In addition, many of the central values within a particular micro-culture can be identified in this way.

> I mean it don't matter if you lose a fight, so long as you don't back down. I mean, you could end up in hospital but so long as you didn't back down you'd made your case. I mean there's a lot of this not wanting to be called a coward in it. When you're 16 or 17, before say you're courting steady and that – that's the time you don't like being called a coward. And it's one thing that hurts you more than anything else, you know.

Whilst such a methodology opens up profitable areas of social research, there are, however, considerable limitations to the approach. There are traditional problems relating to issues of sampling and investigator effects. At a more fundamental level, however, is the problem of identifying the extent of distortion and exaggeration within accounts. The offering of an account is itself a social act. And, like all other social acts, it can serve in the process of image management and presentation of self. Thus, an individual may seek not only to provide an insight into his or her own social action but also to "gloss" that insight in order to enhance his or her own image.

In the case of male informants we have found many examples of a duality of rhetoric within the accounts offered. While offering a view of their aggressive behavior as constrained by tacit social rules – thus rendering it largely ceremonial and ritualized rather than seriously injurious – at the same time they allude to acts of bloody destruction and macho violence. Consider this short discussion with a group of Millwall soccer fans:

Fan B: It's a shouting match . . . it starts off with, but, you know, it gets kind of emotional don't it . . . REally good Millwall supporters, right, they can't stand their club being slagged down you know, and it all wells up, you know, and you just feel like hitting someone.

Interviewer: How many people actually get hurt in those kind of things though?

Fan A: When we played Everton in the FA Cup I spent two weeks in hospital. I got seven busted ribs and a broken nose.

Fan B: No, that's exaggerating. The young fellas, you know, they're giving each other verbal and that, you know, and they're running each other down, that's all harmless fun you know, even if they have a little chase and chase one another round the ground . . . but when it comes to people bringing out knives, that's out of order.

Fan A: But it's changed, it's changed, everything comes out now. All right, fair enough, when we go away, I'll admit it, I do people in the eyes with ammonia, so what? I got done at Everton, and since I've been there I've carried that ammonia with me all the time. There's no way I go away without that ammonia.

Fan C: Where is it now then?

Fan A: Today I haven't got it, right?

Fan C: Aah, I don't believe you. I don't believe you. If you take it everywhere why ain't you got it today?

Fan A: 'Cos I haven't been home to get it. Straight, that's the truth.

Whilst the accounts methodology raises serious problems concerning the conduct of research and interpretation of results, we see it as being an essential first stage of our research procedure. The aim is not so much to collect analysable data *per se* as to provide the basis for the design of empirical instruments which have salience and relevance as well as being amenable to conventional analysis.

Research on female aggression began with the collection of accounts in a variety of contexts and involved mainly lower-class teenage girls, some of whom were members of "distinct" sub-cultural groups (for example, "punks", "skinheads"). They were interviewed using a small tape-recorder and accounts were subsequently transcribed into a computer data base. This allows voluminous material to be coded for content and context, and for recurring themes, situations and events to be identified.

The most striking feature of this initial account-elicitation stage was that the role played by females in youth cultures appeared to be far from "marginal". No longer did they seem to be locked into what has been termed "structured secondariness" and no longer was their culture so insulated against outside inspection.

This increased centrality can be detected in a number of ways. First, in most social settings there is less spatial demarcation between girls and boys. Unlike in the days of the Teddy boys, females tend not to huddle together around the peripheries of dance-hall bars. A more important indicator is, perhaps, the pattern of social talk and exchange – a pattern which is less concerned with sexuality and more to do with shared problems such as unemployment or who buys the next half pint of lager. When the Sex Pistols sang "Sex is boring, sex is boring" and when the myth of youth affluence was finally laid to rest the conditions for more balanced gender roles within lower-class youth culture were established.

There is room here to present only a few examples drawn from a considerable volume of tape-recorded material. However, a number of interesting points can be highlighted. Younger girls (under 16 or so) tended to think that, although fighting was wrong, it was still essential to stand up for oneself and to use violence if necessary. Schoolgirls listed racist remarks, insults to the family and jealousy over boyfriends as common forms of provocation. Highest on their list, however, was "rumour-spreading" or sexual insult. It was agreed that it was wholly justifiable to use physical violence in the defence of one's sexual reputation: "If someone slags you off – calls you a tart or something you've got to be able to do something about it."

Older girls differed in the primary reasons they gave as the causes of fights. They fought more often with complete strangers than with peers with whom there had been a steady build-up of animosity. Justifications offered often involved a sense that a particular "territory" had been violated or that someone had made a direct challenge by staring or laughing at the girl involved.

> I get girls and blokes who just keep staring continuously or if I roll up my sleeves and they see my tattoos they start staring again and that gets me narked, it gets me really mad and I say to my husband, "If they keep staring I'm going to ask them what they are looking at", and he says, "Leave it, don't start trouble", and I'll sit there and give them a few looks back, like a warning and if they still don't stop I go over and see them, have a word and sit back down, and if they still carry on, then I drag them outside.

This kind of situation arose quite frequently in a local "punk" pub, when the members of another sub-cultural group (Teds, for instance) would arrive to "take over" and oust the punks from "their" pub. These older girls seldom gave a sexual insult as a reason for starting a fight. Perhaps they are no longer bothered by what remains a highly sensitive area with the more insecure, younger girls. Certainly, at this later stage, the girls seemed to be less influenced by their male contemporaries.

The two groups also differed in their general attitudes towards open displays of aggression. While all the girls agreed that the ability to fight was necessary in order to maintain self-respect and status amongst one's peers, the younger ones could not summon the same enthusiasm for fighting as expressed by the older, more experienced girls: "I don't enjoy fighting that much, but if I have to, I will . . ."; "I don't think you choose to fight but you've got to fight if someone is going to pick on you . . . ." Often closely identifying with a particular sub-cultural group (skinheads, punks, or whatever) the older girls described the excitement and enjoyment involved: "I do [enjoy fighting], I love it, I get all scared but as soon as I'm into it . . . You let all your feelings out when you're kicking someone and gets rid of your depression. All the things you've had arguments about . . . ."

The ambiguity of schoolgirls' feelings about aggression often makes interviewing them on the subject very difficult. Angela McRobbie has commented upon the seeming desire of girls to mislead the researcher on every possible occasion, and our experience with younger girls bears this out. The girls' conflict lies in the desire to express aggressive feelings while at the same time being aware that overt aggression is not generally accepted as a feminine characteristic. The older girls, however, displayed little inhibition in describing aggressive encounters, and were not disturbed by being described as "unfeminine". This attitude is often reflected in styles of dress and comments about traditional concepts of femininity.

> Getting on for two years, I've been a skinhead. . . . It's different – it's good – like [wolf whistles] down the road when you've got the pencil skirt on – I don't like that sort of thing. I hear, "Ah, you stupid bitch." I love that and I say, "Fuck off, you cunt", you know, I don't care . . . .
>
> I was in Selfridges toilets once and I got kicked out because they thought I was a boy. . . . I had to get out – it was funny . . . .
>
> This bloke says to me, "Come here", and I says, "What?" and he says, "Are you a female or a male?" I says, "Female." So he says to this other bloke, "Give me 50p", because they bet on me as to what I was . . . .
>
> Birds are not supposed to fight, are they? . . . Because they are supposed to be all ladylike and wear skirts and nice high heels and go flirting around and things like that, aren't they?
>
> As long as the bloke I'm going out with thinks of me as a bird, that's OK . . . .

Another difficulty facing the researcher in eliciting acounts of actual fights is that of allowing for inevitable exaggerations. Research into female aggression must depend largely upon oral accounts, because girls have seldom used the public arenas available to men for the expression of hostility. While their male peers fight in bars or on football terraces, girls tend to fight in private. This makes the witnessing of female aggression very difficult; hence the researcher's dependence on the accounts girls themselves offer.

The accounts offered by girls contained many embellishments and in many cases levels of violence were seriously exaggerated. In this sense a number of our informants were very similar to their male contemporaries, using distorted accounts of their aggressive exploits as part of the business of image management and the establishment of a tough reputation. In extreme cases, a large amount of manifest (and checkable) "bullshit" was introduced. This quite clearly indicates the lack of taboos about expressing physical aggression in these contexts. But there seemed to be an important sex difference here as well. Within groups of boys a certain level of embellishment and exaggeration is generally accepted. They conspire, in a sense, to accept conventional rhetoric because it makes fairly mundane events sound more exciting. But this pattern of distortion is itself rule-governed. Pure bullshit, distortion which goes beyond the acceptable limits, will generally be deemed out of order and the perpetrator exposed to derision or some other sanction. In the case of girls we detected no such limits. So, whilst their *action* might be constrained by social rules and a tacit sense of acceptable conduct, their social *talk* about the action seemed not to be. We suggest that this might be owing to the fact that such talk is generally less frequent and routine among girls and is less tied to personal experience of aggressive encounters.

One very striking feature of the accounts offered was the way in which girls acknowledged the existence of a traditional stereotype of female aggression, and indicated that it might be representative of the way some women fight. But they strongly denied its applicability to them personally. "Bitch fighting", as it is called, went on, but not one girl would admit regularly using these tactics herself. Punching and kicking were the tactics the girls, in both age groups, described themselves as using. Scratching and biting were modes of fighting considered to be low in status and high in personal injury, and were therefore placed firmly outside the boundaries of acceptable fighting behavior.

R: I had a fight with this bird and she tried to cover her hair – I had no hair – and you scratch – and you don't do much. That's not what I call a fight – I like to get my foot in or a head butt or something like that.

Interviewer: So why do you reckon girls fight like that?

R: They always do . . . it's because they don't know what fighting's about.

We should emphasize here that our material is derived from lower-class girls, and particularly, in the case of older girls, from those firmly attached to

Dave and Mary go to the disco.

While Dave is buying some drinks, Mike asks Mary to dance.

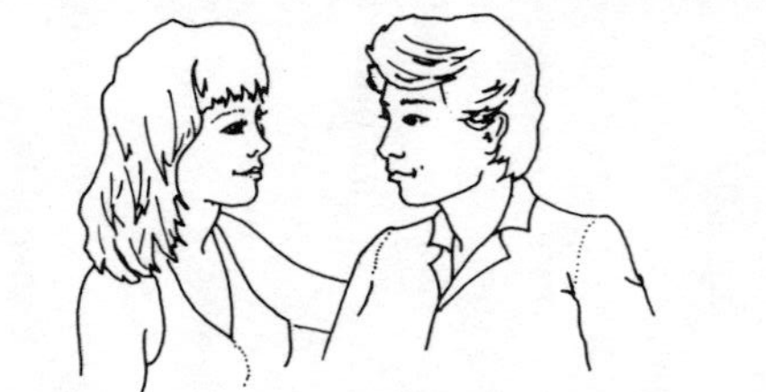

Dave sees them dancing together and suggests to Mike that they step outside and discuss the matter.

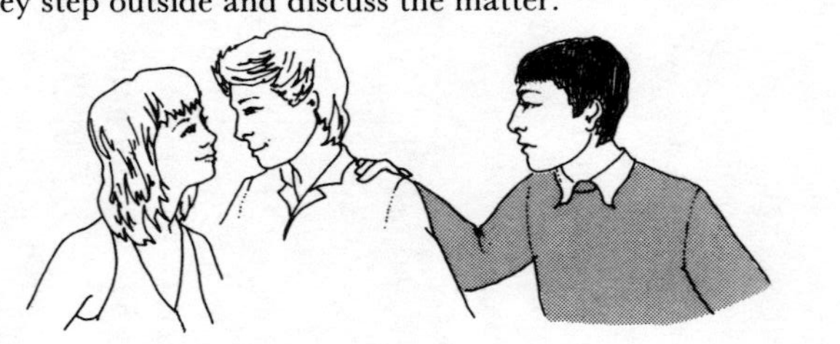

	Mike punches Dave.
	Mike apologizes to Dave.
	Mike refuses to discuss the matter.
	Mike gives Dave a push.
	Mike leaves the disco.
	Mike produces a weapon and threatens Dave with it.
	Mike asks some of his friends to help him out of the situation.
	Mike starts scratching Dave and pulling his hair.
	Mike insults Dave.
	Mike complains to the disco-manager.
	Mike threatens to hit Dave.

What else do you think would happen?

....

....

Figure 1 Example from Conflict–Event Matrix 1

youth-culture groups. Our contact with upper-class girls suggests a large class difference with respect to ideas of femininity and the role of aggression in everyday life. This difference, which has clear historical roots, is now of particular interest given the increasing centrality of lower-class girls in contemporary youth culture.

A sense of rules and conventions relating to aggressive behavior does not emerge from girls' accounts with the same clarity as from boys'. Further work, however, which used a more specific method, was very revealing.

To explore females' concepts of aggression more systematically and to provide a basis of cross-sex comparisons, a technique was developed which had much in common with the repertory-grid method. The aim was to identify and quantify underlying conceptual schemas which relate to behavior in a range of conflict situations. Accounts offered by both male and female informants, contained in the computer data base, were carefully examined and recurring conflict situations and behaviors were identified. These were subsequently embodied in a "conflict-event matrix" (CEM), which, while allowing empirical identification of underlying conceptual schemas relating to aggression, was also in sympathy with an ethogenic perspective.

On the basis of their recurrence and salience, 15 situations were selected from accounts offered by male and female teenagers (median age 16 years). On the same grounds, 11 categories of behavior were selected, but also with regard to their applicability and relevance across all of the situations. Thus, items relating to retreat, verbal abuse, the calling of an authority figure, use of weapon, and so on, were included. Each situation was summarized in simple two- or three-part cartoon scenarios. The behavior categories were tailored to apply to each specific situation whilst still retaining their cross-situational nature. An example from the CEM is shown in figure 1.

Of the 15 situations, 6 involved male characters, 7 involved females and the remaining 2 concerned conflicts between males and females. The scenarios and behavior categories were shown to 81 female and 51 male respondents, who were asked to rate the appropriateness of each behavior in each of the given situations. The use of the term "appropriate" was important in this context, since a major concern was with identifying tacit rule structures. Since social rules are viewed as governing the propriety of action in specific situations, judgments of appropriateness, it was hypothesized, should yield data which reflected underlying rule structures.

Several techniques exist for examining matrix data of the type produced by the CEM. Traditionally, various forms of factor analysis have been used to determine the underlying dimensionality. Increasingly, however, multi-dimensional scaling (MDS) techniques have been adopted. Such methods have been found to be more appropriate to this type of psychological data, and the resulting dimensions are often found to be more readily interpretable than those deriving from a principal-components analysis.

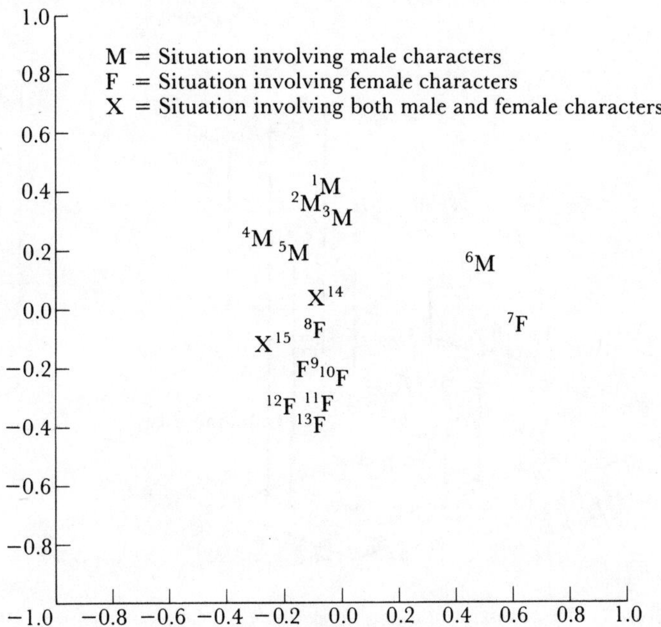

Figure 2 Multidimensional scaling of inter-situation difference (male subjects), Conflict–Event Matrix 1

The rectangular matrices of data for each subject (15 scenarios by 11 behavior ratings) were first transformed into two square Euclidean distance matrices. The first of these contained the distances between scenarios across all behavior ratings. The second was a matrix of the distances between behavior categories across all scenarios. These matrices were subsequently analysed separately for each of the two sexes, using Indscal (Individual Differences Multidimensional Scaling).

The most common application of Indscal is the examination, for a set of objects or stimuli, of the distances between them, given their rating on a set of scales by the subjects. Analysis of the distances between the situations, given the responses on the behavior-rating scales, conforms closely with this approach. Figure 2 shows a two-dimensional solution based on inter-situation distances obtained from male respondents. A clear separation between those situations involving male characters and those involving females can be observed.

The two situations involving both male and female characters lie between the two major clusters. Results obtained from female subjects are substantially similar, although in this case the two situations involving both sexes clustered along with those situations involving males only. We can conclude

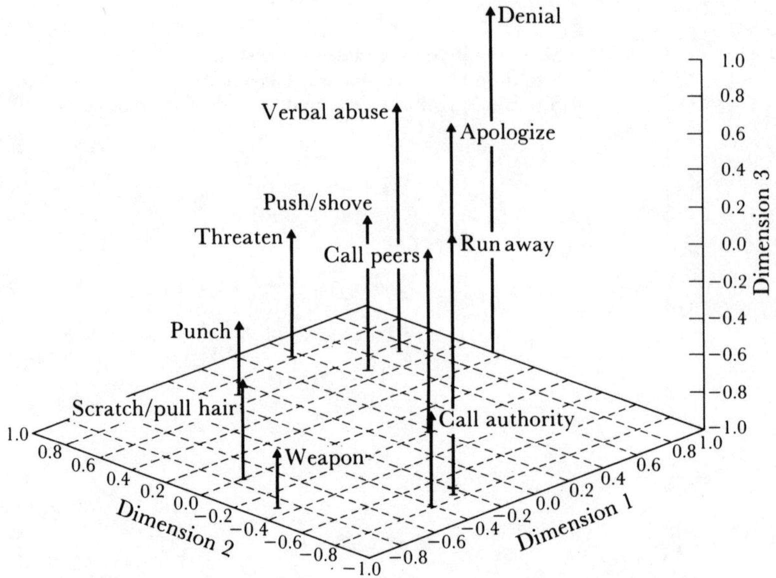

Figure 3 Multidimensional scaling for male subjects, Conflict–Event Matrix 1

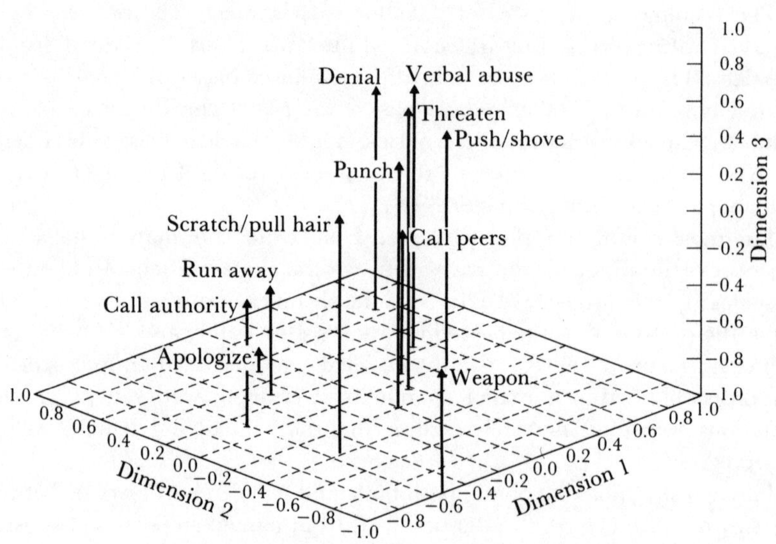

Figure 4 Multidimensional scaling for female subjects, Conflict–Event Matrix 1

from this analysis that both males and females discriminate between situations involving male and female actors in terms of the appropriateness of action by those actors.

A second application of MDS was used to examine the underlying dimensionality of the distances between the behavior categories. This approach is closer to the normal use of factor analysis, the aim being to determine the structure of judgments made by the subjects across all the scenarios. Dimensions resulting from this application can be treated as "conceptual schemas" relating to the appropriate resolution of conflict in the range of situations under consideration.

For both male and female respondents it was found that three-dimensional solutions were optimal in terms of the variance accounted for. Figures 3 and 4 illustrate graphically the results for males and females. The average correlation between respondents' individual data and the group space defined by the three dimensions was 0.73 for males and 0.69 for females. These results were quite satisfactory and indicated a fairly high level of consensus within both groups.

Turning first to the plot for male subjects, the loadings of behavior scales along the first dimension are such that an interpretation in terms of tacit rules seems highly appropriate. At the negative end we observe a cluster of actions regularly deemed to be "out of order" by male informants: using weapons; scratching or pulling hair; calling authority. Conversely, at the positive extreme we find actions generally *prescribed* in conflict situations: denial (of offence or commission of alleged act); verbal abuse or reply; threatening; pushing and shoving. Examination of the mean scores on the scales, based on notions of appropriateness, confirms this interpretation.

At the mid-point of this first dimension lie items related to calling for help from friends, punching and apologizing. Again, such loadings are consistent with previous qualitative research, such actions being prescribed in certain circumstances whilst proscribed in others.

The second dimension obtained from the males' data is significantly correlated with the first ($r = 0.64, p < 0.05$). Inspection of the loadings reveals that, although this dimension has a similar sense of "rules", certain "tougher" actions load more towards the "in order" pole. The use of a weapon is less proscribed, whilst punching is quite definitely prescribed. This suggests a framework of rules for dealing with tough situations. Even here, however, running away is still very much out of order, along with calling authority and apologizing. Thus we might suppose that these "tough rules" would apply to situations where a considerable amount of pride or reputation was at stake.

The third dimension is unrelated to the first two and can be given a quite different interpretation. At the negative pole we find a grouping of items which involve some damage or potential damage to an opponent – punching, scratching, calling on authority, using a weapon. At the positive end are items associated with non-harmful actions – apologizing, denial. This dimension is quite independent of a "violent-non-violent" or "cowardly–brave" continuum owing to the loadings of "running away" and "calling authority".

Thus, we may conclude that the three dimensions reflect a strong conceptual schema, tacitly held by males, which involves not only a sense of rules to guide action in various contexts, but also a concern for the effects of actions on an opponent.

Turning now to the results for female subjects, the most striking feature is the similarity of the first dimension with that observed for males. In fact there is a very high correlation between the two ($r = 0.86$, $p < 0.01$), and a very similar interpretation can also be made. This similarity was not anticipated. Whilst we expected some kind of "general rules" continuum to be present, one so closely resembling that derived from the data for male subjects was quite surprising. We are led to conclude from this that female subjects have equally "orderly" conceptual schemas for attributing a sense of appropriateness to actions in aggressive encounters.

The second dimension, however, was unlike that appearing in the three-dimensional solution for male respondents. Instead, it can be seen as a "hard–soft" or "violent–non-violent" dimension, the acts increasing in physical violence toward the negative pole. The third dimension, in contrast, is very similar to the males' "tough rules" ($r = 0.76$, $p < 0.01$). Note here, however, that scratching is less forcibly proscribed.

The major sex difference therefore, appears to lie in the contrast between the males' third dimension, "harm to other", and the females' second dimension, "hard–soft". Whilst males and females seem to share a distinctive rule framework, females pay more attention to the degree of violence occasioned by the actions, while males consider non-violent acts such as calling the police to be of equal potential harm to an opponent.

Whilst these contrasts are very revealing, it is not possible to pinpoint from this analysis the precise sources of variance between the two sexes. Differences, for example, could be due to male and female subjects responding differentially to either events with male characters, female characters or to both sets of events. What was required, therefore, was an examination of the possible interaction between sex of subject and sex of the characters in the situations. This was undertaken first by computing inter-behavior distances separately across male and female situations and secondly by using a log-linear modelling approach.

From the four sets of three-dimensional solutions obtained in this way (male and female subjects by male and female scenarios) very little difference between male and female subjects was observed with respect to situations involving female characters. A substantial difference, however, was apparent with respect to situations involving male characters. The principal source of difference appeared to lie in the third dimension, which, in the case of male

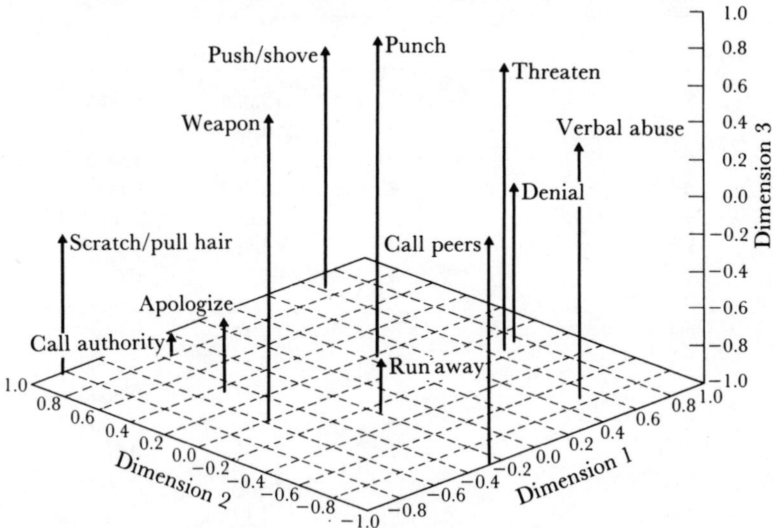

Figure 5 Multidimensional scaling for male subjects of situations involving male characters, Conflict–Event Matrix 1

subjects, could be interpreted as a "macho" dimension. This is shown graphically in figure 5.

This dimension was of particular interest since it reflected well many of the features of males' accounts found in previous research (see Marsh, 1982). A distinct duality of rhetoric had been observed in which routine aggressive behavior was seen as, on the one hand, orderly and constrained by tacit social rules, and, on the other, injurious and violent. From figure 5 we can observe this same duality, two of the dimensions relating well to rule structures, whilst the third suggests that all aggressive acts are conceptually similar and prescribed.

On the basis of inspection of the MDS results it was hypothesized that the major source of differences in conceptual schemas between the two sexes would be found in their attributions of appropriateness to the behavior of males. This was tested using a log-linear analysis of the raw data obtained from male and female subjects (see Everitt, 1973). The variables involved in this analysis were sex of subject (*S*); sex of character in the situation (*C*); behavior category (*B*); and category of appropriateness attributed to the behavior (*A*). The 10-point ratings of appropriateness were reduced to three categories to aid analysis and improve clarity. To test the effects of this reduction, MDS was performed on distances obtained from the reduced data set. The results were almost identical with those obtained from the full set.

Table 1 shows the results obtained with all variables included in the

Table 1 Partial association of factors from Conflict–Event Matrix 1

Effect	*d.f.*	χ^2	*p*
S	1	813.05	0.0000
C	2	2916.44	0.0000
B	10	0.00	1.0000
A	4	1633.76	0.0000
SC	2	0.01	0.9951
SB	10	6.88	0.7369
SA	4	93.61	0.0000
CB	20	0.58	1.0000
CA	8	15.47	0.0505
BA	40	1565.81	0.0000
SCB	20	5.41	0.9995
SCA	8	14.56	0.0684
SBA	40	81.39	0.0001
CBA	80	544.68	0.0000
SCBA	80	109.19	0.0167

S = sex of subject.
C = sex of character.
B = behavior category.
A = appropriateness of behavior.

analysis. Partial associations of the factors were produced using the BMDP4F statistical computer program. Each probability is calculated as the difference between the full *K*th-order model and that which excludes the specified effect. (*K* is the number of factors in the effect.) Of principal interest here is the significance of the saturated model *SCBA*. This indicates that, given the provided set of behavioral categories, both sexes differentiated between events involving male characters and those involving females in attributing scores.

To locate this interaction more specifically, a further analysis was performed in which the data were "conditioned" with respect to the factor of sex of character. In this treatment, data for each value of the factor are treated separately. (The situations involving characters of both sexes were ignored.) Table 2 shows effects for data including only female characters and table 3 shows those resulting from analysis of data relating to male characters.

On the basis of the MDS results it was hypothesized that log-linear analysis of the data relating to female characters would not yield a significant three-factor interaction *SBA*, whilst similar analysis of the data relating to male characters would. This is precisely what was found. The interaction between subject sex, behavioral items and attributed appropriateness is highly significant for situations involving male characters ($p < 0.0001$), whilst for situations involving female characters there is no significant interaction.

Table 2 Partial association of factors from Conflict–Event Matrix 1: data conditioned for level "female" of character–sex variable

Effect	*d.f.*	χ^2	*p*
S	1	379.42	0.0000
B	10	0.00	1.0000
A	4	828.13	0.0000
SB	10	8.23	0.6060
SA	4	68.23	0.0000
BA	40	1092.75	0.0000
SBA	40	49.34	0.1478

S, *B*, *A* as table 1.

Table 3 Partial association of factors from Conflict–Event Matrix 1: data conditioned for level "male" of character–sex variable

Effect	*d.f.*	χ^2	*p*
S	1	325.22	0.0000
B	10	0.00	1.0000
A	4	632.84	0.0000
SB	10	2.48	0.9912
SA	4	31.08	0.0000
BA	40	700.41	0.0000
SBA	40	89.63	0.0000

S, *B*, *A* as table 1.

A further analysis was performed using this technique to confirm the finding, discussed earlier, that in their responses both sexes differentiated between situations involving males and situations involving female. Distinct clusters of both situation types were obtained from matrices of inter-situation distances, no overlap between the two character-sex clusters being found for either male or female subjects. On the basis of this it was hypothesized that a significant interaction *CBA* should be found with the data conditioned for the two values of sex of character in the situations. Tables 4 and 5 show the effects obtained in this way. The first of these was derived from the reduced table containing only data from male subjects, whilst the second derived from female-subject data. It is clear that in both cases the interactions are highly significant ($p < 0.001$), confirming the conclusions drawn from the MDS analysis.

The work described so far relied heavily on accounts from lower-class informants, and the CEMs were administered largely to lower-class respondents. The scenarios themselves would not have had much relevance to

Table 4 Partial association of factors from Conflict–Event Matrix 1: data conditioned for level "male" of subject–sex variable

Effect	*d.f.*	χ^2	*p*
C	2	1813.52	0.0000
B	10	0.00	1.0000
A	4	1281.55	0.0000
CB	20	1.13	1.0000
CA	8	28.17	0.0004
BA	40	1112.42	0.0000
CBA	80	431.78	0.0000

C, B, A as table 1.

Table 5 Partial association of factors from Conflict–Event Matrix 1: data conditioned for level "female" of subject–sex variable

Effect	*d.f.*	χ^2	*p*
C	2	1102.56	0.0000
B	10	0.00	1.0000
A	4	438.68	0.0000
CB	20	0.12	1.0000
CA	8	3.06	0.9304
BA	40	534.87	0.0000
CBA	80	222.92	0.0000

C, B, A as table 1.

respondents from other classes. There was thus the possibility that conceptual schemas relating to aggression might provide evidence not only of precise sex differences (and similarities), but also of class differences and class–sex interactions.

To explore these patterns of variation, further source material in the form of accounts was required in order to develop a CEM which had relevance and salience to both lower- and upper-class males and females. Numerous accounts were collected in local schools, and, unlike in the previous study, what we might call more "ordinary" informants were involved. These were interviewed individually and in small groups. The voluminous material was again transcribed into a data base and examined using specially developed software.

From this material a second CEM was designed, and administered to a larger sample of teenagers representing both sexes and classes. Here the scenarios were presented in short-story form, rather than cartoons, and the range of situations and some of the behavior categories were somewhat

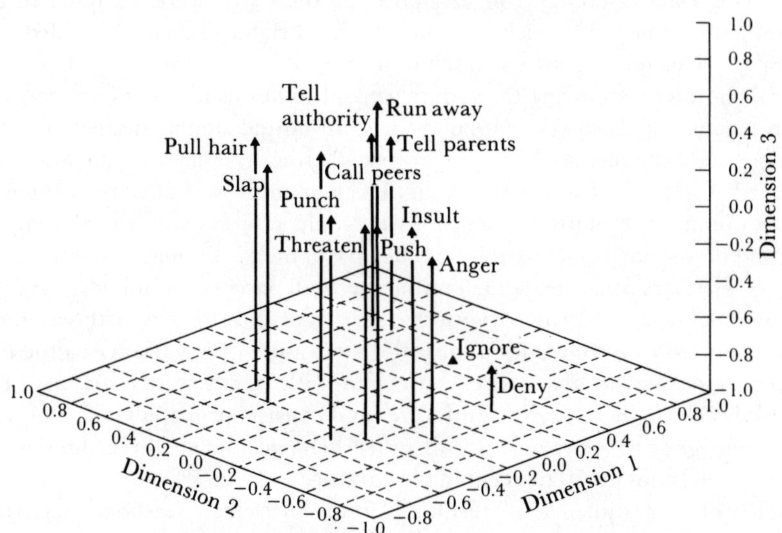

Figure 6 Multidimensional scaling for male subjects, Conflict–Event Matrix 2

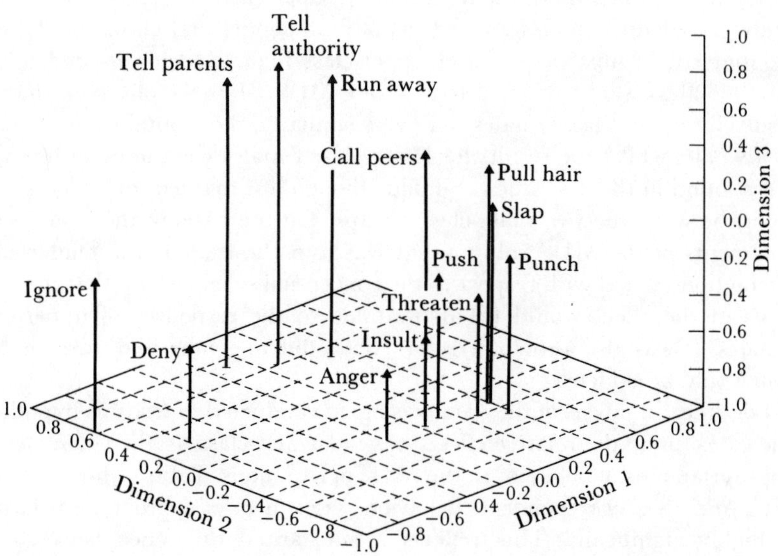

Figure 7 Multidimensional scaling for female subjects, Conflict–Event Matrix 2

different. Data obtained from responses to the CEM were analysed in the manner described previously, except that the variable of class was added.

Space does not permit us to detail all the results of this study. Figures 6 and 7, however, show the three-dimensional solutions for males and females (irrespective of class). We can again see substantial similarities between the conceptual schemas held by the two sexes, although they are not so clearly related as in the first study, which employed mainly lower-class respondents.

Examining the plotted dimensions for male subjects we can see that the second dimension is most strongly reflective of the traditional rules structure, with behaviors such as telling authority and parents, running away and scratching being contrasted with anger, denial, insulting and threatening. This dimension accounts for almost the same amount of variance as the first where assertive behaviors are contrasted with non-assertive actions. The third dimension is less easy to interpret and consists principally of a contrast between ignoring/denying and all other behaviors. The three dimensions together account for 59 per cent of the variance.

The plot of dimensions resulting from the female respondents' data suggests rather different conceptual schemas from those found in the earlier study. The first dimension suggests an assertive–non-assertive continuum, whilst the second reflects a violent–non-violent schema. The third dimension, however, is very similar to the "rules" dimension found earlier. (The three dimensions account for 67 per cent of the variance in the original data.)

The differences between the results from the first and second studies, it was felt, could be due to the inclusion of upper-class subjects in the second study. To identify the relative effects of both gender and class, the data for the four sub-groups (lower- and upper-class males and lower- and upper-class females) were subjected to separate MDS. Here we observed that the results for upper-class females were very similar to those obtained for females as a whole, whilst the results for lower-class females were more in line with those found in the first study. Similar, though less marked, differences were found between the two male class groups. On the basis of these subjective judgments of the MDS solutions, it was hypothesized that a gender–class interaction existed with respect to the conceptual schemas and that the main locus of the effect would be attributable to the responses of upper-class females. It was also anticipated that effects due to gender and class on their own would be evident.

Log-linear analysis of the data was again conducted to test this hypothesis and to examine the relative effects of gender and class on the assessment of appropriateness of behavior in the range of situations. Table 6 shows that the effect *SBA* (Sex of respondent, Behavior, Assessment of appropriate behavior) is highly significant. This reflects a substantial difference between the observed and expected frequencies in the three-way table. The effect *CBA* (Class, Behavior, Appropriateness) however, is also highly significant, as is

Table 6 Partial association of factors from Conflict–Event Matrix 2

Effect	*d.f.*	χ^2	*p*
SCA	2	50.42	0.0000
CBA	24	227.33	0.0000
SCBA	24	50.64	0.0013

S = sex of subject.
C = social class.
B = behavior category.
A = appropriateness of behavior.

the interaction *SCBA* (*S*, sex of subject; *C*, class; *B*, behavior category; *A*, appropriateness of behavior).

Table 7 shows the interaction *CBA* for the two sexes separately. Although the association is highly significant in both cases, the effect is far greater for females than for males. Thus we can conclude that upper- and lower-class females differ from each other in their responses more than do lower- and upper-class males. The precise nature of the effect was identified by constructing sub-tables for each behavior item (i.e. conditioning by behavior) and calculating the relative chi squares for each cell. It was found that in the case of the "insult" item, for example, the bulk of the interaction was accounted for in the upper-class-female low-appropriateness cell. Upper-class females, it seemed, assessed the appropriateness of insulting another person, across all the scenarios, lower than did respondents in the other three sub-groups. Similar effects were found for the other assertive and aggressive behaviors, with the exception of items normally deemed "out of order" in the traditional rule framework. Upper-class females tended, for example, to rate "telling parents" and "calling peers" as more appropriate across the range of situations than did the other groups of respondents. The same held for the appropriateness of "pulling hair".

In a further analysis the data were analysed separately (i.e. conditioned) for each character-sex category. Here it was found that, when males featured in the scenarios, there was a significant interaction between gender and class on the assessment of appropriate behaviors. When the characters were females, the interaction was not at all significant. Inspection of the marginal sub-tables showed that the bulk of the first interaction was accounted for by upper-class girls rating the appropriateness of tough and assertive behaviors by males lower than did the other three sub-groups of respondents. This fits well with the finding from the first study that gender differences were greatest when the behavior of males, rather than of females, was being assessed.

These results would seem to have quite important implications. Although clear gender differences were found to exist, those attributable to social class

Table 7 *Partial association of factors from Conflict–Event Matrix 2: data conditioned by subject–sex variable*

Effect	*d.f.*	χ^2	*p*
For female subjects: *CBA*	24	210.18	0.0000
For male subjects: *CBA*	24	73.32	0.0000

C, *B*, *A* as table 6.

were also highly significant. The fact that strong gender–class interactions were also found suggests that the relationship between aspects of aggression and gender might be considerably more complex than earlier studies have suggested.

To explore possible sources of mediation between gender and social class, on the one hand, and conceptual schemas of aggression, on the other, an attempt was made to develop salient measures of both the sources of self-esteem and the extent to which esteem was gained in particular areas of everyday life.

Although self-esteem has certainly not been ignored by researchers since James (1890) first placed it within the province of psychology, there remains a basic lack of agreement on both conceptual and methodological levels. This, however, has not hindered the production of ways of measuring self-esteem. As Wylie's review (1974) indicates, the number of self-esteem measures currently in use is extremely large. Most of these have been developed within the attitude framework and involve the construction of Likert-type scales. Few of the empirical findings have proved robust enough to withstand either methodological criticisms or replications (witness, for instance, the contradictory findings about the effects of sex and race on self-esteem). With the exception of projective techniques, almost all the measuring-instruments assess self-esteem through reliance on subjects' feelings about themselves in situations which are chosen *a priori* by the researcher. Subjects are therefore required to respond by evaluating themselves in areas which may not be salient to them.

Our research on self-esteem has tried to avoid this pitfall by again using a two-stage methodology, starting with group discussions with samples of adolescents to ascertain what situations and social contexts were salient to them. Based on these interviews, two questionnaires were developed: the Aspiration Measure (AM), indicating how important the context or relationship was for the individual; and the Perceived Achievement Measure (PAM), assessing how successful he or she was in their achievement. Following James's formula "self-esteem = pretensions/successes" (1890), our investigation was concerned with both aspects of self-esteem. We then looked at the links between the sources and degrees of achievement of self-esteem and the scores on the CEM.

The interview-sample was drawn from several secondary schools in Oxford, and consisted of over 100 young people of both sexes, aged 14–18. Both upper- and lower-class youngsters were well represented in the sample. Group discussions involving 4–10 subjects per group were held during class time, and tapes, transcribed and finally coded by key words according to content (i.e. theme, situation and relationship). From these codings we were able to select the most frequently occurring themes and situations and these were incorporated into the two questionnaires. The AM consisted of 26 items covering the evaluations by others which adolescents regarded as most important to them: for instance,

> How important is the following to you? . . .
>
> That teachers approve of you? . . .
> That your parents take your views seriously? . . .
> That your friends think you are clever and intelligent?

Subjects were asked to respond on a five-point scale ranging from "Not at all" to "Very important".

The second questionnaire, the PAM, was also derived from the transcribed material. 96 questions dealing with interactions with others comprised this measure. A five-point scale was again used to measure the subjects' responses. Examples of the questions are: "How often do you apologize to your parents even when you know you are right?"; "How much do teachers pick on you?"; "How much do your friends tease you because of the music you like?"

These two questionnaires were administered, about two weeks apart, to the sample of 233 who had completed the CEM. The results were subjected to factor analyses using oblique rotation. The AM yielded seven significant factors, accounting for 57.9 per cent of the variance. Three of the factors (31.4 per cent) were associated with the family context. This supports previous findings (Coopersmith, 1967; Rosenberg, 1963, 1965; Bachman, 1982) demonstrating the central role of parents in their children's self-esteem.

The other factors from the AM involved peer relationships (independence from others, social affiliation and friendship, heterosexual relationships) and intellectual evaluation. These are summarized in table 8. Although both gender and class differences were found in relation to several of these factors, these will not be reported here in detail.

The oblique factor structure underlying the 96-item PAM indicated 17 significant dimensions, accounting for 61.5 per cent of the variance. Of these factors, six focused on achievement in relationships with parents; nine,

Table 8 Oblique rotated factors and factor loadings for Aspiration Measure items (N = 233)

Item no.	Item	Loading
	How important is the following to you?	
	Factor 1 Pleasing mother/parents (21.1%)	
1	That you feel your mother trusts you?	0.42
3	That you try to please your mother?	0.90
10	That you try to please your parents?	0.65
	Factor 2 Intellectual evaluation (8.3%)	
15	That you think of yourself as clever and intelligent?	0.77
22	That your friends think you are clever and intelligent?	0.62
	Factor 3 Heterosexual relationships (7.8%)	
16	That people think you are attractive to the opposite sex?	0.65
25	That you have a chance to meet and spend time with the opposite sex?	0.69
	Factor 4 Social affiliation (6.5%)	
14	That you can tell your friends how you feel?	0.54
19	That you are able to argue with friends and not lose them as friends?	0.50
21	That you and your friends get on well with your best frend and her/his other friends?	0.59
26	That people of the same age from your own or other schools like you?	0.42
	Factor 5 Parental support in arguments (5.4%)	
2	That your mother backs you in an argument against other family members?	0.74
6	That your father supports you in an argument against other family members?	0.78
	Factor 6 Father/parental disinterest (4.9%)	
5	That your father shows concern and encourages you?	−0.60
7	That your father takes your views seriously?	−0.82
9	That your parents show concern and encourage you?	−0.51
17	That your parents take your views seriously?	−0.60
	Factor 7 Independence from peer group (4.0%)	
18	That people think you can take care of yourself in a fight?	−0.44
23	That your friends think you are the same as they are?	−0.43
24	That you are not seen as teacher's pet by school friends?	−0.62

Percentages in parentheses are the common variances of the factors.

relationships with peers; and one, relationships with teachers. The remaining factor concerned intellectual evaluations. These 17 factors were further factor-analysed, using the same oblique rotation. Ten of the first-order factors were incorporated into four higher-order factors, which accounted for 67.6 per cent of the second-order variance, as shown in table 9.

Table 9 Oblique rotated higher order factors and factor loadings on Perceived Achievement Measure (N = 233)

First-order factor	*Factor loading*
Higher-order factor 1	
Dutifulness towards parents (21.6%)	
1 Guilt towards parents	0.61
2 Concern not to upset parents	0.55
Higher-order factor 2	
Rejection by peers (17.8%)	
3 Teasing by peers	−0.51
4 Snobbishness	−0.61
Higher-order factor 3	
Negative peer regard (16.0%)	
5 Intellectual evaluation	−0.67
6 Lack of sexual attractiveness	0.42
Higher-order factor 4	
Positive authority evaluation (12.1%)	
7 Teacher evaluation	0.43
8 Independence from peers	0.40

Percentages in parentheses are the common variances of the higher-order factors.

Once again, concern over the relationship with parents emerged as the dominant dimension, accounting for 22 per cent of the higher-order common variance. This factor involved concern for parents' feelings and guilt about misbheavior. We have given this factor the label "dutifulness". Both sex and class differences were found here. Girls and working-class youth gave significantly higher scores on dutifulness to parents.

The second factor involved the respondents' impressions of peer evaluations. Both lower-order factors (reputation for snobbishness and being teased by peers) load negatively on this dimension and were infrequently reported for all groups.

The third higher-order factor was more complex, with first-order factors loading on both poles. At one end we find positive intellectual evaluation, whilst the other pole represents lack of sexual attractiveness. Boys were significantly more concerned about being sexually unattractive, whilst girls indicated significantly less success in being evaluated as clever and intelligent. The latter was also true for lower-class youth.

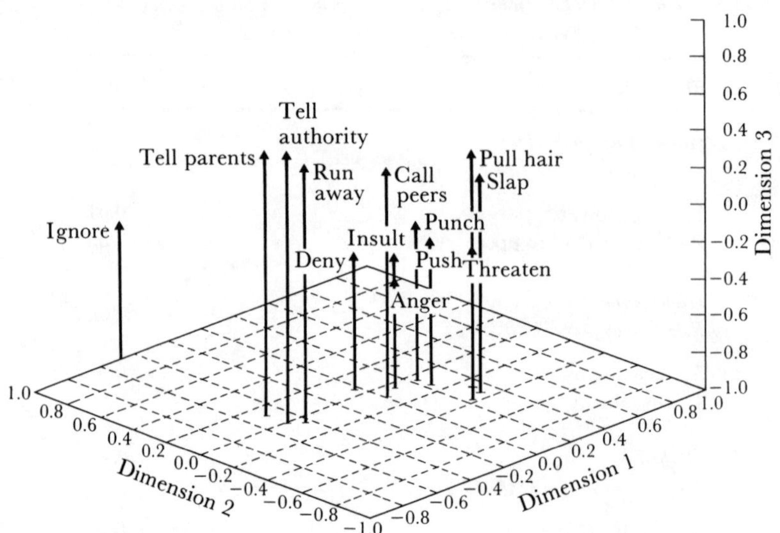

Figure 8 Multidimensional scaling for all subjects, Conflict–Event Matrix 2

The fourth factor, shows a positive association between teacher evaluation and independence of peer presure. This higher-order factor indicates the achievement of self-esteem through the evaluation of those in authority. Girls reported significantly greater success in this than did boys, but social-class differences were not found on this factor.

Our concern at this stage was with the relationships between subjects' scores on the AM and PAM measures and their responses to the CEM (i.e. to what extent were measures of self-esteem related to conceptual schemas of aggression?). The CEM data for males and females of both social classes were now subjected to a single MDS, in contrast to the separate analyses according to sex and class reported above. The three-dimensional solution produced is shown in figure 8.

The dimensions shown in figure 8 are slightly less easy to interpret than those found in analyses of data sub-sets, reflecting a higher level of variation within the full set of data. None the less, interesting correlations were found between factor scores on the AM and PAM and subject weights on the CEM dimensions.

Significant relationships between PAM higher-order factor 4 (independence from peers and perceived positive evaluation by teachers) and the three dimensions of the CEM were found. CEM dimension 1 focuses on confrontation at the positive pole and retreat and passivity at the opposite end. The significant negative correlation obtained demonstrates that those who perceive themselves as independent of peer pressure and also as liked by teachers more commonly see retreating from conflict with peers to be appropriate. These youngsters, having greater success with impression management in relation to authority, view passivity as more acceptable in peer interactions. Girls on average were found to have significantly higher scores on PAM factor 4.

The CEM dimension 2, which had "ignore" at the positive pole and "pull hair/slap" at the negative end, was also found to be significantly related to PAM factor 4. Subjects with high weights on this dimension were those located towards the positive end of PAM factor 4, whilst those with low weights felt that they had a greater reputation for standing up for themselves.

Those youngsters whose self-esteem is invested in their reputation for fighting are likely to perceive even stereotypically female ways of fighting as more status-enhancing than ignoring a conflict.

CEM dimension 3, which can be labelled "rule-governed assertive behaviour", is likewise associated with the positive pole of PAM factor 4. It appears that individuals for whom the conceptual schema reflecting underlying social rules is most salient see themselves as independent of peer pressures and positively evaluated by their teachers. They tend to proscribe acts such as calling for help from authority figures and running away, and prescribe constrained assertive behaviours. These ideas of appropriate responses in conflict situations, however, cannot be attributed simply to the need for peer acceptance.

A similar finding emerged with regard to the factor of dutifulness, on which girls and lower-class youth scored higher. Those for whom the rule-governed assertive-behavior schema is most salient are also the ones most concerned to maintain good relations with their parents. It may be that high scorers are more aware of the rules underlying social interactions generally.

Unsurprisingly, social affiliation (AM factor 4) was positively associated with ignoring conflict (CEM dimension 2). It is to be expected that, for those who see personal friendships as highly important, ignoring conflict is considered the appropriate response in conflict situations.

AM factor 3, concern over heterosexual relationships, was positively related to rule-governed assertiveness (CEM dimension 3) and negatively associated with ignoring conflict (CEM dimension 2). Boys scored significantly higher on factor 3 than did girls.

Whilst a number of significant relationships between measures of self-esteem and conceptual schemas were found, it has to be stressed that the correlations were fairly modest, thus accounting for relatively small amounts of variance. None the less, it is interesting that measures relating to relationships with parents and teachers are directly related to ideas about conflict resolution. Further refinements of both the AM and the PAM are currently being developed, and their relationship with conflict resolution in a wider range of contexts, including those within the family, is being investigated.

In conclusion, the CEM approach has highlighted the conceptual schemas for aggression held by British teenage males and females of both the broad social classes. Whilst sex differences were found to exist, there were also some striking similarities in the schemas held by the two sexes. The fact that class was found to be a strongly interacting variable leads us to question some of the results reported, for example, in the review by Maccoby and Jacklin (1974). Observed differences among upper-class subjects may not necessarily reflect those existing between lower-class males and females. In addition, it is possible that female members of lower-class sub-cultures differ even from other lower-class females in their ideas about appropriate behavior in conflict situations.

It is also possible that some features of the measures relating to the sources and attainment of self-esteem, especially those which were found to vary with sex and class, may have the status of mediating variables between sex and conceptual schemas of aggression. Further work in this area is clearly required. We can, however, suggest at this stage that sex differences in aggression might be very much more complex than the extant literature on the subject would seem to indicate.

REFERENCES

Bachman, J. G. 1982: Family relationships and self-esteem. In M. Rosenberg and H. B. Kaplan (eds), *Social Psychology of the Self Concept*, Arlington Heights, Ill.: Harlan Davidson.

Campbell, A. 1984: *The Girls in the Gang*. Oxford: Basil Blackwell.

—— 1986: Self-report of fighting by females. *British Journal of Criminology*, 26 (forthcoming).

Coopersmith, S. 1967: *The Antecedents of Self-Esteem*. San Francisco: Freeman.

Everitt, B. 1977: *The Analysis of Contingency Tables*. London: Chapman and Hall.

Harré, R. 1977: The ethogenic approach: theory and practice. In L. Berkowitz (ed.), *Advances in Experimental Social Psychology*, vol. X, New York: Academic Press.

—— 1979: Accounts, action and analysis. In M. Brenner, P. Marsh and M. B. Brenner (eds), *The Social Context of Method*, London: Croom Helm.

—— 1979: *Social Being*. Oxford: Basil Blackwell.

Harré, R. and Secord, P. F. 1972: *The Explanation of Social Behaviour*. Oxford: Basil Blackwell.

James, W. 1890: *The Principles of Psychology*. New York: Henry Holt. Repr. New York: Dover, 1950.

Maccoby, E. E. and Jacklin, C. N. 1974: *The Psychology of Sex Differences*. Stanford, Calif.: Stanford University Press.

Marsh, P. 1978: Life and careers on the soccer terraces. In R. Ingham et al., *Football Hooliganism: the wider context*, London: Interaction.

—— 1978: *Aggro: the illusion of violence*, London: J. M. Dent.

—— 1982: Rules in the organization of action: empirical studies. In M. Von Cranach and R. Harré (eds), *The Analysis of Action,* Cambridge: Cambridge University Press.

Marsh, P., Rosser, E. and Harré, R. 1978: *The Rules of Disorder.* London: Routledge and Kegan Paul.

McRobbie, A. and Garber, J. 1976: Girls and subcultures: an exploration. In S. Hall and T. Jefferson (eds), *Resistance through Rituals,* London: Hutchinson.

Rosenberg, M. 1963: Parental interest and children's self conceptions. *Sociometry,* 26, 35–49.

—— 1965: *Society and the Adolescent Self-Image.* Princeton, NJ: Princeton University Press.

Wylie, R. 1974: *The Self Concept: a review of methodological considerations and measuring instruments,* vol. I. Lincoln, Nebr.: University of Nebraska Press.

6

Some Varieties of Human Aggression: Criminal Violence as Coercion, Rule-Following, Impression Management and Impulsive Behavior

Leonard Berkowitz

TWO DIVERGENT PERSPECTIVES

Interpretations of human aggression have long differed as to how much of this behavior is involuntary, controlled with relatively little thought by factors within and outside the individual, and how much is deliberate and calculated in pursuit of a particular objective. At one extreme, theorists in the behaviorist tradition have focused on aggression as a more or less automatic response to internal and/or external stimuli. Good examples can be found in learning-theory-guided analyses of why certain people are especially likely to be targets for aggression. According to Miller (1948; see also Berkowitz, 1962), both the frustration-induced instigation to attack the perceived source of the frustration and the fear of doing so generalize from the perceived frustrater to other persons in terms of their perceived similarity to the provocateur. Hostility is then displaced onto those individuals who are sufficiently similar to the frustrater to evoke aggressive responses but are not so much like the tormentor that they elicit equally strong restraints. Adding to this line of thought, I have suggested (Berkowitz, 1974) that people who are associated with previously obtained reinforcements for aggression are also likely to draw aggressive reactions from those who for one reason or another are inclined to be aggressive.

As yet another example of this mode of analysis, I have noted (see, for example, Berkowitz, 1974) that many homicides result from uncontrolled outbursts of emotion in which the aggressor evidently does more harm than he intends. This is illustrated by an observation once made by a veteran homicide detective in Dallas, Texas, about many of the murders he had encountered. "Murders", he said, "result from little ol' arguments about nothing at all . . . . Tempers flare. A fight starts, and somebody gets stabbed or shot . . ." (Mulvihill and Tumin, 1969, p. 230). It would seem, then, that many murders are "spontaneous acts of passion" caused by trivial issues rather than the result of a thought-out determination to slay the victim. The murderers are presumably affected to a considerable degree by environmental stimuli so that they react with more intense aggression than they would otherwise exhibit.

Opposed to this behavioristic position and the image of the person as a puppet reacting unthinkingly to environmental pulls, other theorists have maintained that aggressors usually know what they are doing when they attack someone. They presumably strike at their target to achieve a desired end. Analyses of criminal violence as conformity to sub-cultural norms (for instance, Wolfgang and Ferracuti, 1967) or as impression management (for example, Felson, 1978) are illustrative of this latter perspective. For this line of thought most aggression has a particular aim, gaining social approval. The aggressors theoretically believe that the significant people in their lives expect them to retaliate against those who have offended them, or would look with favor at such retaliation, and hit out at those who have insulted them in order to win the esteem of their audience. Applying this type of reasoning to the Dallas homicide detective's observations, we should say that the killings took place because the murderers believed they had been humiliated by their antagonists, and that they attacked in an effort to save face or restore a desirable conception of themselves in their own and others' eyes (see also Felson, 1984).

These two perspectives have some points of agrement. For one thing, with a few notable exceptions (for example, Bandura, 1973; Buss, 1961), most proponents of each approach basically define aggression as a deliberate attempt to hurt someone. Thus, even the behavioristic camp generally regards aggressors as having a goal – the infliction of injury (see Berkowitz, 1981). On the other side, even those emphasizing the purposive and thoughtful aspects of aggression acknowledge that violence is sometimes uncontrolled, as when a person goes beserk in intense rage. Furthermore, both approaches recognize the substantial degree to which aggression is affected by situational influences, although they differ in how they conceive of these influences. As noted earlier, writers in the behavioristic tradition typically stress conditioned responses to stimuli in the surrounding situation, while most advocates of the opposing position view aggression as an interaction guided largely by the actual and anticipated behavior of others.

Overriding these similarities, prototypic versions of these two perspectives differ in how much of a role they assign to the operation of involuntary influences in the display of aggression. This is not to say, however, that the formulations emphasizing the aggressors' pursuit of particular objectives are in complete agreement s to what goals are sought. At this point it might be helpful to look at some of the major conceptions of purposive aggression in the social sciences. I shall suggest that each formulation has some validity, since humans can have a variety of motives when they attack someone and that acts of aggression are not all prompted by the same motive (besides the desire to injure the victim). Then, after this brief overview, I shall consider how well two of the best-known conceptions of criminal violence seem to deal with the accounts of aggressive incidents given by violent offenders. I shall argue that some of the violent acts described by these men were at least partly impulsive, so that their behavior was not always directed toward the attainment of some goal.

GOALS OF AGGRESSION

Instrumental and hostile aggression

Although almost every theoretical account in this area now defines aggression as the intentional injury of another, there is also a widespread agreement that the aggressor need not be primarily interested in inflicting harm or destruction. As a case in point, experimentally oriented social psychologists now generally distinguish between two kinds of aggression: *instrumental* (or incentive-motivated) aggression, and *hostile* (or angry or avoidance-motivated, or irritable or aversively-stimulated) aggression (see, for instance, Feshbach, 1964; Rule and Nesdale, 1974; Zillmann, 1979). It is only this latter type of aggression, instigated by some provocative or annoying or unpleasant occurrence, that theoretically is chiefly oriented toward doing harm. By contrast, in instrumental aggression the attempt to injure is part of an attempt to achieve some other goal, such as to gain money or win social approval.

Employing this distinction, I have argued that many acts of criminal violence are examples of hostile rather than instrumental aggression. The offenders in these instances lash out at their victims in rage and with little thought of the consequences or what they might achieve other than the injury of their targets. In one of my studies (Berkowitz, 1978), 65 British men convicted of assaulting another male were interviewed about the incident for which they had been arrested. Contrary to the instrumental conception of aggression, very few of the offenders said they had thought about other people's opinion of them when they had hit their opponent. Most reported that their antagonist had struck first, or had insulted them in some way, so that they lost their temper. Their main intention, they indicated, was either to injure the one who had provoked them or (somewhat less frequently) to escape from the unpleasant situation. I shall have more to say about this study later.

Another British investigation also testifies to the advisability of differentiating between hostile aggression and other forms of fighting. As part of the Cambridge Study in Delinquent Development (West and Farrington, 1977) 389 male youths aged 18–19 from a working-class area of London were asked to describe the "most vicious" fight in which they had been involved. The accounts given by the two-thirds of the sample who described such an incident were then sub-divided into those cases where the teenager had fought alone (54 per cent of those describing a vicious fight) and those where he had fought alongside others. When Farrington, Berkowitz and West (1982) examined these accounts, they found that a much greater proportion of individual fights than of group fights were instances of hostile aggression; the youths who had fought alone were more likely to report that they had been provoked, had lost their temper and had initiated the battle. By contrast, most of the boys involved in group fights indicated they had gone to the aid of a friend, had used weapons and had inflicted physical injuries. Whereas the individual fights were likely to be angry outbursts, these group battles tended to be more deliberate and calculated and were much more in line with the boys' aggressive attitudes and lifestyle. At the very least, these results suggest that the aggression displayed in individual encounters is often quite different from the aggression exhibited in gang battles, and that analyses based on group incidents should not necessarily be applied freely to fights between individuals.

Aggression as coercion

While a great many theorists might accept the distinction just advocated, not all of them would agree that the primary goal in the presumed instances of hostile aggression was to hurt the opponent. A number of researchers maintain that the aggressor's chief aim, even when provoked, is to influence – that is, coerce – the victim. He may hurt his opponent physically or only threaten to do so, insult him verbally or attempt to deprive him of some values resource; and he may do these things either in the heat of anger or in an unemotional pursuit of other objectives. But, whatever he does, his fundamental aim supposedly is to influence the other person's behavior (Patterson and Cobb, 1973; Tedeschi et al., 1974).

Perhaps the most consistent exponents of this thesis, Patterson and his associates (Patterson, 1976; Patterson and Cobb, 1973) base their formulation chiefly on field observations of aggressive youngsters in natural settings. On recording how these children had acted toward their siblings and parents in their homes, the investigators found that the children exhibited a wide spectrum of aversive behaviors, apparently in order to control the behavior of the others in their family. They hit, but they also frequently expressed disapproval, often reacted negatively to the others' wants and requests, and engaged in a good deal of teasing, all presumably in attempts at coercion. These behaviors evidently were frequently reinforced by their victims' reactions. Thus, a boy would be relatively likely to repeat his aversive actions if his victim complied with his wishes in some way.

Of course, it is also possible to interpret these coercive behaviors as attempts to achieve power and dominance over others. A number of researchers have looked at family violence in these terms, holding that many males who beat their wives does so in order to assert their dominance over the women.

Normative considerations

The most popular sociological interpretations of aggression employ normative considerations. The usual version of this line of thought maintains that much violence, even of a criminal nature, is basically only conformity to the norms of a certain segment of society (see, for example, Wolfgang, 1959, 1981; Wolfgang and Ferracuti, 1967). Interestingly, a few psychologists have taken just the opposite tack and have insisted that one of the chief features distinguishing aggression from other forms of behavior is that this action is typically viewed as counter-normative, a serious departure from socially approved modes of conduct (Bandura, 1973; Tedeschi et al., 1974). Other writers bring in social rules by maintaining that the aggression is punishment for a perceived wrong: the aggressors think they have been treated illegitimately in some way, become furious, and seek to punish those who wronged them (Felson, 1984).

I shall not take the time here to discuss the conception of aggression as behavior that has been labeled as illegitimate (see Berkowitz, 1981). Further, I can offer only a few comments here about aggression as a reaction to some perceived misdeed. For one thing, many instances of instrumental aggression obviously have to be excluded: the stereotypic Mafia "hit man" tries to kill his victim without necessarily believing that the victim has wronged him personally. He is just doing a job. Then, too, while many angry aggressors believe they have been mistreated, this perception sometimes only parallels the instigation to aggression produced by exposure to an aversive event, and is not always the direct cause of the instigation. Aversively stimulated aggression can arise without the perception of being wronged. Thus, in a number of laboratory experiments (see Berkowitz, 1983), university students displayed relatively intense aggressive reactions after being exposed to decidedly unpleasant conditions, even though they did not regard the aversive stimulation as a "rule violation".

For our purposes it is more important to examine the view of aggression as conformity to sub-cultural norms. This formulation, initially advanced to explain group differences in homicide rates (Wolfgang, 1959), has now been extended to cover the broad spectrum of anti-social aggression (Wolfgang and Ferracuti, 1967; Schur, 1969). It contends that certain segments of society, especially disadvantaged groups at the bottom of the socio-economic hierarchy, possess values, assumptions and expectations that facilitate the display of aggression. This sub-cultural belief system presumably first defines certain encounters as provocations, so that the members of these groups are easily affronted, and then prescribes aggression as the appropriate response. According to Wolfgang, "Quick resort to physical combat as a measure of daring, courage, or defense of status appears to be a cultural expectation . . ." (1959, p. 189). The men living in this sub-culture of violence supposedly attack others mainly because their groups' rules call on them to react this way to a perceived affront. Failure to adhere to these expectations could bring punishment, at least in the form of a decline in the other group members' regard for them.

This formulation is now widely accepted and some of its proponents seem to believe it is the only reasonable explanation for criminal violence. One writer put the argument this way: if the violent offenders are not mentally ill, their aggression must be "an appropriate form of behavior in a fairly wide variety of situations" (Schur, 1969, p. 129). In other words, unless criminals are seriously disturbed, they will act in a basically rational manner, and so their aggression must be carried out in pursuit of a reasonable objective – probably social approval. Here again is the denial that any significant human behavior – aggression in this case – can be expressed involuntarily.

Nevertheless, however popular this notion might be among social scientists, a number of observations raise serious questions about the adequacy of the sub-cultural thesis as a *general* explanation of criminal violence. For one, my British study mentioned earlier (Berkowitz, 1978) obtained little support for this conception. When the prisoners were queried about the violent incident that had led to their arrest and conviction and were asked why they had assaulted their victim, 70 per cent of those replying indicated they had mostly wanted either to hurt their antagonist (almost 42 per cent) or had sought safety. None of the respondents said he had wanted to protect or enhance his reputation or tried to gain the approval of others.

Of course, it could be that aggression was not generally approved in these offenders' social circles, but the sub-cultural notion would have us believe that lower socio-economic groups having high rates of criminal violence would also hold values and attitudes favoring violence. Recent evidence contradicts this assumption. Surveys of the attitudes, beliefs and values actually possessed by people at the bottom of the socio-economic order have shown that they tend to disapprove of violence; violence is a problem and threat for them as it is for the more privileged groups in society (Erlanger,

1974). And, furthermore, even violent offenders themselves do not necessarily subscribe to the machismo values postulated by the sub-cultural formulation (Ball-Rokeach, 1973).

Impression management

Another conception of aggression, closely related to the sub-cultural analysis, sees the aggressors' behavior as an attempt to manage other people's view of them. As Felson has summarized this position, the impression-management formulation generally assumes "that much of human behavior is designed to obtain favorable reactions from an audience" (1978, p. 205). A person who is insulted or threatened presumably fears that any onlookers will think less well of him because the insult has given him an "unfavorable situational identity". One way for him to nullify this imputed negative identity is to show his strength and courage (p. 207), and so he will try to retaliate against his antagonist, especially if he views the insult suffered as deliberate and unwarranted (p. 208). Moreover, since the retaliation is primarily intended to impress an audience, there is a greater likelihood that the offended party will attack the insulter when onlookers are present than if no one else is around, assuming that the audience favors aggression (p. 209).

THE STUDY'S FOCUS

The succeeding sections report an assessment of how well the impression-management analysis applies to criminal violence. As in my earlier British study, incarcerated men who had been convicted of a serious violent assault were interviewed about the aggressive event and their reactions to it. Unlike in the previous investigation, however, the men were Scots in Scottish jails, because I sought a population that theoretically would heighten the chances of finding impression management. Descriptions of Scottish violent criminals, such as the autobiography of Jimmy Boyle and Patrick's report (1973) of his dealings with a Glasgow gang, generally characterize working-class Scots as being more apt to pursue a "macho" public identity than their English counterparts. Acording to sub-cultural and impression-management analyses of criminal violence, then, a relatively high proportion of the offenders' working-class peers should favor the use of violence in resolving social conflicts. The imprisoned men should therefore be likely to explain their aggression as an attempt to look tough and "manly" to whatever onlookers were present. The principal question was whether such an attempt at impression management was indeed common in this Scottish violent-offender sample.

SAMPLE

Seventy-one men convicted of a violent assault were interviewed in five Scottish prisons by three interviewers.[1] Two of the investigators, graduate students in criminology at Edinburgh University, conducted all but six of the interviews, while the others were obtained by a Belgian criminologist fluent in English. In all cases the questioning was guided by a previously established interview schedule, although the investigators occasionally deviated from the prearranged items if they believed the flow of conversation would be disrupted by a rigid adherence to the schedule. As a consequence, we have fewer than 71 responses to some of the questions.

All of the criminals in the present sample had committed relatively serious acts of violence, but none had committed homicide. Approximately half of the men (36) had been arrested for doing bodily harm to another male during an altercation. Others committed violence against one or more men in the course of a robbery (four cases) or in resisting arrest (ten). The remaining cases had been involved in fights with either one woman (six), members of both sexes (nine) or someone in their own family (six). Tallies of the interview responses revealed that there were relatively few systematic differences between the 36 man-*versus*-man "pure aggression" cases and the others, either in background or in reaction to the incident, and so this report is based on the entire sample of 71 offenders.

By and large, the incident was relatively fresh in the respondents' minds. Fifty-seven per cent of those questioned about this matter indicated that the crime had occurred less than a year before the interview, and in only one case had more than two years gone by.

The crime had also occurred when the men were fairly young. Forty per cent of those asked about their age were younger than 18 when the incident had happened, and 49 per cent had been between 18 and 21. No one was over 29. None the less, despite this youthfulness, most of the sample had a history of brushes with the law. Ninety-seven per cent of the 62 asked about their arrest record had been arrested before, 81 per cent more than five times.

The respondents' home background seems to have been conducive to the development of an anti-social behavior pattern. For one thing, their fathers typically had had only a semi-skilled or unskilled occupation when the respondents were growing up (about 65 per cent); but, more important, and whatever the fathers' occupational level, their family lives had been somewhat unsettled: 94 per cent of the 62 cases asked about this matter revealed that their parents had separated for some time, while almost 60 per cent said that their mother and father had had many arguments or had even had fights. On top of the potential for violence produced by this unstable family life, many of the respondents' parents also could have served as aggressive models for their sons to emulate: 90 per cent of the 60 cases asked about their parents' behavior reported that one or both of them had displayed at least some physical aggression in conflicts outside the home. Not surprisingly, the boys were inclined to be aggressive themselves, and 69 per cent of those who had been questioned about their disputes with others said they had been involved in fights. Only 14 per cent of the respondents talking about their reactions to arguments reported that they did not become angry or aggressive.

Just as it cannot be claimed for the previous study that it was based on a representative sample of English violent offenders, so no claim for representativeness is made for the Scottish sample. However, a good proportion of the participants in this investigation appear to be similar in important respects to many other violent offenders, and it is reasonable to ask how these men described the assaults they had committed. Society had penalized them for this behavior, but why had they attacked their victim? Had they been motivated to present themselves in a favorable manner to the others around them?

INTERVIEW PROCEDURE

The procedure followed in obtaining, recording and analysing the interviews was similar to that employed in the earlier study (Berkowitz, 1978). Officials in the Prisons Department of the Scottish Home Office provided the names of prison inmates who had been recently convicted of a violent offense. These persons were contacted by the staff at their prison and asked whether they wished to take part in a study of how people "get into trouble with the law". The inmates agreeing to participate in the investigation were then met individually by the interviewer in the prison room that had been set aside for our use and were questioned. Each interview was tape-recorded with the respondent's consent. As in all studies of this type, we cannot be sure that the answers the men gave were entirely accurate. Nevertheless, even if the respondents had distorted their reports, consciously or without realizing what they were doing, it is worth knowing how they accounted for their conduct. These accounts might reveal what they regard as the major influences on their behavior.

Two trained judges independently read each interview typescript, guided by a coding-scheme virtually identical to the one employed with the English interviews. If the judges, psychology undergraduates, did not agree in the coding of any particular interview, they went over the typescript again until agreement was reached. Two types of coding were carried out, as in the earlier study: first, the respondents' replies to each question were categorized into one of several possible response classes (usually between three and five), and then a count was made of the occurrence of some 41 different ideas during the course of the interview.

CONTEXT OF THE INCIDENT

At the start of the interview each participant was told to describe the incient that had led to his present conviction, and he was then asked a series of specific questions about this situation and his reactions to it. The answers indicated that many of the assaults had the same background as the violent crimes studied by Sparks (1974) in London, Wolfgang (1959) in Philadelphia, and Pittman and Handy (1964) in St Louis. Thus, as was common in these other investigations, most of the offenses had been committed at the weekend (about 65 per cent of the cases), and an even larger number had been committed at night (83 per cent). Since most of the incidents had occurred in a familiar location such as in or near a place of entertainment (approximately 38 per cent of the cases questioned), or in or near the respondent's home (26 per cent), we are not surprised to find that the participants were typically accompanied by someone they knew: most frequently a male friend or relative (50 per cent of those asked), but sometimes a woman relative, friend or acquaintance (about 16 per cent). Furthermore, also in keeping with the other research, alcohol seems to have played a role in many of the assaults; 68 per cent of the men asked about this matter reported being drunk at the time, and another 21 per cent said they had been drinking. However, unlike the pattern generally found in homicide studies but very similar to the earlier English results (Berkowitz, 1978), the victim was usually a stranger (54 per cent) or a slight acquaintance (16 per cent).

THE INCIDENT AND REACTIONS TO IT

The participants' descriptions of the incident suggested that their assaults had been primarily reactions, most often to a direct verbal or physical attack (36 per cent of those questioned) or to the other person's having blocked their activity in some way (10 per cent). Less frequently, the incident began with a more subtle threat such an argument or the other's boastfulness (17 per cent). Another sizable fraction of the assaults arose when the men went to the aid of a friend (approximately 17 per cent – the same proportion as in the English sample).

Whatever the origin of the fight, the incident apparently intensified fairly quickly and the respondents struck at their opponent. In most cases their reaction was consistent with the definition of aggression as a deliberate attempt to injure someone (see introductory section). When they were specifically asked whether they had wanted to hurt their antagonist, 48 per cent replied in the affirmative. Injury was not the only objective, however.

Most of the others had probably attempted to protect themselves, since over a third of those queried about what they had tried to accomplish said that they had sought safety. Only about 12 per cent of the questioned sample indicated a concern with protecting their reputation or trying to gain approval.

Much the same pattern of concerns is revealed in the ideas the men had expressed in the course of the interview. The idea count showed that a substantial proportion of the men (49 per cent) had talked about wanting to hurt someone when they discussed their objectives in a fight. The next most frequent ideas in this discussion of aggression aims had to do with a desire to protect oneself (37 per cent of the sample) or to ensure one's safety (25 per cent). Far fewer respondents mentioned wanting some form of self-satisfaction (17 per cent) or social approval (3 per cent).

All in all, we have an impression of many of these men striking out in rage, giving relatively little thought to the long-range consequences of their action. When they were asked if they had believed they would win the fight, over half (52 per cent) said yes. Nevertheless, 36 per cent reported that they had not thought at all about what would happen, and even those anticipating victory might have automatically assumed the positive outcome without much thought. The tallies of the ideas expressed during the interview contribute to this picture. For one thing, when they discussed their violence, 76 per cent of the respondents talked about impulsive assaults, while only 18 per cent mentioned highly controlled and planned aggression. The former type of aggression might have been somewhat more familiar to this sample. In keeping with all this, the notion of restraining violence apparently was not especially salient, since only 11 per cent said anything about such restraints.

What weapon did the assailants use? When they were asked this question, about a third of those replying reported attacking their opponent only with their own hands and/or feet, while another third said they had used a knife (a frequently employed weapon in the United Kingdom), and 28 per cent indicated they had used any available object. In a telling contrast to American assaults, only 3 per cent of the men acknowledged using a gun.

Now that the men had the time to think back – from the perspective of their jail cells – they typically were not happy about what had happened. A specific question about their present feelings regarding the incident showed that over two thirds felt bad about it, while 22 per cent said they had only neutral feelings. This pattern of answers is paralleled in the idea tallies. Sixty-two per cent of the participants talked about feeling bad about the incident's outcome, while only 24 and 28 per cent said that their aggression had been justified or that they now felt good about what they had done.

ANY EVIDENCE OF IMPRESSION MANAGEMENT?

The last-mentioned observations provide little comfort for the impression-management interpretation of criminal violence. Nor, considering everything, is there better evidence in the other statements made during the interview.

As I noted in the introductory section, impression-management theorizing basically assumes that many people see themselves as acting in front of an audience. In accord with this assumption, 62 per cent of the respondents said they had been aware of other persons when they attacked their victim. (However, they had not noticed any particular kinds of people more than others, and men, women, friends, acquaintances and strangers were all mentioned with approximately equal frequency as this audience.) Moreover, those saying they had been aware of others also were more likely to mention during the interview that others would learn of their behavior (39 per cent of the "aware" group, as against only 24 per cent of those not aware of others).

None the less, there are no indications that the "aware" men had acted substantially differently from the others. As an example, on determining whether the respondents had said something about caring what others would think of them, we found that this concern was relatively prevalent in both groups: 86 and 81 per cent of the "aware" and "unaware" groups, respectively. Nor were the "aware" participants more likely to talk about controlled and purposeful aggression rather than impulsive aggression; the idea of controlled aggression was relatively infrequent in both groups – 18 and 19 per cent, respectively – whereas slightly more of the "aware" people had mentioned impulsive aggression – 84 as against 77 per cent. This idea count also yielded little evidence that the people who were aware of the presence of others were especially inclined to believe that their audience would approve of aggression. The tally of how many respondents had talked about others approving aggression showed that approximately a quarter of both the "aware" and the "not aware" men had mentioned such an approval. In other words, where impression-management thinking suggests that violent people are apt to believe that the others around them generally favor aggression, the interviews indicated that this idea was not especially salient in our sample of violent offenders, and was definitely not more common in those who were conscious of having an audience.

But, perhaps most important of all, these two groups did not voice the differences in aggression aims that would be expected from impresion-management theory. According to this conception of criminal violence, violent offenders presumably want to maintain a public reputation as tough and manly, and thereby gain approval, when they think they have been observed by an audience. However, contrary to such a contention, the examination of the ideas expressed by the men revealed that both the "aware" and the "not aware" respondents had given relatively little thought during the interviews to either social approval or their reputations. Furthermore, when the men were explicitly asked what they had tried to accomplish in attacking their victim, very few of the mentioned wanting to protect their reputation or obtain approval. What differences there were between the "aware" and "not aware" respondents actually showed a different pattern of concerns: those conscious of being observed were more likely to say they had wanted to hurt their opponent (38 per cent, compared to 25 per cent of the "not awares") and were much less likely to have wanted safety (28 as against 42 per cent).

THE OFFENDERS' PROPENSITY TO VIOLENCE

If the observations just reported offer little support for an impression-management account of criminal violence, they are very much in keeping with the view of violent offenses spelled out in my study of English assaults (Berkowitz, 1978). I had suggested there that many of the violent offenders we interviewed had explosive tempers: they seemed to be easily angered by perceived threats to their self-esteem, and, unless they detected clear-cut signs telling them it would be best to hold back, tended to become enraged fairly quickly. Weak in self-restraints, they then often lashed out in fury against some perceived antagonist, oblivious to the possible long-term consequences of such an action.

The description offered of the men in the Scottish sample is consistent with this portrait. A good proportion of our offenders had grown up under conditions that were conducive to the development of long-standing aggressive dispositions: relatively unstable family lives, with parents who might have served as aggressive models. Also supporting the existence of such a violent inclination is the finding that many of the respondents became angry during the course of arguments (almost two thirds of those questioned reported this reaction). They apparently were infuriated fairly easily.

As suggested earlier, the reason for this relatively high proportion of angry reactions might be that the men's egos were readily threatened. We can also see this possibility in their high frequency of aggressive responses to insults. When they were asked what they did when they were insulted, over half (54 per cent) indicated they resorted to physical violence, while 28 per cent said they only insulted back, with or without anger. Only 14 per cent reported acting non-aggressively in these situations, either "talking it out" or by defusing the incident in some way. Furthermore, and contrary to the rule-following conceptions of violent conduct, the offenders did not seem to believe that their aggressive reactions to insults were required by social rules.

The question, "What is the best way for men to act when they are insulted?" showed that most of the sample viewed a violent response as undesirable (only 13 per cent of those asked said that this was the best way to act). Most of the respondents were not even in favor of a return insult (only about 12 per cent advocated it). The remainder basically held that the best response was either to "talk it out", ignore the insult or withdraw from the situation.

If most of these people did not believe it was a particularly good idea to react violently to an insult, why, we might then ask, did so many of them exhibit just this kind of response? I have already proposed the answer: they attacked impulsively, with relatively little consideration of what might happen afterwards. There is still more evidence of just such an explosive tendency. In one question they were asked to say whether they usually thought of the consequences when they hit someone in a dispute. Fully 82 per cent of those asked indicated that they never stopped to consider the possible outcome of their aggression. They typically were too furious and their self-restraints were often much too weak for them to stop and think of the future. All of this can be summarized very simply. The violent offenses I have been discussing here were often emotional outbursts, and people in a rage are rarely thoughtful.

SOME CONCLUDING REMARKS

Pride and self-consistency

A few final comments are in order to round out this overview of analyses of criminal violence. One point has to do with the role of the self. Generally speaking, impression-management theory, along with other conceptions of the functioning of the self in social behavior, assumes that people strive to enhance their self-value. However, unlike these other formulations, impression-management thinking tends not to recognize that people often want to look good to themselves as well as to others. They may want to make a favorable impression on some audience, but they themselves are also an audience; they observe their own conduct, and in this self-observation frequently want to live up to and even enhance their images of themselves (see, for instance, Scheier and Carver, 1982).

The everyday notion of "pride" basically involves just this kind of striving. In part at least, we are "proud" when we think well of ourselves, as well as when we believe others appreciate us, and we frequently seek to preserve our good opinion of ourselves. Hans Toch's (1969) description of the "self-image promoter" also points to this desire to maintain and protect a cherished self-conception. Exaggerating a tendency that many persons possess, the "self-image promoter" evidently is very quick to interpret other people's behavior as a threat to the way he wants to view himself, even if no one else is aware of this challenge. He then goes out of his way to assert himself, essentially insisting to himself that he *is* the kind of individual he would like himself to be.

But, having acknowledged this striving for self-consistency, it is important to repeat a point I made in discusing my Scottish observations. The aggressive reactions sometimes exhibited by those whose self-conceptions are threatened are not necessarily always a deliberate attempt to assert an image of toughness and manliness. The perceived threat in itself may be so disturbing, especially to persons lacking a firm view of themselves, that they become enraged and strike out in fury. They may say afterwards that they had wanted to show the offender that they were "somebody to be reckoned with", but in actuality it was the pain of the threat that generated their aggression. Unpleasant events generally produce aggressive inclinations (see Berkowitz, 1983; Zillmann, 1979).

Inflicting injury as the goal of hostile aggression

In discussing the goals of aggression, I examined some of the objectives angry persons might have when they attack their victims. It must be stressed, however, that, whatever other aims the aggressors might possess, they are seeking to hurt their antagonist. The goal of hostile aggression (which might also be termed angry or irritable or aversively stimulated aggression) is to injure the perceived source of the displeasure.

Recent experimental findings have demonstrated the goal value of injuring the target for those who are angry (Baron, 1977). One study, for example, found that, whereas non-angry subjects were especially reluctant to punish a peer when the punishment would be very harmful to him, those who were angry with their target were more punitive the more the punishment would hurt the other (Rule and Nesdale, 1974). Other evidence shows that strongly angered persons are also more punitive than they otherwise would be if they find that their aggression is inflicting pain on their victim. The pain cues apparently indicate to them that they are approaching their goal, the appropriate injury of the one who provoked them, and this stimulates them to even stronger aggressive reactions (Baron, 1977). This last point now brings us full circle to where I began: the heightened aggression stimulated by the pain cues is at least partly involuntary. While the angry subjects in this research wanted to hurt the one who had offended them, they were not aware that the signs of their victim's pain were stimulating them to attack even harder.

NOTES

1 My special thanks go to Professor Derek McClintock and his staff and students at the School of Criminology, Edinburgh University, for their generous hospitality and assistance. This study would not have been possible without their expert knowledge and skill.

REFERENCES

Ball-Rokeach, S. J. 1973: Values and violence: a test of the subculture of violence thesis. *American Sociological Review*, 38, 736–49.

Bandura, A. 1973: *Aggression: a social learning analysis*. Englewood Cliffs, NJ: Prentice-Hall.

Baron, R. A. 1977: *Human Aggression*. New York: Plenum.

Berkowitz, L. 1962: *Aggression: a social psychological analysis*. New York: McGraw-Hill.

—— 1974: Some determinants of impulsive aggression: role of mediated associations with reinforcements for aggression. *Psychological Review*, 81, 165–76.

—— 1978: Is criminal violence normative behavior? Hostile and instrumental aggression in violent incidents. *Journal of Research in Crime and Delinquency*, 15, 148–61.

—— 1981: The concept of aggression. In P. Brain and D. Benton (eds), *Multidisciplinary Approaches to Aggression Research*, Amsterdam: Elsevier/North Holland.

—— 1983: Aversively stimulated aggression: some parallels and differences in research with animals and humans. *American Psychologist*, 38, 1135–44.

Buss, A. 1961: *The Psychology of Aggression*. New York: Wiley.

Erlanger, H. S. 1974: The empirical status of the subculture of violence thesis. *Social Problems*, 22, 280–92.

Farrington, D. P., Berkowitz, L. and West, D. J. 1982: Differences between individual and group fights. *British Journal of Social Psychology*, 21, 323–33.

Felson, R. B. 1978: Aggression as impression management. *Social Psychology*, 41, 205–13.

—— 1984: Patterns of aggressive social interaction. In A. Mummendey (ed.), *Social Psychology of Aggression: from individual behavior to social interaction*, Berlin: Springer.

Feshbach, S. 1964: The function of aggression and the regulation of aggressive drive. *Psychological Review*, 71, 257–72.

Miller, N. E. 1948: Theory and experiment relating psychoanalytic displacement to stimulus-response generalization. *Journal of Abnormal and Social Psychology*, 43, 155–78.

Mulvihill, D. J. and Tumin, M. M. 1969: *Crimes of Violence*. Washington, DC: US Government Printing Office.

Patrick, J. 1973: *A Glasgow Gang Observed*. London: Eyre Methuen.

Patterson, G. R. 1976: The aggressive child: victim and architect of a coercive system. In L. A. Hamerlynch, L. C. Handy and E. J. Mash (eds), *Behavior Modification and Families*, vol. I: *Theory and Research*, New York: Brunner/Mazell.

Patterson, G. R. and Cobb, J. A. 1973: Stimulus control for classes of noxious behaviors. In J. F. Knutson (ed.), *The Control of Aggression: implications from basic research,* Chicago: Aldine.

Pittman, D. J. and Handy, W. 1964: Patterns in criminal aggravated assault. *Journal of Criminal Law, Criminology, and Police Science*, 53, 462–70.

Rule, B. G. and Nesdale, A. 1974: Differing functions of aggression. *Journal of Personality,* 42, 467–81.

Scheier, M. F. and Carver, C. S. 1982: Cognition, affect and self-regulation. In M. S. Clark and S. T. Fiske (eds), *Affect and Cognition,* Hillsdale, NJ: Lawrence Erlbaum Associates.

Schur, E. M. 1969: *Our Criminal Society*. Englewood Cliffs, NJ: Prentice-Hall.

Sparks, R. 1974: Criminal victimization in three London areas. Unpublished manuscript, Institute of Criminology, Cambridge University.

Tedeschi, J. T., Smith, R. B., III and Brown, R. C. Jr 1974: A reinterpretation of research on aggression. *Psychological Bulletin,* 81, 540–62.

Toch, H. 1969: *Violent Men: an inquiry into the psychology of violence*. Chicago: Aldine.

West, D. J. and Farrington, D. P. 1977: *The Delinquent Way of Life*. London: Heinemann.

Wolfgang, M. E. 1959: *Patterns in Criminal Homicide*. Philadelphia: University of Pennsylvania Press.

Wolfgang, M. E. 1981: Sociocultural overview of criminal violence. In J. R. Hays, T. K. Roberts and K. S. Solway (eds), *Violence and the Violent Individual*. Jamaica, NY: Spectrum.

Wolfgang, M. E. and Ferracuti, F. 1967: *The Subculture of Violence: towards an integrated theory in criminology*. London: Tavistock.

Zillmann, D. 1979: *Hostility and Aggression*. Hillsdale, NJ: Lawrence Erlbaum Associates.

PART II

Situational Correlates of Aggression

7

Overview

John J. Gibbs

An obvious but important point is that violence is not equally distributed among person–situation combinations. Boys are more violent in gyms than are old ladies at card parties. If you are looking for a fight, you would be better off bellying up to the bar in a waterfront joint than sampling the vegetarian paté in a fern bar. The chapters in this part of the book explore several situations, broadly defined, that generate either a disproportionate amount of violence or kinds of violence that especially concern us.

It is difficult to characterize as a whole the chapters that follow. A wide variety of situations are discussed by scholars from different disciplines, and the chapters reflect several methodological and theoretical perspectives. The lack of a common paradigm or framework makes it hard for the reader to extract common themes and identify generalizable observations, but the diversity means that the reader is introduced to the full range of methods and perspectives.

Despite their diversity in several areas, the authors of the following chapters do share a common approach. Each, to some extent, looks at violence as a process or transaction instead of as a consequence of combinations of individual characteristics. Each author describes an enabling environment or situation that encompasses the interaction between perceptual sets and the environmental material they work with to shape violent behavior. The implicit purpose of each chapter is to describe an opportunity structure and the eyes that see the opportunity. In transactional terms, the authors are describing the market places where buyers and sellers come together to do the business of violence.

As in other respects, there is variation in the extent to which the authors emphasize the transactional approach. In chapter 8, Anne Campbell clearly conveys the transactional message. She tells us that we cannot make sense of acts independent of the context or setting in which they take place, and we cannot make sense of the setting without knowing its meaning to those in it. Indeed, settings and persons are inextricably linked as human environments or arenas in which actions are forged in interactions between persons. The interactions reflect individual goals and class values and norms. The actions once produced do not merely disappear like so many sparks from a fire. They become part of the constantly changing human arena. They become the fuel that keeps the furnace of human interaction going.

The arena that Campbell explores is the street. The street in a central setting in the life of the lower-class man. It is a place where appropriate values and manly comportment are learned and manhood is confirmed and maintained. The street is the setting in which the concerns of men – smartness, sexual prowess, drinking-ability and manliness – are played out in social talk, which under certain conditions leads to violence. Campbell emphasizes that, in order to understand these violent encounters, we must step into the shoes of the lower-class man and walk his walk on his streets. We must see through his eyes how moves and counter-moves by protagonists on the street translate into threats to central concerns that, if the sequence goes far enough, require a violent response.

Chapters 9–11 deal with a factor that has long been associated with violence – alcohol. Drinkers and drinking-places are commonly thought to spawn more violence than people involved in other activities in other settings. Mothers warn their children about the perils of strong drink and frequenting bars, and the current litany of social ills and personal catastrophes connected to alcohol rivals that of the temperance movement.

Our collective consciousness concerning alcohol has been raised, and we are aware of the dangers of drinking. It has been linked to violence on the roads, in homes and in schools, but alcohol's most obvious connection is to the violence in and around bars. Although there is no doubt in most minds that the connection is strong the nature and extent of the alcohol–bar-violence association has not been adequately examined.

In chapter 9, I present a conceptual model and a research strategy to explore the link between alcohol and bar-room violence. I begin the chapter by discussing the contributions and limitations of survey and experimental studies of alcohol and violence. The problems with these studies, as I see it, are conceptual and descriptive impoverishment.

Borrowing from the previous work of some of the contributors to this volume, most notably Toch, Berkowitz and Felson, I suggest that, in studying bar-room violence, we should keep in mind that most incidents are characterized by a sequence of escalatory moves and counter-moves between protagonists. I also suggest, on the basis of work by Toch, Felson and others, that we recognize the importance of self-image and impression management in studying violent encounters.

Once the sequential and escalatory nature of violent interactions and the role of self-image have been accepted, the obvious conclusion is that the probability of violence can be increased by factors which (1) affect self-image, such as threats, challenges and insults; (2) facilitate the first exchange in a sequence that could culminate in violence – for instance, misunderstandings and actions that are seen as arbitrary; or (3) make it less likely that de-escalatory actions such as appeasement and explanation, will be taken. Alcohol is one such factor.

Pernanen's model of the effects of alcohol on perception and cognition is used to suggest how alcohol contributes to those sequential interactions that result in violence. Alcohol, through its restrictive effects on both primary and secondary cognitive appraisal, (1) influences the individual's perception of the situation – he is more likely than when sober to see the actions of others as arbitrary or challenging; and (2) affects his assessment of his resources for dealing with the problem – he is more likely than when sober to consider an aggressive (i.e. regressive) solution, and his evaluation of his physical prowess may be inflated.

I view the bar as the context or human environment within which both drinking and violent and other interactions occur. Bars vary in the environmental features or qualities that facilitate or control both drinking and violence. Bar-room characteristics such as the clarity of rules for dispute resolution, the age and class composition of the clientele, and the predominant customer needs the bar serves shape behavior, especially the behavior of customers with certain dispositions.

Chapter 10 is based on interviews with almost 200 bar-tenders and bar-owners in the United States and Ireland. Felson, Baccaglini and Gmelch describe the characteristics of bars and their customers that are associated with violence. They report that the reasons respondents furnish for incidents of both physical and verbal aggression are similar in both American and Irish bars. Refusal to serve a patron is by far the most frequently reported reason for a dispute.

Felson, Baccaglini and Gmelch see the transaction between the barman and the patron as one in which issues of social control are likely to arise, and control issues are rife with opportunities for conflict. They point out that the customer who is refused service may consider it an insulting breach of the rules of social conduct, and retaliate to punish and save face.

It is not surprising in light of the above finding that Felson and his colleagues report that the bar-room characteristic most strongly associated with incidents of both verbal and physical aggression is the age of the clientele. Not only are young people generally more aggressive in most societies, as the authors point out, but they are also the most likely to be refused service in bars, because (1) they are not of legal drinking-age or they are suspected of not being old enough; (2) they are incapable or ignorant of proper comportment when drunk; or (3) bar-tenders feel that rule enforcement is more appropriate with younger than with older customers.

The authors report that the personal characteristics which distinguish participants in fights from other customers are sex, class and patronage. Those involved in physical aggression are more likely than their less aggressive counterparts to be (1) male, (2) working-class and (3) infrequent customers. The incident characteristic that is best able to discriminate between episodes of physical and verbal aggression is age. Disputes involving younger patrons are more likely to escalate into physical confrontations than are those involving older customers.

The study presented by Felson, Baccaglini and Gmelch is important not only for its findings, but also because it is an example of research that takes person, situation and context variables into consideration. The results of their study also suggest many important areas for further investigation, such as interactions between bar-tenders and youthful customers, that should be explored using a variety of methods.

In chapter 11, Ann Teresa Cordilia explores alcohol-related robberies from a criminological perspective. She points out that criminologists have traditionally studied historical or genetic rather than situational factors. There is, however, convincing evidence that situational, not historical, factors play a central role in some kinds of crime. What is needed, she proposes, is an analytic tool that can help researchers determine if historical or situational factors play the predominant role in certain kinds of crime. Cordilia takes the first step in developing such a tool by providing lucid descriptions of two schemas or hypothetical accounts of criminal acts.

In her first schema, historical factors are predominant. Here, factors such as personality and personal needs produce the motivation which leads the offender to the situation in which the criminal act is committed. In contrast, the offender in the situation-predominant schema does not seek a situation that will facilitate the commission of a crime. He enters the situation for other reasons (such as companionship), and the motive for the crime grows out of the situation (for instance, maintaining the group or increasing group cohesion).

Cordilia offers robbery arising out of a group drinking-context as an example of a crime that fits her situation-predominant schema. She supports her model and vividly brings it to life with interview excerpts and descriptions of drinking-group robberies from several sources. Her developmental use of these materials paves the way for systematic content analysis of descriptions of drinking-related robberies and a formal test of her schema in the future.

Cordilia draws on the literature from a diversity of areas to help explain and generate hypotheses about several issues that emerge from the application of her situation-predominant schema to drinking-group robberies. For example, she explores the motives of the offenders and the dynamics of the group by using observations contained in the literature on delinquent groups as a model, and she uses Pernanen's model to shed light on the role played by alcohol in the genesis of group crime.

The description of group robbery presented by Cordilia clearly illustrates how one kind of violence emerges from the intersection of the personality (for instance, socially inadequate) and needs (say, companionship) of the individual with the demands of the situation (for example, drinking and maintaining group cohesion).

Chapters 12 and 13 center our attention on the contribution of organizations and institutions to violent situations. In chapter 12, Robert Johnson illustrates the awesome proportions violence can take when it becomes incorporated into an institutional strategy for achieving goals. Such violence not only has obvious and devastating effects on its victims, but also works in more insidious ways by robbing of their humanity those who carry out violent tasks.

Johnson draws from a wide range of institutional settings – the military, police, prisons, factories, "death row" and death camps – to develop his framework for understanding institutional violence. He finds and describes the common threads that tie a seemingly diverse group of institutions and organizations into a meaningful and coherent whole.

The key factor in promoting and sustaining violence for institutional purposes is dehumanization of both the victims and agents of the organization. The result is that personal factors play a minor role in institutional violence, as compared with other kinds of violence, and situational factors predominate. Indeed, as Johnson sees it, one aim of the organization is to produce a "situational self" that is free of the moral restraints which under normal circumstances inhibit violence. Depending on the major activity of the organization, this situational self either will respond violently to certain situational cues or will fail to interfere when completion of organizational tasks will obviously result in harm to others or even oneself.

The dehumanization necessary for violence is brought about by recruiting those who are most susceptible to certain situational factors and providing situational socialization to foster the development of the situational self. This requires the appropriate combination of authorization, bureaucracy, isolation and insulation. The organization must manipulate situational factors in order for situational socialization to occur.

The picture of our institutions painted by Johnson is not totally bleak. He argues that if dehumanization, which facilitates violence, can be promoted by the institutional environment, then humanization, which restricts violence, can be fostered by making changes in the institutional environment. He suggests that introducing the principles of participatory democracy into some of our institutions is one way to promote a sense of individual responsibility and reduce unnecessary violence.

As members of an organization whose purpose is commonly considered social control, the police encounter potentially violent situations more often than those in most other occupations. In chapter 13, James J. Fyfe stresses that, in order to understand police reactions to these situations, we must go beyond personality and explore the occupational and organizational forces that shape the police officer's perception of the situation. Fyfe also points out that the role of the police and the characteristics of the situations they encounter contribute to the potential for violence in their work.

As Fyfe see it, the role of the police, from the broadest perspective, is to provide human service. Their job differs from those of other human-service providers in that their encounters with clients are more urgent, involuntary and public. These situational factors are linked to potential violence. Police officers should be aware of the influence of these factors if they are correctly to read or diagnose a situation and take actions to diminish the chances of unnecessary violence.

Fyfe coins the term "split-second syndrome" to characterize the unenlightened and heavy-handed approach some officers take to dangerous situations. Encouraged by an organizational philosophy that police are men of quick and decisive action, they take action before a proper diagnosis of the situation can be made. The result is often unnecessary violence. However, if one views the violence from the restricted perspective of the split second – a perspective that is part of the police organizational fabric and shared by some members of the public – the violence appears justified.

Fyfe's major point in his chapter is that the police should expand their perspective on dangerous situations beyond the split second. Once the point of the split second has been reached, the situation is out of the control of the officer. Officers should concentrate on the factors that culminate in split-second situations. They should explore how dangerous situations unfold, and take note of what these situations have in common and the contributions of officers to these situations. With these data available, officers can prepare for dangerous situations so that they do not culminate in split-second judgments.

Fyfe's chapter demonstrates the important practical applictions of broadening our perspective on violence beyond personality. He clearly makes the case that police can reduce violence and save lives by expanding their view of dangerous situations and exploring their actions from a situational perspective.

The last two chapters contain discussions of two areas that have drawn widespread attention in recent years – family violence and sports violence. The home was at one time considered a sanctuary in which one escaped or held at bay the pressures of the outside world. In recent years, however, under the increasing scrutiny of researchers from many disciplines, the home and family have been found to engender situations that lead to conflict and violence. In chapter 14, Robert J. Powers reviews the forces and conditions that shape aggression and violence within the family.

Powers reviews the systematic research and clinical observations concerning the functions, forms and determinants of family violence. His descriptions of bidirectional and transactional models of family violence are particularly useful for understanding violence within the family context, and his examples of family situations that lead to violence clearly illustrate that family violence is the result of an interactive process.

In chapter 15, Jeffery H. Goldstein takes a critical look at what some consider an increasingly violent trend in sport, and he reviews the theory and research on the effects of witnessing sporting-events. Some of the evidence Goldstein reviews suggests that situational factors can influence fan violence. For example, he cites studies that demonstrate a link between aggressive acts by players and aggressive acts by spectators. He points out that there are greater changes in pre- and post-game measures of aggressiveness among fans at sporting-events that feature body contact than there are among fans who watch non-contact sports.

As has been emphasized by other authors in this volume, Goldstein argues that the meaning and expectations held by the spectators of an event affect the impact. This means that, in order to understand, predict and control sport-related violence, we must view the significance of the event and the purposes it serves from the perspective of the fan.

The purpose of this overview has been to provide the reader with a chart of the richly diverse methodological and theoretical terrain he or she will be traversing. No apology is offered for the diversity. It reflects current thinking on situational aspects of violence, and indicates the sort of issues that theory and research must address in the future.

8

The Streets and Violence

Anne Campbell

INTRODUCTION

Aggression, like telephone calls and love-making, requires co-operation between at least two people. It is a piece of social interaction which depends, like most others, on processes at once too familiar and too opaque to be readily discernible. As social psychology has turned its attention to the requirements and signals of interactional patterns, social scientists have begun to spell out processes that seem at once obvious and yet are manifestly too complex for us to program into successful computer simulations. We have begun to recognize the way in which eye contact is used to regulate turn-taking in conversation, the way in which spatial distance can discomfort us, the importance of routinized scripts in many interactions and the way in which language is interpreted as a function of its syntax and inflection, as well as its semantics (see, for example, Argyle et al., 1982). We all know how to "do" a conversation and therefore at some level must have a grasp of these conventions and usages, yet we find it almost impossible to make explicit the complex cues and symbols that we are interpreting.

The notion of aggression as a form of interpersonal transaction is a relatively new one. Not only have we largely failed to see it as a process rather than an outcome, but we have also fallen into the belief, common in criminology, that "bad" outcomes must have "bad" causes – so we continue to search for the predictors of aggression in static intrapersonal attributes such as under-controlled hostility or defective ego strength. When we move into the area of situational analyses, we fall into the same static trap by manipulating factors in the laboratory – the presence of a gun, exposure to an arousing film – and watching their impact upon a person's willingness to write a negative evaluation of a stranger with whom he or she has no ongoing relationship.

The factors that researchers studying interpersonal processes have found to be important are the setting, the relationship between the participants, their mutual goals for the interaction, and the extent to which they share a similar cultural understanding of the propriety and meaning of social actions. The problem is that these factors cannot be conveniently pulled apart for the purposes of analysis, however much our social-science instinct tells us to partition the variance. People and situations are not logically independent of one another in the real world. For example, a young male and a given street do not come together by happenstance. He is there because he lives there or because his friends do. His neighborhood and his streets have been part of the socialization process that has contributed to his personality. The person and the street may be intimately related from the very beginning of any aggressive episode which takes place. The street is not separable from its inhabitants. Although it is possible to imagine a street devoid of persons, the specific as opposed to generic meaning of a street depends intimately upon the type of people who frequent it and the things that they do on it. Fifth Avenue and the Lower East Side in New York are certainly different architecturally, but the social importance of their architecture inheres in its ability to inform us of the kind of people who are likely to live there. If we accept the notion of aggression and violence as an interpersonal process, then we must also reject the simplistic belief that aggression results from the main effects and interactions of the independent variables – the people and the setting. Thus violence cannot be understood as what happens when certain classes of people and a certain street come together, the two jointly producing aggressive actions. The street and the people in it are a function of the past history of that street in terms of the violence that occurs in it. It is for this reason that some people avoid certain locations while others seek them out. Nor does time conveniently freeze itself in the real world. A social setting can change over time, as anyone who has witnessed a cocktail party become a male drinking-contest in the wee small hours of the morning can testify. The behavior or effect we try to explain is part of a bidirectional relationship over time with the causes that produce it.

The dynamic quality of social interaction (and aggression as a form of such interaction) remains problematic only if we continue to treat it as an asocial output rather than as a process deployed over time and requiring the joint action of at least two participants. To tackle the problem from this point of view, it seems reasonable to start by focusing upon settings and actors with a reputation for violence, and then examine the aggressive interactions in their own context and as far as possible through the eyes of the participants themselves. The significance of the street as a location for aggression can only make sense if we examine the backgrounds, culture and roles of the people who frequent it. Without them the street is no more than concrete and tar.

The problem of putting aggressive behavior back into the real world and into its proper social context is complicated by the lack of reliable data. Statistics from the Uniform Crime Reports and National Crime Panel are fraught with problems of both reliability and validity. Nevertheless, these figures represent about the only compass we have for discovering the places and people who are involved in aggression and violence in the United States.

Assault is a city crime. Its reported rate is ten times higher in cities than in rural areas (Harries, 1974). Not all areas of a city are equally likely to be the setting for assaults. They occur most frequently in low-income neighborhoods and are committed principally by blue-collar and lower-income groups (Pittman and Handy, 1964; Mulvihill and Tumin, 1969; Blau and Blau, 1982). Assault is also a predominantly male crime: only about 15 per cent of reported assaults are by women (Brown et al., 1984). It is also committed more by the young than by the old, and the victims too tend to be young. The rates for blacks aged 16–24 are considerably higher than for whites. While blacks constitute 12 per cent of the population of the United States, they are responsible for 46 per cent of violent crime. Violence remains a principally intra-racial crime. Black males of all ages die from homicide at a rate that is six times that for black females or white males. Assault often occurs between acquaintances and friends and this is equally true of homicide. In 1981, 30 per cent of homicides were committed by friends or neighbors of victims, as compared to 17 per cent committed by family members and 15 per cent by strangers. This trend becomes even stronger if we examine the relationship between perpetrator and victim as a function of motive for the killing. The killer was a friend or acquaintance of the victim in 75 per cent of incidents which were precipitated by romantic rivalry or disputes over money or property. Perhaps most importantly for our purposes, the majority of assaults (53 per cent) occur in streets, parks or other outside locations near the home of the victim, as opposed to inside the home (14 per cent), in a non-residential building (12 per cent), school (12 per cent) or elsewhere (14 per cent). In cases of manslaughter, 30 per cent take place on the street (Brown et al., 1984).

These figures are not without problems. Violence in the home is under-reported and under-prosecuted. Violence which occurs in bars and taverns is likely to be dealt with by the management, who are often reluctant to call in the police. Violence in schools is also likely to be dealt with by internal disciplinary actions. More problematically for this argument, it is not only assault which happens on the street: rape, robbery and personal larceny also occur there. To paraphrase Wille Sutton, maybe crime occurs on the streets because that is where the victims are. Assault, however, is different from other crimes in that it frequently occurs between individuals who know one another, and the aggression is less obviously instrumental than in crimes such as robbery. Of all assaults on acquaintances, only 14 per cent are felonies or suspected felonies. The remainder are motivated by personal arguments. Given that acquaintances meet in a number of locations, from each other's homes to bars, why should the streets be the setting for aggression? My answer – that aggression occurs there because that is where those involved spend the most time – is less glib than it may appear, as a closer examination of the reasons for this pattern and of the meaning that the streets assume for the men in poverty-level families should demonstrate.

WHO OWNS THE STREETS?

The streets with which we are here concerned are those in the poorest urban environments. These streets are primarily black and Hispanic neighborhoods and they are male territory. The women run the home, struggling to maintain their income and to raise their children. Though they may have live-in arrangements with their men, role segregation remains high and the men spend a good deal of time on the streets (Rainwater, 1967). In a number of American states evidence of a male in the house means that the woman loses her eligibility for welfare benefits, so his presence is likely to be concealed. Women frequently feel that a male must earn his place in the home by making some financial contribution, and if he is unable to do this he may find himself welcome only at certain convenient times. The streets represent the most likely source of easy money for men who are jobless or irregularly employed. More than any of these things, it is the mutual understanding that the apartment is the woman's territory and the street the male's that tends to keep him on the street (Liebow, 1967).

While the male may be discouraged from remaining at home all day and getting under the woman's feet, his presence on the street often produces conflict. The streets are full of threats to domestic tranquillity; loose women who threaten to lure the man away; confidence tricksters who want to relieve him of what money he has; impecunious friends requesting long-term loans; drug-sellers; drinking-partners; and numbers runners[1] with their seductive promises of easy money. Against these threats, the woman tries to budget their money, maintain her sexual attractiveness, and raise her children to a better life away from the dangers of the street. It is the women who most often assume the role of the upholders of morality in the community. Men are seen as "no good". They all have a "bit of the dog" in them and are prone to the opportunities for irresponsibility which the streets present. Young girls are taught that the street is no place for a decent woman, and those who too frequently violate this rule are considered to be irresponsible mothers or promiscuous women.

Ghetto men have been sub-divided by a number of writers into distinct types. Liebow (1967) writes of street-corner men in Washington whose employment patterns are sporadic and who often rely upon their relationship with a woman to provide shelter, food and companionship. They may be involved in marginal law-breaking such as selling or buying stolen goods, stripping abandoned buildings and selling marijuana. Some may receive disability payments. Their existence is eaked out day to day, the focal point being the fifteenth of every month, when the woman's welfare check arrives. "Boss players", by contrast, are young men who have made it in the ghetto world. They dress with ostentatious style, eschew heavy labor and straight jobs, drive expensive cars, and represent what Glasgow (1981) calls the "Machiavelli of the ghetto system ... the functional intelligence of the streets". Their major income is from pimping and they take pride in the fact that they use sex to control their women – in contrast to the street-corner men, who are controlled by their women's need for sex (Curtis, 1975). Glasgow also describes "strong-arm studs", whose income comes from well-planned burglaries outside the immediate neighborhood and who carry and use weapons. In contrast to them are those who engage in local burglaries, which are rarely planned in advance and in which the men take any household appliances they can find, regardless of their street value. Lewis's description of (1965) of mainland Puerto Rican family life accords some importance to local men who earn their daily living by doing the rounds of local families collecting numbers money. On the street too may be youth gangs, hanging out, drinking with the older men, and flying their colors.[2] Increasingly, these groups are likely to be involved in local drug sales, operating within the compass of a few blocks (Campbell, 1984).

Most writers concur that, because there is rarely a stable male figure in the home, young males in these neighborhoods are likely to undergo their socialization chiefly on the streets (Glasgow, 1975; Liebow, 1967; Miller, 1958; Schulz, 1969). While mothers may strive to protect them from it, the struggle is often futile. Overcrowding in the home and the boy's desire to associate with his peer group will naturally draw him there. It is on the street that he gains exposure to adult role models and seeks to demonstrate his masculinity. The mother's attitude to his street life is often highly ambivalent, as Curtis notes: "In addition, the female head and other women in the family may suggest in an undertone that some overt masculine expressions are necessary coping devices, despite their ostensible enmity to such behavior. Worse than a no-good man is a cissy" (1975, pp. 31–2).

Street-corner life for most of these men involves staving off the boredom of poverty and unemployment. It is in this context that talk takes on a central role. It provides the main source of entertainment, and its expressive function allows the men to control and monitor their self-image. A number of ethnographers have pointed to the significance of smartness (Miller, 1958), "rapping" (Glasgow, 1980), verbal ability (Hannerz, 1969) and signifying[3] (Abrahams, 1964). As Glasgow describes it,

> Hour after hour of bullshit is what the perpetual argumentative discussions appear to be. In these debates any and every subject is material for discourse so

> long as it involves a certain degree of controversy. . . . The rapping usually occurs between two people at a time, while the other group members observe. These arbiters establish the rules, act as judges of Black character and Black style, and ultimately determine whether there is a victor. A winner is not easily determined and the group is not hasty in deciding, since the substance of the debate may be secondary to its socialization function. Very often the protagonists are "beautifully" engaged, the observers encourage them by interjecting opinions, "signifying" and generally abdicating their role as arbitrators, while exhorting the protagonists to demonstrate their ability. (1981, p. 98)

A second concern among this all-male group is the demonstration of sexual prowess. This happens chiefly in the world of talk, where the men present themselves to one another as accomplished lovers and like to see their relationship with their live-in woman as an indicator of their superior sexual and exploitative ability. Liebow (1967) notes that in many cases this is in fact no more than a crafted public image to compensate for the male's economic reliance on the female. They distinguish, however, between "nice" and "not nice" women and see the latter as a natural target for their exploitation. As Liebow summarizes their philosophy, "A man should take anything he can get when he can get it" (1967, p. 145). To reject the advances of a woman is tantamount to a public admission of emasculation (Campbell, 1984), and this outlook is responsible for a considerable amount of domestic fighting as well as aggressive confrontations between the two women involved. Another important aspect of manhood is the ability to drink large quantities of alcohol (Liebow, 1967; Miller, 1958). Days passed on the street are punctuated by trips to the local store to purchase beer or, where money allows, stronger forms of alcohol. Thus, as the day continues, the level of drunkenness goes up, tending to increase the vehemence of the verbal battles.

Coolness (Glasgow, 1981), autonomy (Miller, 1958), commanding respect (Hannerz, 1969) and machismo (Wallace, 1978) are also central to the preoccupations of the men. Deprived of the standard economic means for establishing dignity, they have to demonstrate it by the way in which they handle themselves on the street. "Coolness" involves knowing how things work, maintaining control and refusing to allow others to determine or influence one's life. It means remaining a free spirit in a world which persistently seeks to tame, crush or restrict you. As Glasgow notes, "Because cool is such an essential attribute and maintaining it has such an important effect on his ego, the ghetto youth would sooner go down than blow his cool, even in a situation where he has to retreat and the particular game is considered lost" (1981, p. 97).

There is no starting- and finishing-time for street life. It is an ongoing party that changes its character constantly as individuals join and leave in the course of the day. The streets are above all public places. Unlike in someone's home, those present are not beholden to their host, nor are they required to constrain their behavior out of respect for someone else's property or territorial rights. The street therefore represents an area that is "up for grabs" in terms of control and territorial rights. The police often represent the main rivals for ownership of the neighborhood, and it is clear from ethnographic accounts that the men deeply resent the harassment they suffer while simply hanging out on their own "turf". Young gang-members often conduct long-term feuds with the local police who harass and search them. Their presence is a personal affront to the gangs who also provoke the police by shouting abuse as they drive by. The police are seen not as remote representatives of a peace-keeping institution but as men who represent a direct power challenge to the gang-members (Campbell, 1984). If the police are seen as outsiders, so too are neighboring gangs who enter the gang's territory. The wearing of gang colors through another group's turf is seen as a sign of disrespect, and is enough to provoke direct confrontation. Increasingly, the intrusion of other gangs may mean an attempt on their part to move in or take over local drug sales in the area. The motivation for violence thus becomes economic as well as expressive.

The public nature of the streets also ensures the almost continuous presence of an audience. The demonstration of valued personal qualities requires a public arena. As the soccer terraces may serve such a function for British working-class youth (Marsh et al., 1978), the streets provide the stage for urban American teenagers. The socialization of maleness requires feedback from others and most specifically from other males. The establishment and maintenance of public face is learned, tried out and improved. The audience, besides providing evaluation and approval, serve to regulate the interactions which occur. They serve as arbitrators and mediators in disputes as well as instigators on occasion. Older males will intervene to "stop this bullshit" where aggression seems to be inappropriate. Young males will often goad one another into more and more extreme states of outrage about some real or imagined slight as they tell it over and over again to each other. Above all, the street is male. It is where masculinity is won and lost, and, in the marginal economic position occupied by these men, it is the approval of other males that is most central.

THE DYNAMICS OF VIOLENCE ESCALATION

Some writers have begun to examine the temporal sequencing of interactional moves by the participants. The idea is that commonalities across different aggressive episodes are the surface manifestation of underlying rules of social behavior that may be shared by a particular culture (Collett, 1977). This might be conceptualized as a branching-tree diagram moving through time. Each overt move is recognized by the other as carrying a particular social message and opens up a number of possible counter-moves. The number of such moves, however, is not infinite, because social action is constrained by rules, expectations and norms which are enforced by particular groups in specific circumstances. At the most trivial level, for example, questions tend to produce answers (or, at least, the subsequent act is interpreted as an answer), and commands usually lead to compliance or to an account of non-compliance.

Two analyses are pertinent here, although both address aggression generally rather than on the street specifically. Felson (1982, 1984) examined reported incidents of conflict where the respondent variously felt anger but did nothing, became involved in an argument, was involved in a physical fight, and used a weapon in a fight. Luckenbill (1977) examined the sequence of events leading to criminal homicide. Thus the two studies taken together provide a continuum of outcome seriousness. Just as assaults and homicides are very similar in terms of contextual factors, they are equally similar with respect to their interactional dynamics.

What behaviors lead to violence? In his study of criminal homicide, Wolfgang (1958) notes that the violent incidents often stemmed from domestic disputes (14 per cent), jealousy (11.6 per cent) or altercations over money (10.5 per cent). However the single largest category of precipitating incident was "trivial" behavior such as jostling, cursing or insulting. The use of the term "trivial" to describe behavior eventuating in murder seems to result from the tendency to seek information on these critical issues from official files and police reports, which, compiled by outsiders and abstracted for bureaucratic convenience, look only at immediate, behavioral factors. Above all, our acceptance of the term "trivial" indicates our inability as outsiders to interpret and make sense of the semiotic significance of opaque social events. However, the term is unfortunate in that it tends to suggest that the only plausible explanation of the disproportionately violent reaction is poor self-control or some other psychological problem. Both Luckenbill and Felson, however, provide more concrete examples of the kinds of actions that precipitated the initial verbal aggression. They include annoying behavior; comments that were interpreted as a direct attack on the integrity of the other party; failure to discharge an obligation or to comply with a command; ignoring; causing another's loss; boasting; inappropriate demeanor; infidelity; and taking or violating another's property. In and of themselves such affronts are not sufficient to account for the violent outcome; the explanation lies, rather, in the whole chain of events, in which behavioral choices are increasingly constrained toward violence. Nevertheless, more detailed analysis of these precipitating events provides a picture of those "deviant" acts within a culture that constitute sufficient grounds for the escalation of aggression. The norm-violating individual is less likely to be the aggressor in the engagement that follows than is the person who attempts to implement control over the deviant act. The norm-enforcer issues a reproach or an order to cease the offensive action, to make redress, to give some account of the deviant behavior or to leave. The typical response to this is non-compliance. (Subsequently, some form of account may be offered but it is generally too late. The effectiveness of account-giving as a de-escalator of aggression depends, according to Felson, on its occurrence before a reproach has been issued.) Following this come insults which in turn provoke threats, ultimately culminating in physical attack (in those situations in which an attack is made). This is followed by submission and by mediation by third parties present.

By no means do all such disputes end in physical violence. Liebow provides a vivid example of an exchange that contains all the elements of threat, insult and invitations to fight but where the mediating-effect of a third party together with a cooler head on the part of one protagonist averts violence. Nevertheless, the public persona of both parties is clearly at stake and, while the argument begins over a debt, it ends as a character contest:

> Tally reminded Richard of all the times he had lent Richard money.
>
> Richard said he always paid him back and demanded to know if he owed Tally anything.
>
> "Yes", said Tally. "You remember, you owe me a dollar from last week when you wanted to get back in that crap game."
>
> Richard told Tally not to go away. He ran inside and came back out with a dollar bill and threw it at Tally.
>
> "Now we're even", he said. "I don't owe you nothin' and you don't owe me nothin'. And Tally, I want to tell you one thing: don't ever step across my door again. If you ever put one foot in my house Tally, I'll kill you, I swear to God."
>
> "And Jackson", Richard continued, taking out his knife again and waving it in Tally's face, "don't ever think you're going to catch me without this. From now on whenever you see me, daytime, nighttime, or any other time, I'm always going to have somethin' on me."
>
> Despite the knife, Tally stayed within arm's length. "Richard, I ain't afraid of you and I ain't afraid of your knife. But I ain't mad at you, Richard, so I don't want to fight you. But don't make me mad."
>
> "Get mad then", said Richard. "I'm mad. You get mad, too, and then let's have it out." Richard said that he wasn't afraid of the police, that he had been in jail before and had gotten out and if he was in again he'd get out again.
>
> "Maybe you would," said Tally, "but you'd have to go out and scuffle to get them dollars." Tally slapped his back pockets with both hands. "But not me", he said. "I always carry that stuff with me. I always got some right here. I don't have to scuffle for mine. I always got it."
>
> Richard mumbled something weakly and unintelligibly. He was hurt. I tugged at Tally's arm and he let me pull him away from the corner. As we walked away Richard's shouts followed us. "You're yellow, Jackson, you're yellow. You're a yellow black mother." (Liebow, 1967, pp. 186–8)

It is possible to conceptualize the escalation of violence in terms of impression management. Reproaches, insults and threats assign the person challenged a negative identity and he has little alternative but to save face by counter-attacking (thus in turn challenging the other's right to cast such aspersions and simultaneously asserting his worth as an individual). The challenging of rule violations and willingness to "call out" the challenger, however, are not identical in different cultural groups. Many rule infractions are ignored, especially among the middle class, who are likely to respond with embarrassment or humor to untoward behavior.

Two factors suggest themselves as important in this respect. One is the extent to which the individual's general self-esteem depends upon his public identity in the situation to hand. Among marginal economic groups, whose members spend much of their daily life on the same street with the same acquaintances, the individual has less opportunity to establish multiple social roles and so salvage self-esteem by moving from one to another. In addition, among these groups the values which have been so well described by ethnographers become central in interpersonal conflict. Concern with autonomy and independence may augment the belief that the attacker has a right to point out shortcomings and rule violations. But, by the same token, the victim may feel that he is equally entitled to resist any attempts to influence or coerce his behavior. Threats and insults are likely to determine a narrower range of responses in a setting where masculinity and tougness are often equated. Concern with sexual prowess as a measure of worth is likely to enhance the seriousness of acts of infidelity or promiscuity by sexual partners. Ability in repartee means that insults suggesting that the other person is stupid, slow, ignorant or unsophisticated are likely to result in a severe loss of self-esteem.

The previously mentioned research by Felson failed to reveal significant differences between interactional patterns resulting in different degrees of violence, and the sequencing of acts is strikingly similar to that provided in Luckenbill's analysis of homicides. If we cannot distinguish these outcomes on the basis of interaction routines, we must look to other factors in the situation which more reliably discriminate between verbal abuse, a fist fight and a killing.

THE BOUNDARY CONDITIONS OF FIGHTING

There is high consensus from ethnographic accounts as well as from interview data and analysis of official records, that fights often result from acts which are interpreted as slights to dignity or personal integrity. These slights take on a particular significance amongst economically marginal males:

> Quick resort to physical combat as a measure of daring, courage or defense of status appears to be a cultural expression, especially for lower socio-economic class males of both races [black and white]. When such a culture norm response is elicited from an individual engaged in social interplay with others who harbor the same response mechanism, physical assaults, altercations, and violent domestic quarrels that result in homicide are likely to be common. (Wolfgang, 1958, pp. 188–9)

Although Wolfgang sees the fact that death may result from such interchanges as inevitable, other writers have drawn attention to the fact that most fights do *not* result in death (Marsh et al., 1978). In-group fighting between familiars would be highly maladaptive if it frequently resulted in fatalities. Indeed, if it did, certain sectors of society would have eliminated themselves through genocide by now. If the aim of these fights is to demonstrate courage, status and dignity, there is no reason to kill the opponent. It has been suggested by a number of writers that the "fair fight" is one cultural solution to the problem of large-scale in-group killing (Fox, 1977; Morris, 1967; Marsh et al., 1978). Analogies (not homologies) have been made with animal behavior, where "ritualized" or "limited war" strategies have long been observed in intra-specific fighting. It seems plausible that, in human socialization, children are taught that some forms of aggressive behavior are unacceptable and that it is desirable to "fight fair". Norms of fairness apply to the choice of adversaries, the form of aggression used, the number of opponents involved, and the signals which preclude further attack. Thus it is generally considered unacceptable for males to attack females. (This is not to deny that they frequently do, and the growing number of wife-abuse cases amply documents this. The point here is that it is not considered a normatively appropriate way of demonstrating manhood and courage to other males.) It is not regarded as fair for a large number of people to attack a single individual. Nor is it appropriate to continue an attack when the opponent is clearly injured or defeated. The usual form for a fair fight is with fists, and the introduction of weapons (especially if the other person is unarmed) confers an "unfair" advantage to one party.

Such a compilation of norms is intuitively satisfying, but, clearly, if they represented an adequate description there would be no cases of death resulting from fights triggered by personal affronts. These norms are frequently violated and this requires explanation. A number of studies which have compared the circumstances, participants and interaction patterns of assault and homicide have suggested that very few differences exist between them. Indeed, it has been argued that the only dividing-line is the speed with which the ambulance arrives to get the victim to hospital. However, closer inspection reveals two factors which reliably differentiate assault from homicide (Felson and Steadman, 1983; Pittman and Handy, 1964).

In homicide, a higher proportion of assailants and victims had been drinking alcohol prior to the interaction than in assault cases. A number of theories have been advanced with respect to the effects of alcohol on aggression (see the following chapter). One line of research suggests that the primary effect of alcohol is to heighten the general level of sympathetic nervous-system arousal and that this reduces cognitive control over behavior (Boyatzis, 1977; Zillman, 1979). Others have maintained that the effects of alcohol on the central nervous system are more direct, reducing information-processing capacity and resulting in a tendency to attend to only the most salient cues in the environment (Pernanen, 1976; Taylor and Leonard, 1983). For example, aggression in intoxicated subjects can be lowered by restating non-aggressive norms (Jeavons, 1980) and by focusing the subject's attention on his own behavior by placing a video camera in the room (Bailey and Leonard, cited in Taylor and Leonard, 1983). However, if the environmental cues are aggression-enhancing, then a high level of aggression is anticipated. In the case of street violence, we should expect that minimal aggressive cues such as an antagonistic but friendly verbal dispute might be interpreted as aggression in conditions where the protagonists had been drinking, especially when observers make salient to the participants aggression-producing cues ("Are you going to let him say that about you?"). The accompanying reduction in information-processing capacity might be expected to diminish attention to social norms and increase the difficulty of conforming behavior to these rules.

A different point of view has been taken by others, who highlight the social meaning of being drunk. For example, MacAndrew and Edgerton (1969) have proposed an acquired-disinhibition model of alcohol effects. They suggest that the ingestion of alcohol acts as a discriminative cue signalling that socially uninhibited behavior will not be subject to negative sanctions. Being drunk may therefore act as a mitigation for acts that if performed sober would be subject to disapproval. Indeed, Scott and Lyman (1968) maintain that drunkenness is one of a battery of justifications and excuses which we habitually employ to extricate ourselves from moral responsibility. Rather than acting as *post hoc* accounts of deviant behavior, it may be that they also operate prospectively to legitimate future acts in the manner of an internal disclaimer. As Taylor and Leonard describe it, "Drinking occasions are perceived as a time-out from normal social rules" (1983, p. 92). Being drunk legitimizes the violation of the normal rules of a fair fight.

A second critical factor discriminating assault and homicide is the use of weapons. The presence of a weapon opens the way for a single assault to become an aggravated assault, but beyond that, the availability of a gun has been found to be more closely associated with homicide and that of a knife with aggravated assault. The number of handguns manufactured in and imported into the United States in the 1970s exceeded the total for the previous six decades combined (Wright et al., 1981). However, according to

Gallup polls the number of households reporting the ownership of guns has not appreciably changed for the last two decades (Cook, 1982). This must cast some doubt on the veracity of self-report in this area and tends to suggest that many guns change hands illegally (Burr, 1977). Zimring (1968) distinguishes between gun use where the motive is unambiguously to kill and incidents where a weapon may be used but the intent is not to cause death. He found that a single shot was fired in about two thirds of gun murders in Chicago, and that, for every death caused by a bullet in the brain or chest, 1.8 victims with the same type of wound did not die. He concludes that victims die not because of differences in the gunman's intent but because of chance differences in the precise location of the wound. Even where a gun was used in an aggravated assault, death resulted in only 14 per cent of cases. In comparison, death resulted from only 4 per cent of knife attacks. The point is that the use of a gun in an assault situation does not necessarily betoken the user's intent to kill the victim. In most cases the user does not continue to fire after injury has been inflicted (Cook, 1982). The mere availability of the gun combined with willingness to use it (which may be augmented after alcohol consumption) tends tragically to increase the rate of death in these situations where the initial intent was not lethal. The nature of the interaction between alcohol, the natural boundaries of fair fights between acquaintances and the availability of guns is one that clearly requires more attention.

The very nature of this relationship is one that may well alter over time. For example, the increasing availability of weapons doubtlessly diminishes adherence to fair fight norms. In this connection, Maynard-Smith and Price (1973) offer an interesting analysis. As animal behaviorists, they examined a variety of aggressive forms in terms of their value as evolutionary stable strategies. Instead of offering the classic group-survival explanation of "limited war" (or, in our terms, "fair fights"), they argued that such a strategy may be the most adaptive and least injurious for the *individual* under attack. While speculative the study does suggest some interesting analogies to the problem faced by those living in neighborhoods where guns are readily available in deciding the appropriate response to threat. Maynard-Smith and Price examined two forms of aggression (conventional fair fights and lethal violence) in terms of various aggressive strategies that the combatants might pursue: "Mouse" (always uses conventional), "Hawk" (always uses lethal), "Bully" (uses lethal as first move, responds lethally to conventional moves, but responds with conventional moves to lethal moves by his opponent), "Retaliator" (uses conventional on first move thereafter duplicates the action of his opponent) and "Prober–Retaliator" (uses conventional if his opponent uses conventional, but occasionally uses lethal; after a lethal move, he abandons it if the opponent responds in kind but continues if the opponent continues to respond conventionally). These strategies were fed into a computer simulation where the probability of serious injury from a single lethal move was set at 0.10. Fortunately for present purposes, this figure is not far from the 0.14 probability of death resulting from the use of a handgun in an assault. Under these circumstances, Retaliator is the single most successful survival strategy for an individual who faces an opponent whose strategy he does not know. Such a model strongly argues for the advantage of owning and carrying a weapon in a situation where the opponent may use one. Interestingly, a change from 0.10 to 0.90 in the value of serious injury from a lethal move changes the most effective strategy to Hawk. If we entertain the notion that the higher figure reflects people's *subjective* estimation of the likelihood of dying from a gunshot wound, then the model suggests that, where individuals hold this belief, the single best strategy is to employ a gun before your opponent can do so. Of course, this would predict that over time the use of a lethal weapon, in a community where they are readily available to others, will increase. The introduction of guns to an environment which previously had none and employed "fair fight" tactics is likely to escalate the use of such weapons, ultimately resulting in the abandonment of fair-fight rules. The close correlation between gun availability and homicide has been noted frequently (Cook, 1982) and precisely such a pattern of change from fair fights to hit tactics with guns has been noted in youth-gang behavior over the last 20 years as guns have become more readily available (Miller et al., 1961; Miller, 1975; Short, 1976).

SOME REMAINING PROBLEMS

I have described how the street, its inhabitants and its culture can be seen as forming a setting for violence. I have also suggested that these factors are not static but truly interactive over time. The argument is deficient, however, in failing to account for individual differences. Although the temporal stability of aggressive behavior within individuals is not as high as many personality theorists would have hoped, studies have reported correlations up to 0.60 over several years (Olweus, 1979).

In the past, the study of individual differences has in fact been the study of individual commonalities. Groups of individuals are defined (united by some conceptual label or a personality-test score) and are compared with other groups of people, who form controls. The explanatory schema for these differences in aggression has been in terms of physiological factors (for example, psychopaths' low level of autonomic responsivity to stress) or personality factors (over- and under-controlled hostility, sensation-seeking, extraversion, and so on). The person is not only denied true individuality but is removed from the situations in which his aggression is expressed. A more adequate approach would be to examine the interaction of the person with the environments that evoke violent behavior from him. Though more time-consuming and less generalizable, this approach has been pioneered. Toch's work examining the social context in which violence manifests itself (1969) and Kelly's theory of personal constructs (1955) were far ahead of their time. The recent critical re-examination of personality (Endler, 1982; Mischel, 1973) has underlined the point that one of the most stable aspects of individuals resides in their cognitive styles – in both the complexity and the type of constructs which they use to make sense of the world. The examination of the social interpretations placed upon conflict situations may prove to be at the heart of individual differences (see chapter 3 above). If these truly are individual, we may have to abandon the desire for parsimony and simplicity which lures us into the development of typologies or groups. Commonalities may be more evident than we suppose at the level of interaction routines, since they fall in the public domain and thus are subject to the normative pressures of audience reaction. But what routine is selected is likely to depend heavily upon what the individual believes is really going on in the situation.

The examination of aggression as an interpersonal process rather than as an output from some intra-psychic black box can only be performed effectively within the context in which it is occurring. The orderliness which we hope to uncover is the overt manifestation of two individuals who "read" social signals in the same way. (This is not to deny that occasionally aggression may result from a lack of shared understanding when two people from different cultures misinterpret the meaning of words and actions.) It presupposes that, once meaning is decoded, a reduced number of options are available in the next interactional turn. If, for example, you are called a liar, you may admit the fact or question the other's right to reach such a conclusion or make such an allegation. It is true that you may select some improbable next move, such as asking about the other's vacation or ordering another drink, but this in itself will carry meaning, since it will almost certainly be seen as changing the subject and thus implying guilt or social discomfort. The nature of the rules (indeed, the way action itself is read) is likely to depend upon the culture and social setting in which the action takes place. The variability of these contextual factors is relatively unexplored and can only be uncovered by immersion in the culture itself or with the help of a native "interpreter".

Such an analysis will shed light on routine aggression but may not illuminate actions which are considered "crazy" or "weird" by the host community. (Indeed, academics tendency to dismiss the motives for lower-class violence as "trivial" is a good example of this loss of insight. Asked what had led to a particularly hostile interchange at an academic conference, they would probably be able to provide itemized examples of how different statements were "read" as implying that the researcher had invented data, deliberately misinterpreted previous tudies or taken the wrong political attitude to his work. To street-corner men these same statements would remain opaque and probably seem "trivial".) Street gangs find their own inter-gang aggression quite natural and can quite easily interpret for outsiders the meaning of wearing colors in the wrong territory. However, they clearly recognize some acts to be deviant – for example, a sniper firing randomly into a crowd or the rape of a young child. These actions are outside the boundaries of normal violence and so are remarkable even to those who routinely engage in a high level of aggression. The explanation of these sorts of acts may require a very different kind of approach. In the meantime, the attempt to systematize and make overt the implicit knowledge about aggression held by members of a given community will not be any easy task. But it will place routine aggression, which has always been with us as a necessary and functional part of our history, firmly in the province of meaningful social exchange and finally remove it from the domain of psychological disturbance.

NOTES

1 "Numbers runners" are individuals who collect money wagered illegally on the appearance of certain numbers in some statistical listing or tabulation published in a daily newspaper or racing form. Organized criminal networks generally act as the brokers for such bets.

2 Colors are sleeveless, denim jackets on the back of which the gang name and insignia are emblazoned. To "fly colors" means to wear the identifying jackets provocatively into the territory of a rival gang.

3 To signify is to use non-verbal signs of approval or solidarity. The most frequent form of signifying is the offering of an open palm by one person which in turn is slapped by the hand of the other person. When this is done with the hands above the head, it is called a "high five". It indicates strong support, agreement or appreciation.

REFERENCES

Abrahams, R. D. 1964: *Deep down in the Jungle*. Harboro: Folklore Associates.

Argyle, M., Fumham, A. and Graham, J. A. 1982: *Social Situations*. Cambridge: Cambridge University Press.

Blau, J. and P. 1982: The cost of inequality: metropolitan structure and violent crime. *American Sociological Review*, 47, 114–29.

Boyatzis, R. E. 1977: Alcohol and interpersonal aggression. In M. Gross (ed.), *Advances in Experimental Medicine and Biology*, vol. 85B: *Alcohol Information and Withdrawal 1116: studies in alcohol dependence,* New York: Plenum.

Brown, C. 1972: The language of soul. In T. Kochman (ed.), *Stylin' and Rappin' Out*, Urbana: University of Illinois Press.

Brown, E., Flanagan, T. and McLeod, M. (eds) 1984: *Sourcebook of Criminal Justice Statistics – 1983*. Washington, DC: US Government Printing Office.

Burr, D. E. S. 1977: *Handgun Regulation (Final Report)*. Tallahassee, Florida: Bureau of Criminal Justice Planning and Assistance.

Campbell, A. 1984: *The Girls in the Gang*. New York: Basil Blackwell.

Collett, P. 1977: *Social Rules and Social Behavior*. Oxford: Basil Blackwell.

Cook, P. 1982: The role of firearms in violent crime: an interpretive review of the literature. In M. Wolfgang and N. Weiner (eds), *Criminal Violence*, Beverly Hills, Calif.: Sage.

Curtis, L. 1975: *Violence, Race and Culture*. Lexington, Mass.: Lexington Books.

Endler, N. 1982: Interactionism comes of age. In M. Zanna, E. Tory Higgins and C. P. Herman (eds), *Consistency in Social Behavior*, Hillsdale, NJ: Lawrence Erlbaum Associates.

Felson, R. B. 1982: Impression management and the escalation of aggression and violence. *Social Psychology Quarterly*, 45, 245–54.

—— 1984: Patterns of aggressive social interaction. In A. Mummendey (ed.), *Social Psychology of Aggression: from individual behavior to social interaction*, Berlin: Springer.

Felson, R. B. and Steadman, H. S. 1983: Situations and processes leading to criminal violence. *Criminology*, 21, 59–74.

Fox, R. 1977: The inherent rules of violence. In P. Collett (ed.), *Social Rules and Social Behavior*, Oxford: Basil Blackwell.

Glasgow, D. G. 1981: *The Black Underclass*. New York: Vintage Books.

Hannerz, U. 1969: *Soulside: enquiries into ghetto culture and community*. New York: Columbia University Press.

Harries, K. 1974: *The Geography of Crime and Justice*. New York: McGraw-Hill.

Jeavons, C. 1980: The effects of alcohol and a norm on aggressive behavior. Master's thesis, Kent State University.

Kelly, G. 1955: *The Psychology of Personal Contructs*, vol. I and II. New York: Norton.

Lewis, O. 1965: *La Vida: a Puerto Rican family in the culture of poverty*. New York: Vintage Books.

Liebow, E. 1967: *Tally's Corner*. Boston: Little, Brown.

Luckenbill, D. F. 1977: Criminal homicide as a situated transaction. *Social Problems*, 25, 176–86.

MacAndrew, C. and Edgerton, R. 1969: *Drunken Comportment: a social explanation*. Chicago: Aldine.

Marsh, P., Rosser, E. and Harré, R. 1978: *The Rules of Disorder*. London: Routledge and Kegan Paul.

Maynard-Smith, J. and Price, G. 1973: The logic of animal conflict. *Nature*, 246, 15–18.

Miller, W. B. 1958: Lower class culture as a generating milieu of gang delinquency. *Journal of Social Issues*, 14, 5–19.

—— 1975: *Violence by Youth Gangs and Youth Groups as a Crime Problem in Major American Cities*. Washington, DC: US Government Printing Office.

Miller, W. B., Geerz, H. and Cutter, H. 1961: Aggression in a boys street corner group. *Psychiatry*, 24, 283–93.

Mischel, W. 1973: Toward a cognitive social learning reconceptualization of personality. *Psychology Review,* 80, 252–83.

Morris, D. 1967: *The Naked Ape.* New York: McGraw-Hill.

Mulvihill, D. J. and Tumin, M. M. 1969: *Crimes of Violence.* Washington, CD: US Government Printing Office.

Olweus, D. 1979: Stability of aggressive reaction patterns in males: a review. *Psychological Bulletin,* 86, 852–75.

Pernanen, K. 1976: Alcohol and crimes of violence. In B. Kissin and H. Begleiter (eds), *The Biology of Alcoholism: social aspects of alcoholism,* New York: Plenum.

Pittman, D. and Handy, W. 1964: Patterns in criminal aggravated assault. *Journal of Criminal Law, Criminology and Police Science,* 55, 462–70.

Rainwater, L. 1967: Crucible of identity. In T. Parsons and K. Clark (eds), *The Negro American.* Boston: Beacon Press.

Scott, M. and Lyman, S. 1968: Accounts. *American Sociological Review,* 33, 46–62.

Schulz, D. 1969: *Coming up Black: patterns of ghetto socialization.* Englewood Cliffs, NJ: Prentice-Hall.

Short, J. F. 1976: Gangs, politics and the social order. In J. Short (ed.), *Delinquency, Crime and Society,* Chicago: University of Chicago Press.

Taylor, S. and Leonard, K. 1983: Alcohol and human physical aggression. In R. Green and E. Donnerstein (eds), *Aggression: theoretical and empirical reviews,* vol. II, New York: Academic Press.

Toch, H. 1969: *Violent Men: an inquiry into the psychology of violence.* Chicago: Aldine.

Wallace, M. 1978: *Black Macho and the Myth of Superwoman.* New York: Dial Press.

Wolfgang, M. E. 1958: *Patterns in Criminal Homicide.* Philadelphia: University of Pennsylvania Press.

Wolfgang, M. E. and Ferracuti, F. 1967: *The Subculture of Violence.* London: Tavistock.

Wright, J., Rossi, P., Daly, K. and Weber-Burdin, E. 1981: *Weapons, Crime and Violence in America: a literature review and research agenda.* Amherst: University of Massachusetts, Social and Demographic Research Institute.

Zillman, D. 1979: *Hostility and Aggression.* Hillsdale, NJ: Lawrence Erlbaum Associates.

Zimring, F. 1968: Games with guns and statistics. *Wisconsin Law Review,* 1113–26.

9

Alcohol Consumption, Cognition and Context: Examining Tavern Violence

John J. Gibbs

INTRODUCTION

There is a substantial amount of evidence from surveys of victims, offenders and prisoners that alcohol is a component of many acts of criminal violence (Collins, 1980; Pernanen, 1976) and there is a growing body of experimental data which indicates that the association between alcohol and aggression is not direct (Pernanen, 1981; Blum, 1981). The probability that drinking in an experimental setting will result in increased levels of aggression is dependent on a number of factors. Both who is doing the drinking and the context in which it takes place influence the magnitude of the alcohol–aggression association.

The findings from surveys and experiments clearly suggest that there is an association between alcohol and violence which is influenced by person and context variables. This conclusion seems obvious and plausible. However, when we examine the methods used to gather the data on which this conclusion is based and we attempt to specify and explain the connections between violence, alcohol, person and situation, the link between alcohol and violence becomes less clear.

The lack of clarity is due, in large part, to the nature of the phenomenon: the association between alcohol and violence is complex. The methods typically used to examine the links between alcohol and violence also are problematic. Nearly all the studies to date have relied on either (1) survey data, primarily official records, or (2) experimental data. Both approaches have genuine limitations.

Some of the evidence that has been used to establish the connection between alcohol and violence is based on surveys of violent events described in police records. Typically, the researcher computes the proportion of cases in which the offender or victim or both had been drinking prior to the violent incident, and draws a conclusion about the role of alcohol in violent crime based on this proportion. There are some obvious limitations to this method. One is that there is no assurance of a statistical association between violent crime and drinking until (1) the proportion of incidents of violence involving drinking is compared with the proportion of incidents of some other behavior that involve drinking in comparable groups, or (2) we determine if violent or aggressive behavior varies with drinking within the same group. For example, it is possible, although not probable, that, if committing a homicide were compared with writing a homily, we might find the same percentage of each group had been drinking.[1] Or, we could find that people who are drunk when they get into fights are just as likely to be drunk when they cheat at cards, call old friends, or buy a bunch of flowers on the way home from work.

Another problem with surveys of official records is the measure of the independent variable. In most cases, the measure of the amount of alcohol participants in the incident had consumed is not precise (Collins, 1980, p. 21) and there is little information on the effects of the alcohol consumed on the functioning of the offender(s) and victim(s). Usually, the police can find out only whether or not participants in a crime had been drinking. For this reason, the alcohol variable in most studies of police records is a dichotomy (i.e. drinking or no drinking), and the association between violence and increasing levels of alcohol consumption cannot be determined.

The same holds true for measuring the effects of alcohol on various cognitive functions. It may be that violence typically occurs after at least one of the participants has reached a level of intoxication at which cognitive functioning is impaired. However, because judgments about the level and effects of the intoxication of offenders and victims are typically not reported to and recorded by the police, the influence of degree and effect of intoxication on violent crime cannot be assessed from police records.

Experimental studies, the other approach to examining the association between violence and alcohol, have gone a long way toward specifying the conditional and interactive nature of the association. However, their value is limited because of some of the features of the method. The most obvious limitation is the contrived and artificial nature of the experimental conditions: they may not be accurate representations of what occurs in natural settings. The effects of a certain amount of alcohol in a controlled experimental setting may be very different from its effects in a more complex, real-world setting. One researcher (Sui, 1979) has gone so far as to suggest that researchers who conduct alcohol experiments should report not only the probability of their results if the null hypothesis were true, but also estimates of the likelihood that their findings can be generalized to the real world – an external validity coefficient (Blum, 1981).

One reason why experiments on alcohol and violence do not accurately reflect what happens in natural settings is that ethical and practical concerns dictate that measurement of both the dependent variable (aggression) and the independent variable (alcohol) to be limited to a certain range (Pernanen, 1981). Generally, the expression of aggression in the experimental setting is restricted to mild forms and only small quantities of alcohol are consumed. One can hardly generalize from these experimental conditions to the real world of "blind" drunks and rages. When additional independent variables – threat, frustration, challenge, or insult, for example – are introduced into an experiment to specify the conditional nature of the association between aggression and alcohol, they are seldom as menacing and personal as the real-world forms they are intended to represent. A measure of threat such as overhearing a fellow experimental subject tell the experimenter that he has no qualms about administering a shock to you if he defeats you in a timed task (Taylor et al., 1976) is hardly in the same league as the guy on the next bar-stool, who happens to know your wife, calling her a pig.

One of the impediments to generalizing from experiments on alcohol and violence to the world outside the experimental setting is also one of the great benefits of using the experimental method, i.e. the control that the experimenter has over the composition of the experimental and the comparison groups. Experimenters typically assign subjects to experimental conditions (such as alcohol) and comparison conditions (such as fruit juice) by means of random allocation or matching. Their aim is groups of subjects that are comparable on all important variables except the independent variables of interest. In the real world, people are not randomly assigned to drinking-situations. When, where and how a person drinks – and with what consequences – are determined by a number of factors, including personal preference, social and economic status and cultural affiliation. When an experimenter assigns subjects to groups by randomization or matching, the role that factors such as preference and culture play in the choice of drinking-situation cannot be explored, because the subject does not make the choice (see Argyle, 1977; Wachtel, 1977).

The major shortcoming of the survey and experimental approaches to studying the connection between alcohol and violence has been their inability to provide complete descriptions of violent incidents. This is more than a methodological flaw. It is related to a more fundamental problem – conceptual impoverishment (Collins, 1981).

Clearly, conceptual development and description are related. A detailed description of a phenomenon is often an important first step in explaining it. Once established, the theoretical framework tells us what information to collect, which variables are important, and how the phenomenon under study should be described. Without proper description and measurement, we cannot assess the worth of our conceptual schemes.

Surveys of existing records and standard victimization surveys can tell us that there is an association between violence and alcohol, and that the magnitude of the correlation varies by sub-population as defined by characteristics such as race, income and social class. However, these survey techniques are not well suited to measuring the constructs that explain the association between alcohol and violence in certain sub-populations. Explaining why drinking leads to violence in some groups but not in others may require the exploration of differences in interpretation of events, and explaining why drinking promotes violence in some settings but not in others may warrant detailed situational analysis.

A detailed description of a phenomenon is often an important first step in explaining it. Official records of incidents of violence and other behaviors may not furnish very complete descriptions,[2] especially when participants had been drinking. Gathering retrospective accounts of incidents through the use of standard survey questionnaires may not provide a very accurate or complete picture if the subject had been drinking heavily at the time the incident took place.

Experiments on the association between alcohol and aggression seldom provide descriptions of incidents of violence, because their dependent measure is not the violent incident but usually some measure of the expression of aggression, such as strength of shock administered to another experimental subject or score on a projective test. Most of the experiments in this area also have another flaw: little attention has been given to the subjects' perception of the conditions of the experiment. The experimenter assumes that his interpretation of an experimental condition (threat, say) is the subjects' interpretation. The experimenter may frame his findings in terms of his interpretation (threat) when the subjects' view of the condition may be something other than a threat – for example, a challenge.

The inherent limitations of the two kinds of studies that have been discussed do not mean that these studies are not valuable. They provide some information that could not be gathered by other techniques, and they are the foundation for further methodological approaches that can advance our knowledge of the link between alcohol and violence.

Although a number of approaches will be incorporated into the research strategy presented in this chapter, the central method will be observation of behavior in bars. One reason for this is that I agree with Collins that "if the relationship (or absence of one) between drinking and assaultive crime is to be understood in detail, interpersonal behavioral interactions need to be mapped in detail. Microlevel understanding of behavioral configurations and their determinants is required" (1981, p. 26). The bar is a natural setting where alcohol is consumed and where violent and other interactions take place that are accessible to mapping.

The explanation of the association between alcohol and violence that will be advanced in this chapter is that violence is the product of certain kinds of interpersonal interactions, and alcohol affects perception and cognition in ways that make the occurrence of these kinds of interactions more likely. The bar is the context within which these interactions occur, and it features environmental qualities that can shape both drinking and the expression of aggression.

PERSPECTIVE ON VIOLENCE AND ALCOHOL

The model of violent behavior that is reflected in the research strategy presented in this chapter is based on the work of Toch (1969), Berkowitz (1978), Luckenbill (1977), Felson (1982), Shoham, Ben-David and Rahav (1974) and Hepburn (1973). Although these investigators differ in their data sources, techniques of analysis and academic disciplines, their research shows that violence is typically the culmination of multi-stage interaction between two or more persons that involves moves and counter-moves of an escalatory nature. Their research further specifies that these interaction sequences are initiated and sustained by the perception of at least one of the actors that he has been the target of an insult or that his self-esteem or public image has been threatened or challenged. The following excerpt from the work of Luckenbill illustrates one version of the model derived from impression-management theory (Felson, 1982):

> Criminal homicide is the culmination of an intense interchange between an offender and victim. Transactions resulting in murder involved the joint contribution of the victim to the escalation of a "character contest", a confrontation in which at least one, but usually both, attempt to establish or save face at the other's expense by standing steady in the face of adversity (Goffman, 1967: 218–219, 238–257). Such transactions additionally involved a consensus among participants that violence was a suitable if not required means of settling the contest. (Luckenbill, 1977, p. 177)

Most of those who study violent interactions consider the participants' perceptions an important part of the explanation, and they contend that within each stage of the interaction a move by one participant influences the counter move by the other. Furthermore, they suggest what happens in one stage of interaction influences what happens in the next stage, and it has an impact on whether the interaction culminates in violence. Although there are some differences in the number of stages described and what happens in them, the common portrayal of the violent interaction that emerges from these studies is one in which the protagonists sequentially paint themselves into a less-than-neutral corner. At each stage of the interaction, they manage further to reduce the options open for peaceful resolution of the conflict, thereby increasing the probability of violence, until they reach a point in the script at which anything short of *deus ex machina* will not save the scene from a violent ending.

The description that is required goes beyond the violent incident itself. The explanation of violent interactions requires that we know something about the persons interacting and the setting in which the interaction takes place. Toch points out that

> Violent acts, and violent interactions, do not make sense when viewed in isolation. The dilemmas people encounter are continuing, their personalities are constant, and their ways of relating to others reflect established habits and dispositions. Most violent conduct is no less lawful than other human conduct. If we examine different violent acts committed by the same person, we expect these acts to carry consistent meanings. We expect these acts to serve common needs; we expect them to result from pressures that operate persistently over time. We also expect that consistencies in the person's approach to others can produce situations in which violence always results – sometimes without the person being aware of the fact that he is the instigator of destructive (or self-destructive) games. And finally, some institutions in our society contain features that reliably encourage, provoke, or elicit violent conduct. These forces, also, contribute to shape the patterns of violence, and we must isolate and describe them. (1969, p. 6)

This is where alcohol comes in. Alcohol may be an important factor in describing and explaining (1) the situations a person persistently encounters, and (2) the variation and consistency in his reactions to these situations. Alcohol can play a role as a trait (for instance, alcoholic/non-alcoholic), state (intoxicated/sober), behavior (drinking/not drinking), or setting (drinking/non-drinking). Various combinations of these factors can increase or decrease the probability that a person will be involved in a violent interaction. My drinking-habits, for example, influence the probability that I will be in a place in which others are drinking, and the amount I drink during a particular drinking-episode will shape the interactions I have with others.

The most useful model I have found for explaining how alcohol shapes interactions that result in violence has been developed by Pernanen (1976, 1981). His model is based on a wide range of experimental findings, survey results and clinical observations. Pernanen summarizes his model of the influence of alcohol on violent behavior in the following terms:

> It can be said that the narrowing of the perceptual field with the consequent random determination by a smaller number of cues (and possibly a concomitant preponderance of "inner" cues, or drive states), experienced as significant in the orientation to the situation and the interpretation of the behavior of others, lead to a higher likelihood of violence in drinking situations. Another causative factor is the conceptual impoverishment and decline in abstracting ability under the influence of alcohol, which decrease the likelihood

of use of coping devices that go outside the immediate situation and thus cut down the probability of alternative acts. (1976, pp. 415–16)

He also furnishes a diagram as a summary of his model (see figure 1).

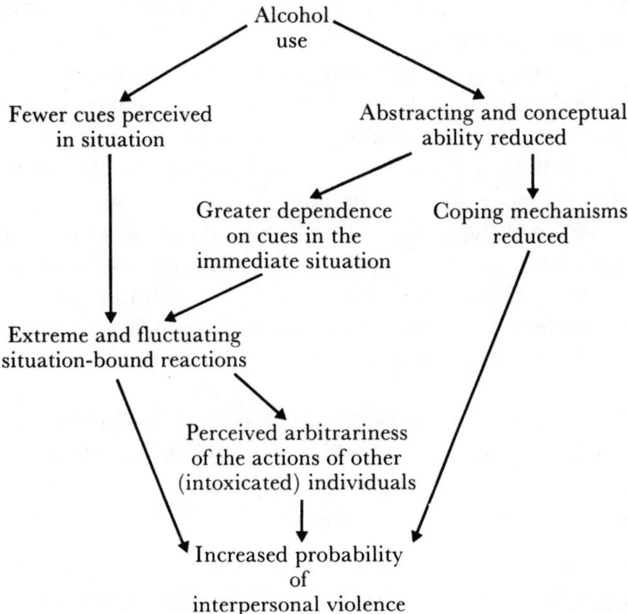

Figure 1 Factors in the use of alcohol leading to an increased probability of interpersonal violence (K. Pernanen, 1976, Alcohol and crimes of violence. In B. Kissin and H. Begleiter (eds), The Biology of Alcoholism: social aspects of alcoholism, *New York: Plenum, p. 416)*

Pernanen's model suggests that alcohol affects what Lazarus and Launier term primary and secondary cognitive appraisal. "Primary appraisal" refers to the person's evaluation of the situation in terms of his well-being, and "secondary appraisal" refers to the person's assessment of the coping-resources available to deal with the situation (1978, p. 302).

Alcohol influences primary appraisal by restricting the perceptual field. When under the influence of alcohol, people are less aware of what is going on around them than they are when completely sober, because they attend to relatively fewer cues in the environment. This means that primary appraisal of a situation is based on less information when a person is intoxicated than when he is sober.

The comparatively less complete representation of the total environment that is perceived when a person has been drinking can result in radical changes in that person's impression of a situation. When assessment is based on a limited number of environmental cues, a change in one of them can translate into a complete modification of one's view of the situation. The person who is intoxicated can be compared to the naïve researcher who has based his conclusions on a small number of cases. A small change in the absolute number of cases in a category can result in a huge change in the percentage of cases in the category, and change his impression about patterns suggested by the data.

When a person's perceptual field is narrowed to the point at which his perception of the situation is based on a few environmental cues, random fluctuations can mean drastic changes in his perception of the situation. This can lead to misunderstanding and conflict. Actions by others may appear inconsistent and arbitrary to the intoxicated person because he does not have a full view of the context in which they are taking place. If the intoxicated person then challenges the actions of others, their explanations for their actions may seen capricious in light of the situation the intoxicated person perceives. The person may feel that a detailed explanation or sincere apology is warranted by an action that others may feel is trivial in the larger context of things.

Arbitrariness and accounts or explanations for behavior (or their absence) have been found to play a role in violence. Pernanen refers to the experimental work of Pastore (1952), Buss (1963) and Epstein and Taylor (1967) to argue that arbitrariness leads to increased levels of aggression:

> aggression that is seen as arbitrary, as being the result of the whim of the aggressor, elicits more aggression than aggression that can be attributed to an acceptable cause or reason. Due to the narrowing of the perceptual field, we can assume that the probability for two individuals to see overlapping cues as relevant in the situation will be less than in a sober sitution (this is strictly statistical reasoning). Thus, the one will more likely fail to see a justification for the other person's action. Consequently, the action of the other person will seem more arbitrary and will thus evoke more aggression, which again has a higher probability of seeming arbitrary, and thus the probability of escalation into physical violence is successively increased over the comparable probabilities in a sober situation. (Pernanen, 1976, p. 415)

Felson's log-linear analysis of descriptions of disputes provided by samples of the general population (N = 245), ex-mental patient (N = 148), and ex-criminal offenders (N = 141) suggests that when explanations are given in disputes they are less likely to result in violence than when accounts are not given:

> The results suggest that when a respondent gives an account during a verbal dispute, the incident is less likely to involve physical violence. An account by the respondent decreases the odds of hitting/slapping vs. verbal dispute 2.9 times. . . . In the final model, accounts by the antagonist were substituted for accounts by the respondent. The results were similar to those from the previous model and again the fit was excellent. . . . An account from the antagonist

> decreases the odds of a physically violent dispute vs. verbal attack 3.0 times. (1982, p. 250)

The findings that have been reviewed so far in relation to Pernanen's 1976 model suggest that part of the association between alcohol and violence can be accounted for by the reduction of the perceptual field produced by drinking. This shrinking of the perceptual field increases the likelihood that disputes will arise and decreases the probability that accounts will be provided and accepted. Pernanen proposes that alcohol also affects how a person deals with what he perceives: that is, alcohol influences secondary cognitive appraisal, which involves assessment of the resources available to cope with a situation.

Alcohol has a dampening effect on intellectual functioning and verbal ability (see Graham et al., 1980, p. 144). When a person is under the influence of alcohol his ability to resolve conflict in a peaceful manner is limited in two ways: (1) he has difficulty accessing and evaluating the appropriateness of existing solutions and developing new ones; and (2) he has difficulty in translating his solution into words that might pacify his antagonist.

The influence of alcohol on conceptual ability also may be responsible for the restricted time perspective that has been observed in drinkers. It has been suggested that alcohol reduces future time perspective and increases concern with the present. The conceptual shrinking that occurs when a person is intoxicated can make current external and internal cues, which may have very little meaning in the larger picture that he holds of his life when sober, seem tremendously important.

Pernanen's model (1976) indicates that alcohol increases the probability of violent behavior by influencing both primary and secondary cognitive appraisal. Lazarus and Launier point out the connection between the two:

> The two forms of appraisal also influence each other. The knowledge that one can overcome a potential danger may make that danger moot; and the knowledge that one is in danger typically mobilizes a search for information about, or an evaluation of, what can and cannot be done (Janis, 1974, refers to this as vigilance). The important point, however, is that secondary appraisal is important in shaping the coping activities of the person under psychological stress, as well as in shaping the primary appraisal process itself. (1978, p. 206)

In a more complex, but less clearly stated, version of his model, Pernanen speculates that the reduction in the perceptual and cognitive fields produced by drinking may result in feelings of control and power:

> To take the reasoning onto somewhat shakier ground, there is probably a greater degree of "mastery" – less ambiguity in situation cues . . . due to the fewer number of cues perceived, cognized, and mentally processed. This may lead to a greater "feelings of power" among males in certain types of social situations . . . . (1981, p. 30)

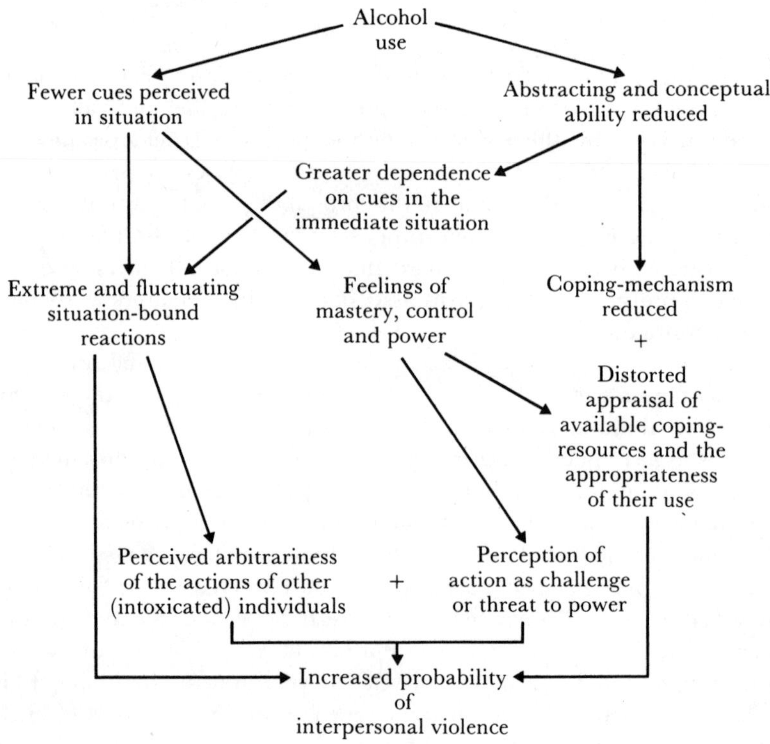

Figure 2 Factors in the use of alcohol, including power concerns, leading to an increased probability of interpersonal violence

The association between drinking and power concerns has been investigated by McClelland and his colleagues, who concluded after a decade of research that

> Men drink primarily to feel stronger. Those for whom personalized power is a particular concern drink more heavily. Alcohol in small amounts, in restrained people tends to increase thoughts of social power – of having an impact on others for their own good. In larger amounts, in supportive settings, and in impulsive people, it leads to an increase in thoughts of personalized power – of winning personal victories over threatening adversaries. Among younger men, particularly in appropriate settings, thoughts of personal power are often expressed in terms of sexual and aggressive conquests. (1972, p. 334)

Pernanen felt he led us to "somewhat shakier ground" by introducing the possibility of connection between the reduction in perceptual cognitive ability associated with alcohol and the feelings of power related to alcohol for some people in some situations. In figures 2 and 3, I intend to take us from

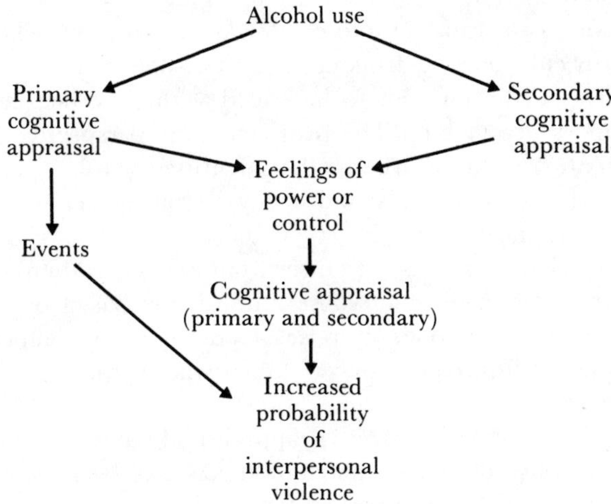

Figure 3 Simplified model of factors in the use of alcohol leading to an increased probability of interpersonal violence

"somewhat shakier ground" to standing squarely on the conceptual fault-line by incorporating feelings of mastery, control and power into Pernanen's 1976 model.

The model appearing in figure 2 shows where feelings of mastery, control and power fit into Pernanen's 1976 model. Figure 3 presents a simplified version of the model presented in figure 2. The model specifies that alcohol produces a narrowing of perceptual and cognitive fields. This produces a relatively uncomplicated view of the situation, whatever that situation may be, which in turn creates a feeling of mastery, power or control over that situation. Unfortunately, as described earlier, this simple view of the situation based on relatively few environmental cues is unstable and subject to rapid changes. This can result in misunderstanding and conflict when the definitions that two or more people hold of a situation change in different directions. The model suggests that the same effect of drinking, i.e. the narrowing of the perceptual field, can produce (1) a feeling of control over a uncomplicated situation, and (2) a situation that seems to change uncontrollably.

A change in a person's sense of power or mastery of his world can translate into changes in primary and secondary cognitive appraisals of events. A man of power has certain rights, privileges, duties and obligations. Events that seem inconsequential to others may require a response from the powerful. A breach of drinking-protocol at the far end of the bar may be an irritant to the average man, but it flies in the face of the powerful man's authority. After all, it is his duty to maintain protocol in his bar–territory.

Misunderstandings that result from changing definitions of the situation owing to drinking can translate into challenges to authority when a man's sense of power is enhanced by drinking, and a person's view of himself as an authority figure or someone not to be trifled with may become the only identity of importance to him. The restricted time perspective mentioned earlier may create a situation where other identities or roles – for instance, responsible employee, loving husband or loyal scout-leader – seem remote and unconnected to the present.

The man who derives a sense of power from alcohol seldom responds to threats with the wisdom of one whose authority is based on more solid ground. The tap-room despot's exercise of power is not tempered by an extended view of the future or a concern about what is the greatest good for the greatest number.

Alcohol affects secondary cognitive appraisal directly and through its enhancement of sense of control and power. As has been described previously, drinking impairs conceptual and abstracting-ability, which reduces the number and complexity of coping-options available. Drinking leads to regressive styles of coping. The drinking man is more likely to deal with threats and challenges directly and physically than is his more sober counterpart, and alcohol-induced feelings of power may color the drinking man's secondary cognitive appraisal or his assessment of the strength of his resources – in this case, his physical prowess. A man may be more likely to implement a physical solution to a problem when he is drunk than when he is sober, because he has a higher opinion of his combative talents when he is intoxicated.

The model described above of the influence of alcohol on interpersonal violence suggests that alcohol influences primary and secondary cognitive appraisal in a way that enhances the drinker's sense of power, which in turn influences the primary and secondary appraisal of subsequent events. The model does not add anything new to our understanding of violent interactions themselves. It simply shows how alcohol can increase the probability of the kinds violent interactions described by Toch (1969), Berkowitz (1978), Luckenbill (1977) and others. As we have seen, alcohol increases the likelihood that the first stage of a violent encounter will occur. In this stage, at least one of the protagonists feels that his identity has ben threatened or that it is incumbent upon him to document or enhance his status in his own eyes and in the eyes of others. Alcohol reduces the chances that tactics of threat reduction such as avoidance and acceptance (Hepburn, 1973) will be used, and thereby increases the probability that the interaction will advance to other stages. The farther the interaction advances, the less likely the use of avoidance or acceptance of threat by either party because the cost to identity becomes too great (Hepburn, 1973).

THE BAR AS A HUMAN CLIMATE

One would predict, given the experimental evidence on the conditional or interactive association between alcohol and aggression, that violence would be more prevalent in some settings in which drinking occurs than in others. The purpose of this section is to explore the violence-promoting and violence-inhibiting features of some drinking-places. Of course, there are many other settings in which violence occurs in conjunction with drinking – for example, the home, which is discussed by Robert Powers in chapter 14.

People drink in bars for many different reasons. They use bars to relax, meet friends, find excitement, gamble, do business and find entertainment. Bars vary in their ability to satisfy these needs, and consequently they vary in the clientele they serve. Combinations of clients and needs are the main determinants of the atmosphere of the bar. There are quiet little places with three-piece bands where lovers meet, and there are dance halls with dirt floors and rockabilly bands where bar-tenders serve buckets of beer through small openings in concrete walls.

The atmosphere of the bar shapes the style of drinking and proper comportment while under the influence of alcohol. It also regulates the amount of aggression that can be expressed and determines which expressions of aggression are appropriate. Some bars feature more structure than others for interpreting and reacting to conflict situations. There are formal rules that limit the possibility for misunderstanding. In some bars, for example, gambling on pool and darts for stakes higher than a drink is not allowed, and money never changes hands between gambling customers. The loser buys the winner either a drink or a beer check. In these bars, the house rules for games are clear, specific and posted, and differences in interpretation are settled by the bar-tender.

There are also informal rules that limit conflict and misunderstanding. For example, in some bars, it is commonly known that the proper behavior when an opponent is playing a shot at the pool table is to step away from the table and keep silent. In bars where standards of conduct at the pool table have not been established, there is a greater chance that disputes will arise over the propriety of certain behaviors.

When conflict does arise, some bars have mechanisms for dealing with it so that the likelihood of escalation into violence is diminished. The bar-tender is seen as the final arbiter in some bars. When misunderstandings occur, the patrons involved are expected to present their sides of the argument to him, and to abide by his judgment.

The role that customers not directly involved in the conflict should play is also clearly established in some bars. For instance, it may be established that those not involved in a dispute should not take sides in it, even if they are invited to do so, but should discourage the protagonists from continuing it. The actions by audiences of disputes have been found to be important in the escalation of violent interactions (see Felson, 1982; Hepburn, 1973). Factors that structure the role of the audience can make the difference between a beery argument and a drunken brawl.

The findings from studies of violence in bars indicate that there is considerable variation between bars. Graham and his colleagues conducted 633 hours of observation (303 observation periods) in 185 bars in Vancouver over a three-month period. They recorded 160 incidents of aggression (47 physical aggression and 113 non-physical), and they collected data on the characteristics of the bars in which they conducted observations. For example, they made observations concerning the characteristics of the patrons their drinking-patterns, the decor of the bar, and the major activities and interactions taking place in the bar. A factor analysis of the characteristics of the settings produced one factor that correlated substantially with aggression ($r = 0.59$):

> This environment was characterized by very permissive decorum expectations, unpleasant, unclean and inexpensive physical surroundings, higher percentages of American Indians and unkempt patrons than in other bars, a tense atmosphere, patrons drinking rapidly and becoming highly intoxicated, downtown location, poor ventilation, shabby decor with no theme, people talking loudly to themselves, tables crowded together in rows and unfriendly barworkers. (Graham et al., 1980, pp. 287–9)

Graham and colleagues report that incidents of aggression during the observation period occurred in 29 of the 185 bars in their sample (15 per cent). These bars included many of what they classified as "skid row aggressive" bars:

> A fairly large proportion of the clientele of this type of bar are people without regular work (unemployed, disabled, retired) or people with illegal work (prostitutes, drug dealers). The bar is frequented by at least one minority group (American Indian, Black, homosexual). Patrons tend to be in and out of the bar all day and use the bar as a "home base" for social and other activities. For many of the patrons, this bar is one of the circuit of bars they visit during the day. . . . There are few limits on acceptable behavior and little pressure for patrons to behave "normally". This accepting attitude seems to be combined with suspicion and hostility ("tense atmosphere"), possibly because of the deals going on. Most of the barworkers are not friendly and avoid interaction with patrons . . . . (p. 290)

The aggressive bars described by Graham and his colleagues certainly do not appear to be places with rules and norms that help structure ambiguous situations which could result in disputes.

As part of a study of pub violence in the United Kingdom, Campbell and

Marsh analysed 2000 questionnaires completed by licensees of Whitbread pubs. One purpose of their study was "to enable analysis of problems and incidents in terms of the characteristics and locale of the public house and with respect to the personal data concerning the licensee" (1979, p. 33).

Approximately 35 per cent of the Campbell and Marsh sample reported one or more fights involving men in their pubs within a two-year period. The comparable percentages for women fighting in pubs and fights outside pubs were 11 and 41. Forty-four per cent of the respondents reported that they had intervened to stop a fight at least once.

Campbell and Marsh combined information on incidents of disturbances by patrons of pubs and interventions by licensees into an index that they used as the dependent variable in their analysis. They conclude that the characteristics that are most highly associated with their index are

> The age of the licensee, the time he has been in charge of a particular pub, his length of time in the trade, his previous experience and his status .... In fact, these effects together can account for a greater degree of variance among pubs than can effects due to the location of the pub or variables relating to the clientele. The locality in which the pub is situated is, of course, an important consideration. But whilst effects due to this variable "swamp" any effects due to characteristics of clientele, the effects due to characteristics of licensee are still highly significant even when the effect of location is partialled out. In other words, within a particular locality, the characteristics of the licensee are the only significantly discriminating factors. (p. 188)

It is noteworthy that, in both the observational study by Graham and colleagues and the Campbell and Marsh questionnaire survey, characteristics of the bar staff were found to be associated with violence. This suggests that they may be important in shaping the context in which violence takes place. Staff may make a significant contribution to the atmosphere of the bar by shaping and enforcing the rules for dispute resolution. The following section presents a strategy for exploring the bar as the context for violence and some of the other factors discussed in this chapter that shape violent interactions.

STRATEGY FOR EXPLORATION

There are a number of questions touched on in this chapter that need to be addressed methodologically. These include (1) why people are more violent in bars than in other settings, if they are more violent in bars; (2) why some bars are more violent than others; (3) why some people in bars are more violent than others; and (4) why some people are more violent in bars at some times than at other times. To develop research designs capable of answering adequately any of these questions would require the production of a major proposal. Here I will be much less ambitious and simply mention a few areas that I think should be explored, offering a few suggestions on how to explore them.

My primary concern is to examine the effects of alcohol on perception and cognition in natural settings and to see what role they play in interactions that end in violence. The first essential, I think, is to obtain complete descriptions not only of the violent interactions in which people are involved, in a given setting, but also of the interactions that do not end in violence. Shoham and his colleagues have pointed out that "a full scale study of violence should include not only a study of the escalatory processes leading towards an eruption of violence (that is, verbal communication, gestures, and mutually-understood symbols), but also a study of the factors which are linked to the avoidance of violence" (1974, p. 418).

It may be useful to observe the same people involved in a variety of interactions in the same settings over an extended period of time. With the exception of Toch's study of violent men (1969), the studies of violent interactions and the studies of alcohol referred to in this chapter have been based on the observation of single incidents. Pervin and Lewis argue that a broader perspective is needed:

> The interactionist perspective, and the work of the ethologist, suggests the need for a broader temporal context than the single act (Rausch, 1977). If we take the process question seriously, then we must be prepared for long-term observations and appreciation of complex relationships. Much of our research to date has involved a freezing of behavior rather than a witnessing of the unfolding of behavior. (1978, p. 18)

If some of the same people are observed in a bar on a number of occasions, it should yield a sample of interactions for each subject that varies in terms of content, level of aggression, length and sobriety of participants. A comparison of interactions of varying levels of aggression for the same subjects should provide some clues to why some interactions escalate into violence while others do not.

Until now, I have been referring to participant observation. Modern technology makes a further step possible: video and audio records of bar-room interactions. Video and audio records of interactions not only would be valuable for mapping the exact sequence of the interactions, but also could be used to gather important phenomenological information. Participants in interactions could be requested to view them and to interpret their actions. They could be asked to describe what they were thinking and feeling at certain junctures in the interaction. Probes could be directed at finding out what options they saw available to them in resolving conflicts, and what assumptions they made about their adversaries in conflict situations. Information could be collected on how much they had had to drink and its effects. Subjects could be directed to describe what they consider the important differences between interactions featuring different levels of aggression.

There are many ways in which such tapes could be used to map the cognitive and perceptual fields of participants in an interaction. For example, they could be used to reconstruct changes in perception and cognition over an evening of drinking. They also could be used in studies of subjects who were not participants in the interactions recorded. They could be used, for example, in a study, such as suggested by Anne Campbell, in which subjects are shown an interaction up to a certain point and asked to predict whether it will end in violence.

There are, of course, a number of practical and ethical problems associated with recording everything that happens in a bar during a certain time period. I am not qualified to comment on the technical problems of doing it, but I have a feeling that there are plenty of them. I do know that such recording would require more money than I will ever see, and I know that obtaining the informed consent of the subjects is a thorny issue. I also know that discussing this issue would take more time and space than I can devote to it here.

It also may be informative to observe subjects in settings other than bars – for example, a cafeteria at work or a lunch room at a mission. Argyle claims that

> each person consists of a set of discrete states and patterns of behavior, manifest in different situations – his or her performance at psychological conferences, at home, as a psychotherapist, etc. It is not possible to generalize across these situations to traits, because totally different aspects of behavior are involved in each case. (1977, p. 363)

Observation of the same subjects in a bar and in another setting would furnish the data needed to determine those aspects of behavior that are drawn out by the bar environment.

Some information about differences in bar-room climates could be gleaned from audio and video records of interactions in a variety of bars. Factors that may be related to violence – rules and their enforcement, for example – could be represented in recorded interactions. Other information on the atmosphere of bars could be gathered by observing and interviewing patrons and/or staff. Bars could be classified by a number of environmental qualities – for instance, characteristics of customers, reasons why customers frequent the bars, presence of competitive games, proportion of customers who are regulars, and clarity of rules and regulations.

NOTES

1 When alcohol consumption is examined by kind of offense there is some evidence that it is more likely to be connected with violent crimes than with property offenses (Collins, 1980, p. 2), and there is an association reported between the seriousness of an act of aggression and alcohol involvement (Gerson and Preston, 1979, p. 309).

2 I am specifically referring to studies of alcohol and violence. As will be shown in the next section of this chapter, those who have designed studies specifically to explore violent interactions have done a commendable job of gathering descriptions of violent incidents from official records and participants in violent encounters (see Toch, 1969; Berkowitz, 1978; Luckenbill, 1977; Felson, 1982).

REFERENCES

Argyle, M. 1977: Predictive and generative rule models of P × S interaction. In D. Magnusson and N. S. Endler (eds), *Personality at the Crossroads: current issues in interactional psychology*, Hillsdale, NJ: Lawrence Erlbaum Associates.

Berkowitz, L. 1978: Is criminal violence normative behavior? Hostile and instrumental aggression in violent incidents. *Journal of Research in Crime and Delinquency*, 15, 148–61.

Blum, R. H. 1981: Violence, alcohol and setting: an explored nexus. In J. J. Collins, Jr (ed.), *Drinking and Crime*, New York: Guilford.

Buss, A. H. 1963: Physical aggression in relation to different frustrations. *Journal of Abnormal and Social Psychology*, 67, 343–8.

Campbell, A. and Marsh, P. 1979: *Final Report to Whitbread Ltd.* Oxford: Contemporary Violence Research Centre, Oxford University.

Collins, J. J. Jr 1981: Alcohol use and criminal behavior: An empirical, theoretical and methodological overview. In J. J. Collins, Jr (ed.), *Drinking and Crime*, New York: Guilford.

Collins, J. J., Guess, L. L., Williams, J. R. and Hamilton, C. J. 1980: *Final Report: a research agenda to address the relationship between alcohol consumption and assaultive criminal behavior.* Research Triangle Park, NC: Research Triangle Institute.

Epstein, S. and Taylor, S. P. 1967: Instigation to aggression as a function of degree of defeat and perceived aggressive intent of the opponent. *Journal of Personality*, 32, 457–72.

Felson, R. B. 1982: Impression management and the evaluation of aggression and violence. *Social Psychology Quarterly*, 45, 245–54.

Graham, K., LaRocque, L., Yetman, R., Ross, T. J. and Giustra, Y. 1980: Aggression and barroom environments. *Journal of Studies on Alcohol*, 41, 277–92.

Gerson, L. W. and Preston, D. A. 1979: Alcohol consumption and the incidence of violent crime. *Journal of Alcohol Studies*, 40, 307–13.

Hepburn, J. R. 1973: Violent behavior in interpersonal relationships. *Sociological Quarterly*, 14, 419–29.

Lazarus, R. S. and Launier, R. 1978: Stress-related transactions between person and environment. In L. A. Pervin and M. Lewis (eds), *Perspectives in Interactional Psychology*, New York: Plenum.

Luckenbill, D. F. 1977: Criminal homicide as a situated transaction. *Social Problems*, 25, 176–86.

McClelland, D. C., Davis, R. and Wanner, E. (eds) 1972: *The Drinking Man*. New York: Free Press.

Pastore, N. 1952: The role of arbitrariness in the frustration–aggression hypothesis. *Journal of Abnormal and Social Psychology*, 47, 728–31.

Pernanen, K. 1976: Alcohol and crimes of violence. In B. Kissin and H. Begleiter (eds), *The Biology of Alcoholism: social aspects of alcoholism*, New York: Plenum.

—— 1981: Theoretical aspects of the relationship between alcohol use and crime. In J. J. Collins, Jr (ed.), *Drinking and Crime*, New York: Plenum.

Pervin, L. A. and Lewis, M. (eds) 1978: *Perspectives in Interactional Psychology*. New York: Plenum.

Shoham, S., Ben-David, L. and Rahav, L. 1974: Interaction in violence. *Human Relations*, 27, 417–30.

Taylor, S. P., Gammon, C. B. and Capasso, D. R. 1976: Aggression as a function of alcohol and threat. *Journal of Personality and Social Psychology*, 34, 938–41.

Toch, H. 1969: *Violent Men: an inquiry into the psychology of violence*. Chicago: Aldine. (New edn Cambridge, Mass.: Schenkman, 1984.)

Wachtel, P. L. 1977: Interaction cycles, unconscious process, and person–situation issues. In D. Magnusson and N. S. Endler (eds), *Personality at the Crossroads: current issues in interactional psychology*, Hillsdale, NJ: Lawrence Erlbaum Associates.

10

Bar-Room Brawls: Aggression and Violence in Irish and American Bars

Richard B. Felson, William Baccaglini and George Gmelch

INTRODUCTION

Conflict in bars is commonly attributed to drinking. It is well known that the consumption of alcoholic beverages is associated with aggression and violence (cf. Pernanen, 1976, for a review). However, conflict in bars may have other sources as well. This chapter focuses on two such sources: (1) the type of clientele that bars attract, and (2) the types of situations that are likely to develop in them.

Bars may create the opportunity for conflict because they bring together in one location young adult males, a violence-prone population. Research shows that males, in general, tend to be more violent than females (cf. Frodi et al., 1977) and that violence declines with age (Wolfgang and Ferracuti, 1967). Therefore, any type of activity that attracts young males increases the opportunity for conflict. This explanation is consistent with the routine-activity approach to crime suggested by Cohen and Felson. According to this approach "the probability that a violation will occur at any specific time and place might be taken as a function of the convergence of likely offenders and suitable targets in the absence of capable guardians" (Cohen and Felson, 1979, p. 590). Thus, to the extent that employees and others are unable to prevent violence, the presence of young males – particularly intoxicated young males – may be important. Of course, bars vary in the extent to which they attract youthful patrons. One would expect that bars with a youthful clientele would experience more conflict than bars serving older patrons. The data from a study of bars in Vancouver suggest that physical aggression is more frequent in weekend night spots with young patrons (Graham and Turnbull, 1978).

We wish to thank Kevin Buckley, Reid Golden, Stephen Light, Ruth Pasquerello and Paul Turner for their assistance in collecting the data, and Allen Liska for his helpful comments.

Another reason why conflict may occur more frequently in bars than in many other locations is suggested by a recent interactionist theory of aggression (Felson, 1981, 1984; Black, 1983). According to this approach much aggression can be interpreted as punishment or behavior aimed at social control. Aggressive episodes often begin when someone believes a violation of a norm or rule has occurred. For deterrence or retribution this person may then punish the rule-violator, usually with some verbal reprimand or insult.[1] While the punishing-agent usually views his behavior as legitimate and justifiable, the target is likely to perceive the behavior as an illegitimate attack, and is likely to retaliate. Retaliation occurs for deterrence and retribution but it also reflects face-saving concerns (Felson, 1978, 1982).

The provocation for the first attack in most aggressive encounters, then, is an alleged rule violation.[2] Therefore, aggression should occur more frequently in situations in which rule violations are more common. Another important variable may be the extent to which the authority of the punishing-agent is recognized by the target. The target is more likely to retaliate when he or she does not recognize the authority of the punishing-agent as legitimate.

Bars may create opportunities for conflict because they are locations in which issues of social control are likely to be problematic. First, drinking increases the likelihood of violations of norms of interaction. For example, intoxicated individuals are less likely to display the tact and politeness required in interaction (see Goffman, 1959). Second, the rules concerning the control of drinking are likely to create conflict. Bar-tenders frequently refuse to serve patrons who are under age, extremely intoxicated or disorderly, and their actions may cause conflict if patrons are angry over not being served. Marsh (1980), for example, reports that fights in English pubs typically begin when the publican refuses to serve patrons, and that publicans who lack social skills in controlling their customers' behavior are more likely to elicit aggression. Finally, the authority of bar-tenders and bouncers may not be recognized as legitimate by patrons. Hence, they may retaliate for what they perceive as unjust treatment.

The social class and race of the clientele may also be associated with the frequency of conflict in bars. Graham and his colleagues (1980), for example, found a greater frequency of verbal and physical aggression in bars that were characterized as having inexpensive physical surroundings, a high proportion of minority customers and a relatively large number of customers whose appearance suggested that they were members of the lower classes. In general, there is evidence of class and race differences in criminal violence (see, for instance, Braithwaite, 1981; Hindelang, 1978). However, studies using self-reports, which tend to focus on less severe violence, do not always show these effects (see, for example, Ball-Rockeach, 1973; Steadman and Felson, 1984). This suggests that these social–demographic variables may have a bearing on whether conflicts escalate and become more serious.

The present study is based on interviews with bar-tenders and bar-owners, and includes four types of analysis. First, we describe the actual content of disputes in order to determine what initiates aggression in bars. We are particularly interested in the role of social control (i.e. attempts by bar-tenders to control patrons) as an instigator of aggression. Second, we examine variables that might affect the frequency of aggression in bars and their use of bouncers. Here we examine whether the demographic characteristics of the patrons (age, sex, race and social class) predict which bars have more fights and which use bouncers. Third, we compare the characteristics of the clients involved in physical conflict with the general clientele of the bars in which the conflict took place. The question here is whether patrons who are young, black, male or from a lower socio-economic status are more likely to engage in conflict. Finally, we examine variables that may cause verbal disputes to escalate into physical violence. Here we attempt to determine whether antagonists are more likely to use violence during a verbal dispute if they are intoxicated, male, young, black or from a lower socio-economic status. This analysis compares the characteristics of participants in verbal and physical incidents, treating the incident as the unit of analysis.

By comparing data from two cultural settings – the United States and Ireland – we hope to examine cross-cultural differences in the incidence and causes of aggression in bars. It is also hoped that the cross-cultural comparison will increase the generalizability of the findings. Ireland was chosen for the study for two reasons. First, Irish bars have often been described in popular literature as places of heavy drinking and frequent brawling. Second, Ireland being a predominantly English-speaking country, it was possible to use essentially the same interview schedule as in the American study, thereby allowing a more tightly controlled comparison.

METHODS

The data were collected through interviews with bar-tenders and bar-owners in 131 bars in Albany, New York, and 67 bars in Ireland, mostly in the capital city, Dublin. Interviews were carried ot primarily by two white American males in the American sample and two Irish females and one Irish male in the Irish sample. Interviewers used the telephone directory and their own knowledge of the areas to contact as many bars as they possibly could from a broad range of social classes and neighborhoods.

Measurement

Two measures of frequency of violence were used. First, respondents were asked, "How many times in the past month has there been a fight here where someone was hit with a fist or an object?" The second measure focused on how recently a fight had occurred. Respondents were asked, "Can you recall a recent dispute here where there was a physical fight involving fists or a weapon? These could involve patrons or employees. We're interested in an incident where you saw what happened and can tell us about it." If such an incident could be recalled, the respondent was asked, "How long ago was it?" The response was coded in number of weeks. Any incident occurring more than one year before the interview was coded 52 (weeks). If no incident could be recalled, the item was coded as 52, indicating that at least a year had passed since the last incident. This assumes that, if no incident could be recalled, none had occurred during the preceding year. It was necessary to make this assumption to avoid a significant loss of data.

The two measures of verbal aggression were similar. First, respondents were asked, "How many times in the past month has there been a bad argument here where there was shouting or insults but no hitting, pushing or physical fighting?" The measure of recency was the same as before, except that the words "a big argument involving shouting or name-calling but no physical violence" were substituted for "a physical fight involving fists or a weapon".

In sum, we had two types of frequency measure for each form of aggression: one based on reported frequency in the preceding month, and one based on how recently during the last year an incident had occurred. The recency measure was more subtle and less subject, one would expect, to a social-desirability bias. On the other hand, the measure is subject to criticism because respondents were asked to remember a recent incident, not necessarily the latest incident.

The correlation between the measure of behavior during the preceding month and the measure of recency during the preceding year was, for the American data, 0.51 for physical violence and 0.36 for verbal aggression. The corresponding figures for the Irish data were 0.16 and 0.10, suggesting problems with these measures in the Irish data. In part, the low correlations may have been owing to the infrequency of these behaviors in Irish bars. Less than 8 per cent of the bars, for example, had had a violent incident in the preceding month. In addition, our interviewers noted a degree of defensiveness in some of the Irish respondents, who may have been afraid that their bar licenses would not be renewed if conflict in their establishments were reported.

We examined six measures of social class:

1 Duncan scores based on the respondent's answers to the question "What are the most typical occupations of the people who come here?" (if respondents named multiple occupations, the mean of these scores was used);
2 the respondent's description of the crowd on Friday and Saturday

nights as mostly working-class, middle-class or upper-class (coded 1, 2, 3, respectively);

3 the price of a draft beer;
4 the price of the house Scotch whisky;
5 the interviewer's estimate of the socio-economic class of the crowd, from "very low" (coded 1) to "very high" (5);
6 the interviewer's rating of the decor, from "not at all fancy" (1) to "very fancy" (5).

A factor analysis revealed a single factor with loadings of 0.46, 0.64, 0.76, 0.87, 0.77 and 0.84, respectively. A scale was constructed omitting the item with the lowest loading.

Respondents were also asked to estimate the percentage of patrons who were male, the percentage who were from the neighborhood and (in the American sample) the percentage who were white. They were also asked to estimate how many patrons they usually served on Friday or Saturday nights, and the average age of these patrons. Liquor consumption was measured by the number of bottles of hard liquor and cases of beer consumed on a typical weekend evening. A scale was constructed based on the sum of these two items after each was standardized. We controlled, of course, for number of patrons when examining the effect of this variable.

There were also a series of questions on the incidents that the respondents could recall. We asked about the sex and age of the participants, their social class (working, middle or upper), how intoxicated they were (not at all, slightly, somewhat, extremely), their relationship to each other (whether they were friends, strangers, acquaintances, husband and wife, or other relative), and whether women were involved. Finally, respondents were asked what the dispute was about.

RESULTS

The contents of disputes

Data on the content of disputes are presented in table 1. These results suggest that fights in American and Irish bars generally occur over similar issues and that the contents of verbal and physical aggressive incidents tend to be similar. None of the differences between verbal and physical incidents or between American and Irish incidents were statistically significant. The most interesting finding in the table is that the bar-tender's refusal to serve patrons was the most frequent source of conflict. Thus a major source of bar-room aggression appears to be the attempt to control alcohol consumption, rather than alcohol consumption itself.

Table 1 Percentages for the content of verbal and physical disputes for both samples

	American		*Irish*	
Content	*Verbal*	*Physical*	*Verbal*	*Physical*
Refusal to serve	22.8	24.1	25.0	30.0
Conflict over opposite sex	5.2	19.0	11.4	10.0
Insults	10.4	12.1	6.8	13.3
Spectator sports	9.1	1.7	2.3	3.3
Games	7.8	5.2	2.3	6.7
Work-related	6.5	6.9	2.3	0.0
Disruptive behavior	6.5	12.1	15.9	10.0
Money/property	6.5	5.2	6.8	6.7
Politics	3.9	3.4	11.4	10.0
Conflict between intimates	14.3	8.6	9.1	3.3
Other	7.8	1.7	6.8	6.7
	100.0	100.0	100.0	100.0
(N)	(77)	(58)	(44)	(30)

Variation across bars

In the following analyses we examine frequency of aggression and violence in American bars as a function of the age, sex, race and social class of the clientele, the amount of alcohol consumed, the number of patrons, and the percentage of the clientele who come from the neighborhood. We predicted that bars that catered to youth, males, blacks and persons of lower socio-economic status would experience more frequent aggressive incidents. In addition, it was hypothesized that the amount of alcohol consumed would be associated with a higher frequency of conflict. One might also expect that, the greater the number of patrons, and thus the greater the number of people at risk, the more frequent the incidents, since crowding itself may result in more aggression. We made no prediction about differences between neighborhood bars. On the one hand, where the patrons know each other, there may be more opportunities for conflict; but, on the other, conflict may be less frequent where there is less anonymity and more effective social control.

The zero-order correlations, means and standard deviations are presented in table 2 and the standardized regression coefficients are presented in table 3. The results suggest that the average age of the patrons is the best predictor of both verbal and physical aggression: the older the patrons the fewer the aggressive incidents, particularly violent ones. Bars with a lower-class clientele were more likely to experience incidents of verbal aggression. However,

Table 2 Zero-order correlations, means and standard deviations

		1	*2*	*3*	*4*	*5*	*6*	*7*	*8*	*9*	*10*
1	Socio-economic status		−0.30	−0.28	0.33	0.10	−0.27	−0.37	0.11	0.21	0.34
2	Percentage non-white			0.21	−0.22	−0.09	−0.19	0.13	−0.06	−0.02	0.04
3	X̄ age				−0.41	−0.15	0.24	0.24	0.30	0.27	−0.38
4	Number of patrons					0.30	−0.06	−0.20	0.04	−0.13	0.36
5	Amount of alcohol						0.05	−0.07	0.09	0.00	0.03
6	Percentage men							0.06	0.01	−0.06	−0.28
7	Percentage from neighborhood								−0.23	−0.01	−0.21
8	Physical violence									0.35	−0.15
9	Verbal aggression										−0.11
10	Bouncer										
X̄		0.155	16.3	32.6	65.1	0.012	64.7	51.8	−0.09	−0.062	0.325
SD		0.345	23.0	9.32	55.4	1.68	15.1	25.1	1.72	1.63	0.466

X̄ = mean of X.
SD = standard deviation.

Table 3 Standardized regression coefficients for American sample where bar is the unit of analysis

	Dependent variable		
Independent variables	*Physical violence*	*Verbal aggression*	*Bouncer*
Socio-economic status	−0.03	−0.31[a]	0.18[b]
Percentage non-white	0.10	0.05	0.08
$\bar{X}$ age	−0.48[a]	−0.34[a]	−0.21[a]
Number of patrons	−0.11	0.12	0.24[a]
Amount of alcohol	−0.11	−0.06	−0.08
Percentage men	0.10	0.08	−0.14
Percentage from neighborhood	0.29[b]	−0.02	−0.06
R^2	0.235[a]	0.179[a]	0.275[a]

R^2 = square of multiple correlation coefficient.
[a] Significant at the 0.05 level or greater.
[b] $p < 0.10$.

socio-economic status did not affect the frequency of physical violence. In addition, neighborhood bars were more likely to experience incidents of physical violence (but not verbal aggression) than bars that drew patrons from further afield. None of the other variables had any significant effects. That is, neither number of patrons, race, percentage male, nor amount of alcohol consumed was related to either verbal or physical aggression.

Social control: the bouncer

Bouncers – persons employed to eject disorderly customers – are uncommon in Ireland. In the American sample, however, 32 per cent of the bars employed bouncers. In order to examine which bars employed bouncers, we regressed a dummy variable (coded 1 if there was a bouncer, 0 if there was not) on the variables described above for the American sample. The results are presented in the last column of table 3. The results suggest that bouncers are more likely to be employed when there are many patrons and when the patrons are young. Socio-economic status also had a marginally significant positive effect, suggesting that higher-class bars are either more concerned with protecting their investment or else are more likely to have the money to employ such persons. No other variable had a significant effect.

As shown in table 2, the correlations between use of bouncers and the aggression measures were negative but statistically insignificant. One would expect that the positive effect of aggression on the use of bouncers would be suppressed by a negative reciprocal effect, since the use of bouncers most likely reduces the frequency of aggression.

Table 4 Characteristics of participants in conflicts and general clientele

	American sample			Irish sample		
	Verbal incident	*Physical incident*	*General clientele*	*Verbal incident*	*Physical incident*	*General clientele*
Mean age	33.9	28.6	31.6	35.5	30.8	35.9
Percentage working-class	0.634	0.671	0.488	0.841	0.853	0.659
Percentage both antagonists male	0.582	0.839	0.439[a]	0.833	0.778	0.459[a]
Percentage regular customers	0.570	0.519	0.692	0.511	0.338	0.788
Percentage non-white	0.783	0.872	0.828	–	–	–

[a] This is the square of the percentage of male patrons in the bar.

Comparison of participants in aggressive incidents with other patrons

Here we compare the characteristics of participants in aggressive incidents with the characteristics of other patrons at the same bars. This will suggest whether or not the former were a representative sample of the general clientele.

Table 4 presents the relevant data for both the American sample (columns 1–3) and the Irish sample (columns 4–6). Columns 1 and 4 describe the characteristics of participants in verbal incidents and columns 2 and 5 describe the characteristics of participants in violent incidents. The mean is computed for the two antagonists in each case. The descriptive statistics for the bar are presented in columns 3 and 6. In the case of the variable "percentage male" we present the square of that percentage in order to obtain the probability that a pair of patrons, chosen randomly from the pool of patrons, would be male. This number can be compared to the percentage of the incidents in which both participants are male. In each case we compare the statistics for the bar with the characteristics of participants using a t-test that allows for correlated means.

The hypothesis that the participants in aggressive incidents would be younger than the general clientele was not supported in the American sample. The participants in physical incidents were slightly younger ($p = 0.16$) while the participants in verbal incidents were actually slightly older ($p = 0.04$). In the Irish sample, participants in violent incidents were likely to be younger than the other patrons ($p = 0.001$) but the participants in verbal incidents were of similar age to the general clientele.

The results for socio-economic status were more consistent. For both Irish and American bars, participants in verbal and physically violent incidents were more likely than the general clientele to be from the working class. Both differences were significant for the American sample ($p = 0.02$; $p < 0.003$). For the smaller Irish sample, the difference was statistically significant only for the verbal incidents ($p = 0.01$; $p = 0.11$).

The results were also clear-cut as regards sex. In both samples, participants in both verbal and physical incidents were more likely to be males than were random pairs of patrons (American verbal, $p < 0.01$; American physical, $p < 0.001$; Irish verbal, $p < 0.001$; Irish physical, $p < 0.001$).

We also attempted to determine whether bar-room violence tended to involve regular customers or not. For verbal and physical aggression, in both American and Irish bars, participants in aggressive incidents were less likely than the general clientele to be regular customers (American verbal, $p < .05$; American physical, $p < 0.001$; Irish verbal, $p < 001$; Irish physical, $p < 0.001$).

Finally, for the American sample we compared the race of participants with the race of other patrons. No significant differences were observed.

In sum, participants in bar-room fights in both the United States and Ireland were more likely to be males and from the working class, and they were less likely to be regular customers than the general clientele of the bar. Irish participants in violent incidents but not verbal ones were likely to be younger than the general clientele. In the American bars, age effects were slight and inconsistent, and race had no effect.

Escalation from verbal aggression to physical violence

Next we compared verbal and physical incidents to determine which variables cause a conflict to escalate from a verbally aggressive encounter to a physically violent one.[3] To carry out this analysis the data set was rearranged so that the incident became the unit of analysis. Each of the 132 American incidents and 87 Irish incidents was coded as 1 if the incident involved physical violence and 0 if it involved only verbal aggression. For each sample of incidents this variable was regressed on the following variables:

1 the mean age of the two antagonists;
2 the mean socio-economic status of the antagonists (working-, middle- or upper-class, coded 1, 2, 3, respectively);
3 how intoxicated they were (coding 4 for "extremely", 3 for "somewhat", 2 for "slightly" and 1 for "not at all");
4 whether both antagonists were male (coded 1 if they were and 0 if they were not);
5 the race of the antagonists (coded 2 if both white, 1 if one white and one black, and 0 if both black;

6 two dummy variables representing three types of role relationships – primary relationships (i.e. relatives and friends), acquaintances and, the omitted category, strangers.[4]

For both samples, the standardized regression coefficients (see table 5) suggested that age was the best predictor of escalation to physical violence. Verbal conflicts were more likely to become physically violent among youthful antagonists. In the American sample, antagonists appeared more likely to become physically violent when they were intoxicated, but this effect was not significant in the Irish sample. Conflicts between males were more likely to lead to escalation in the American sample, while in the Irish sample the sex of the antagonists had no effect. Finally, class, race and role relationship had no effects on escalation in either sample.

Table 5 Standardized regression coefficients where escalation is the dependent variable and the incident is the unit of analysis

Independent variables	*American incidents*	*Irish incidents*
Age	–0.26[a]	–0.26[a]
Socio-economic status	–0.10	–0.04
Intoxication	0.20[a]	0.11
Sex (males)	0.25[a]	–0.08
Race (white)	0.09	–
Primary relations	–0.05	–0.10
Acquaintances	–0.02	–0.21
R^2	0.197[a]	0.114[a]

[a] Significant at the 0.05 level or above.

DISCUSSION

The best predictor of aggression in these data was age. Bars that served youthful patrons were much more likely to experience incidents of verbal and physical aggression, and verbal incidents involving youthful patrons were more likely to become physically violent. Thus, it appears that one of the reasons why aggression occurs in bars is that they are places where young adults congregate and come into contact. However, participants in aggressive incidents were no younger than the general clientele. The finding (in the American sample) that the age of a bar's clientele predicted the frequency of aggression in that bar, but that the participants in aggressive incidents were no younger than the general clientele, suggests a contextual effect: youths are more likely to fight when they are with other youths than when they are among older persons. This is consistent with previous research, which suggests that third parties in incidents of homicide and assault that involve youth are more likely to be supportive of violence and are likely to induce more intense violence (Felson et al., 1981).

The role of intoxication in these incidents was difficult to establish. While, in about a third of the incidents, at least one of the antagonists was described as "extremely intoxicated", the degree of intoxication of non-participants is unknown. There was evidence that participants in physical violence were likely to be slightly more intoxicated than participants in verbal incidents, indicating that persons who are intoxicated are somewhat more likely to use physical violence. However, in contrast to the findings of Graham and his colleagues (1980), variation in alcohol consumption across bars was not associated with the frequency of aggression in those bars.

The most frequent source of conflict involved the anger of patrons over the bar-tender's refusal to serve them. This occurred when patrons were perceived as intoxicated or unruly, or when they were thought to be under the legal drinking-age. Thus it appears that the efforts of employees to control the behavior of patrons elicits an aggressive reaction. This suggests that one reason why alcohol results in aggression in bars, and perhaps elsewhere, is that intoxication and the behaviors associated with it elicit from others a social-control reaction that is perceived as an affront by the intoxicated person, who then retaliates.

This approach also suggests that the development of aggressive interactions may be similar to the development of secondary deviance (Lemert, 1978). The latter approach suggests that deviant careers begin because the social reaction to an initial deviant act – the labeling-process – elicits more deviant behavior. This process has also been described in terms of a deviance-amplification system (Wilkins, 1965). In the case of aggressive interactions, a similar process occurs: the initial deviant act results in punishment – the social response – which then provokes retaliation. However, the developmental process in aggressive interactions is usually situational, occurring within a shorter time frame. And, unlike in the development of secondary deviance, the initial act is usually a different type of behavior from the subsequent act.

Race had no effects on any of the measures of aggression. By contrast, the social class of patrons predicted the frequency of verbal aggression, though not of physical violence, and participants in both types of conflict were more likely than other patrons to be from the working class. However, the social class of the antagonists did not play a role in the escalation of incidents. In general, the results suggest that verbal conflicts are more frequent among the working class, but that class has no effect on escalation.

The findings that participants in fights are more likely to be from the working class and are more likely to be intoxicated are subject to an alternative interpretation. It may be that respondents are more likely to believe that participants in fights are from the working class because of their stereotypes about working-class persons. Similarly, respondents may assume patrons are intoxicated if they become involved in fights, particularly if those fights involve physical violence. We cannot rule out these alternative explanations. However, the evidence is consistent with the literature, which shows that aggression is related to social class and alcohol consumption. In addition, we believe that bar-tenders develop a certain amount of expertise in judging whether patrons are intoxicated or not, since they are required by law to refuse to serve persons in this condition.

In both samples, males were much more likely than females to be involved in verbal or physical aggression. In the American sample, escalation to physical violence was more likely when the antagonists were males, while, in the Irish sample, female participation was low in both types of incidents. The frequency of aggression, however, was unrelated to the percentage of males patronizing a bar.

Most of the findings were similar for both samples. There were two notable exceptions. First, there was a much greater frequency of aggression and violence in American bars than in Irish bars. The stereotype of brawling in Irish pubs appears to be untrue, at least as compared with American bars. Second, there were differences between the two countries in the role of sex. Females were more likely to be involved in verbal incidents in the American sample, and, when males were involved, the incidents were more likely to become physical. In the Irish sample, on the other hand, female participation was uncommon in both types of incident and it did not play a role in escalation.

In conclusion, these findings suggest that alcohol plays a role in bar-room aggression but that it alone does not account for the relative frequency of aggression in this location. In fact, the attempt to control alcohol consumption by refusing to serve certain patrons appears to be the most frequent source of conflict, suggesting that some violence results from issues of social control. While social class has some effects, the frequency with which aggression occurs in different bars is more strongly and consistently associated with the age rather than the social class of a bar's clientele. The findings suggest that one of the reasons that aggression and violence occur in some bars is that they are locations where young adult males, who are susceptible to violence, congregate.

NOTES

1 Sometimes these reprimands involve only mild criticism of the target's behavior.

2 This was found to be the case in a recent study of self-reports of incidents that culminate in verbal and physical aggression (Felson, 1984).

3 Evidence suggests that almost all physically violent incidents begin with verbal aggression (Felson, 1984).

4 A problem of multi-collinearity was apparent in earlier analyses when the characteristics of each participant were considered separately.

REFERENCES

Ball-Rokeach, S. J. 1973: Values and violence: a test of the subculture of violence thesis. *American Sociological Review*, 38, 736–49.

Black, D. 1983: Crime as social control. *American Sociological Review*, 48, 34–45.

Braithwaite, J. 1981: The myth of social class and criminality reconsidered. *American Sociological Review*, 46, 36–57.

Cohen, L. and Felson, M. 1979: Social change and crime rate trends. *American Sociological Review*, 44, 588–608.

Felson, R. B. 1978: Aggression as impression management. *Social Psychology*, 41, 205–13.

—— 1981: An interactionist approach to aggression. In J. T. Tedeschi (ed.), *Impression Management Theory and Social Psychological Research*, New York: Academic Press.

—— 1982: Impression management and the evaluation of aggression and violence. *Social Psychology Quarterly*, 45, 245–54.

—— 1984: Patterns of aggressive social interaction. In A. Mummendey (ed.), *Social Psychology of Aggression: from individual behavior to social interaction*, Berlin: Springer.

Felson, R. B., Ribner, S. and Siegel, M. 1984: Age and the effect of third parties during criminal violence. *Sociology and Social Research*, 68, 452–62.

Frodi, A., Macaulay, J. and Thome, P. R. 1977: Are women always less aggressive than men? A review of the experimental literature. *Psychological Bulletin*, 84, 634–60.

Goffman, E. 1959: *The Presentation of Self in Everyday Life*. Garden City, NY: Anchor.

Graham, K. and Turnbull, W. 1978: Alcohol and naturally occurring aggression. Paper presented at a meeting of the Western Psychological Association, April.

Graham, K., LaRocque, L., Yetman, R., Ross T. J. and Giustra, Y. 1980: Aggression and bar-room environments. *Journal of Studies on Alcohol*, 41, 277–92.

Hindelang, M. J. 1978: Race and involvement in common law personal crimes. *American Sociological Review*, 43, 93–109.

Hindelang, M., Gottfredson, M. and Garafalo, J. 1978: *Victims of Personal Crime*. Cambridge, Mass.: Ballinger.

Lemert, E. M. 1978: Secondary deviance and role conceptions. In R. A. Farrell and V. L. Swigert (eds), *Social Deviance*, New York: Lippincott.

Luckenbill, D. F. 1977: Criminal homicide as a situated transaction. *Social Problems*, 25, 176–86.

Marsh, P. 1980: Violence at the pub. *New Society*, 12, 210–12.

Pernanen, K. 1976: Alcohol and crimes of violence. In B. Kissin and H. Begleiter (eds), *The Biology of Alcoholism*, New York: Plenum.

Steadman, H. J. and Felson, R. B. 1984: Self-reports of violence: ex-mental patients, ex-offenders and the general population. *Criminology*, 22, 321–42.

Wilkins, L. 1965: *Social Deviance*. London: Tavistock.

Wolfgang, M. and Ferracuti, F. 1967: *The Subculture of Violence*. London: Tavistock.

11

Robbery Arising out of a Group Drinking-Context

Ann Teresa Cordilia

INTRODUCTION

Sutherland distinguishes two explanations of criminal behavior: "historical" or "genetic", and "situational" or "mechanistic" (Sutherland and Cressey, 1970). Historical explanations concern "processes operating in the earlier history of the criminal" (p. 74) – for example, "differential association", or exposure to an excess of definitions favorable to violation of the law. Situational explanations, by contrast, are stated in terms of factors which come into play at the time of the crime. For Sutherland, historical factors are crucial, while situational factors are important only in so far as they provide an opportunity for the criminal act.

Following Sutherland, criminologists have generally used historical factors, such as criminal norms or psychopathology, to explain adult crime. Two criminologists however, have called for greater attention to the role of situational causes. In line with his theoretical orientation to crime as a socially created phenomenon, Lemert (1951) has suggested that the causes of crime should be looked for in situational factors rather than in factors "within the skin" of the individual. Gibbons, in response to empirical findings, has also come to the conclusion that "criminological attention ought to shift toward more concern with criminogenic situations" (1971, p. 268). Attempting to categorize prison inmates according to a typology of criminal careers, he found that a large percentage did not fit any category and did not seem very different in their background or beliefs from the non-criminal population. This suggested that there exists "a broad class of offenders who might be labelled 'situtional–casual criminals'" (p. 266).

The author wishes to express her appreciation to Professor John E. Conklin of Tufts University for generously allowing access to interview data from his study on robbery, conducted under the auspices of the Center for Criminal Justice at Harvard Law School.

Situational explanations of crime focus on (1) forces in the immediate situation which are external to the actor, such as crises or pressures; (2) "psychological transformations wrought by situations" (Lemert, 1951); or (3) opportunities for crime. As Gibbons states, "the next etiological task is evaluation of the relative contribution" of historical and situational explanations of particular crimes (1971, p. 193). It is not clear, however, how to weigh the relative importance of historical and situational factors. While situational causes of crime have been described convincingly (Lemert, 1953; Cressey, 1953), no analytical tool has been devised for distinguishing crimes in which such factors play a central explanatory role. An analytical schema is presented here which provides a basis for conceptualizing the relative importance of historical and situational factors. It consists of two causal chains through which crime can occur and is organized around the issue of motivation to commit the crime. In schema A, historical factors are more central, since the motivation to commit the crime predates the crime situation. In schema B, however, the motivation to commit the crime arises within the crime situation; thus situational factors play a more important role.

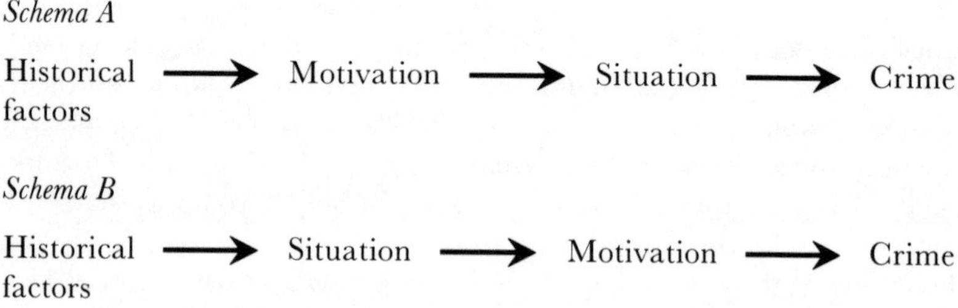

In schema A, historical factors pre-existing the crime situation give rise to criminal motivation. For an example involving Sutherland's differential association, take the case of a professional thief who has been exposed to an excess of definitions favorable to violation of the law. In response, he develops the motivation to earn his living by stealing. On account of this, he looks for or attempts to create situations which will give him the opportunity to commit crime – that is, he looks for accomplices and for victims. Once he has found an appropriate situation, he will steal. However, the motivation to commit the crime has preceded the development of the crime situation. Indeed, as Sutherland states, the situation is important only in so far as it provides the opportunity to commit the crime.

Psychological factors may also provide historical explanations for crime. For example, a person repeatedly involved in assaults on children may be responding to a deep psychological need which motivates him to seek out situations in which to commit the crime. Again, motive precedes situation.

In schema B, by contrast, the actor is neither strongly psychologically predisposed to commit the crime nor strongly committed to pro-criminal norms. He does not enter the criminogenic situation with the intention of committing the crime, nor is he motivated to do so until he is exposed to particular situational influences. Then, the motive to commit the crime arises in response to the demands of the situation. Historical factors play a role in the sense that they determine the likelihood that the person will enter the criminogenic situation. This may be illustrated with reference to juvenile delinquency, the literature on which has paid the most attention to situational explanations for crime. Many theorists do not explain juvenile delinquency by historical causes. Rather, they characterize juvenile delinquents as neither grossly psychologically abnormal nor as strongly committed to pro-criminal norms (Matza, 1964; Short and Strodtbeck, 1974). However, historical factors do help to explain the juvenile's presence in criminogenic situations: the delinquent is available for involvement in these situations since he is isolated and not strongly attached to conventional institutions (Hirschi, 1969; Short and Strodtbeck, 1974; Matza, 1964). Isolation leads the juvenile to gang membership, and juvenile crime can be seen as situationally determined in the sense that it is the outcome of group processes within the gang (Short and Strodtbeck, 1974; Wade, 1967). This occurs in a variety of ways. Cut off from conventional means of gaining status, members gain status in the group through crime and commit crime in response to peer pressure. Crime is also an available and effective means of increasing the cohesion of the gang. Gang-members, being isolated people, are heavily reliant on the gang for social support. However, the gang tends not to fulfill adequately these support needs, since it has low cohesion and low stability (Short and Strodtbeck, 1974; Yablonsky, 1959; Rothstein, 1962). Delinquent action is a way of solidifying the group (Thrasher, 1963; Yablonsky, 1959; Gordon, 1967) and occurs most frequently following low points in group solidarity (Jansyn, 1966). Joining together to commit a crime is a way of "creating instrumental problems demanding cooperative enterprise, thus fostering group cohesion" (Jansyn, 1966).

What types of crimes are better explained by primarily historical factors (that is, schema A) and what types by primarily situational factors (schema B)? While most studies of adult crime have focused on historical explanations, convincing descriptions have been given of situational causes of white-collar crimes such as check forgery (Lemert, 1953) and embezzlement (Cressey, 1953). In addition, Gibbons (1971, 1983) has suggested that short-run criminality and petty crime are more likely to be explained situationally than are serious crime and crime committed in the context of a criminal career. It is proposed here that situational factors can explain an even wider variety of crimes, including repeated serious violent crime such as robbery. Which kinds of robbery can be explained situationally? The key distinction here is between "crime as work", which is amenable to historical explanation, and "casual" crime, in which situational factors figure importantly. Crime pursued as work, as a job, has been described by a number of observers (Conklin, 1972; Roebuck et al., 1983; Petersilia et al., 1977; Letkeman, 1973). Miller categorizes certain criminals as workers whose crimes "are characterized by sufficient degrees of rationality and organization" and who are "oriented toward crime as a primary source of income and toward the criminal role as an important basis for personal identity" (1978, p. 27). By definition, then, historical causes are operative, since criminality is part of the identity of these criminal workers. At the other end of the continuum are casual criminals, also known as "intermittent criminals", "jack of all trades offenders", "disorganized criminals" and "adolescent recapitulators" (Petersilia et al., 1977; Roebuck and Johnson, 1962; Irwin, 1970; Glaser, 1972). They have been characterized as committing occasional, sloppily executed crime and "as vacillating between commitment to conventional and criminal values" (Irwin, 1970, p. 24). Though several commentators have suggested that situational factors such as "disorderly recreational pursuits" (Glaser, 1972) and peer pressure (Irwin, 1970; Roebuck and Johnson, 1962) play a role in causing this type of crime, the process by which a criminogenic situation escalates into crime has not been described. This chapter will describe such a process. The chain of events by which a group drinking-situation gives rise to "casual" robbery and burglary will be delineated using the categories of schema B. The pattern of crime described has characteristics which suggest a similarity to juvenile crime; it bears little resemblance to crime as work.

METHODOLOGY

The pattern of casual crime arising out of a group drinking-situation first came to my attention in the course of a study on the relation between drinking and crime (Cordilia, 1983, 1985). In order to explore this pattern further, qualitative data sources were sought which would provide detailed material on the situational dynamics out of which this kind of crime develops and which would allow us to reconstruct the process leading up to the crime. The model delineated in this chapter was constructed through secondary analysis of the following data sources, all of which provided detailed descriptions of group drinking-situations that culminated in criminal acts:

1 criminal histories of 32 alcoholic prison inmates;[1]
2 interviews with 67 men arrested and imprisoned for robbery;[2]
3 descriptive studies of crime.[3]

Since the data were chosen for their detail on situational dynamics rather than for their representativeness of either the criminal population or the universe of criminal acts, they do not allow us to provide any precise estimate of the prevalence of this pattern of crime. However, the second data source, interviews with men imprisoned for robbery, does make it possible to determine how widespread this pattern is among a random sample of men who were tried, convicted and served time for robbery. Of the 55 respondents who admitted committing the robbery, ten committed crimes which shared the three main characteristics of the crime pattern described here:

1 the robbery was committed by a group of men;
2 the men had been drinking together;
3 the robbery was not planned before the drinking-situation.

Thus, a substantial percentage of the crimes described by inmates imprisoned for robbery fall into this pattern. This fact, plus the frequency with which this pattern is found in criminal histories and in descriptive studies of casual crime, leads us to conclude that it is common enough to warrant further study.

FINDINGS

This section describes, using the categories of schema B, a pattern of robbery found among casual criminals distinguished by the way the crime arises out of a group drinking-situation.

According to schema B (see p. 168), the motive for the crime arises in the situation immediately preceding the crime. Thus, it will first be shown that, in the cases examined, the group-members did not enter the drinking situation with a plan or intention of committing the crime. Second, the nature of the criminal *motive* (that is, the goal to be achieved by participation in the crime) will be described as well as the way it was generated by the situation immediately preceding the crime. Third, the role of alcohol as a catalyst will be delineated. Fourth, the impact of historical factors will be considered briefly.

A cursory examination of descriptions of casual crimes committed by drinking-companions reveals that the drinkers rarely enter the drinking-situation with the intention of committing the crime. Thus, they do not seek out or construct the situation for criminal purposes. In fact, sometimes the crime literally occurs "on the spur of the moment". Far from giving rise to the drinking-situation, the intention to commit the crime seems to arise at the very moment of the crime, as the following quotations illustrate.

> We went to this tavern on the way home. It was cold out. We had a few drinks there and we got to talking to this guy and we asked him if he wanted to go to some other place. So we were walking and the next thing I know we had him in

the alley and I hit him and we took his money and that was it. We didn't discuss it or anything. It just happened that way. We went into another tavern and we were drinking and that's where the police caught us. . . . We had enough money to drink, but on the way somehow we got him in the alley. (Finestone, 1967, p. 580)

He went to a bar and proceeded to get drunk with a friend. After the bar closed, the two were sitting in an alley when a young Black couple passed. Ken grabbed the girl, his friend held the man, and they forced them to return to their car and drive out of town. There, Ken and his friend beat and robbed the couple. They drove off in the couple's car, but Ken was so drunk that he soon crashed into a freeway divider. The police found him unconscious behind the wheel; the friend had fled. (Petersilia et al., 1977, p. 105)

At other times the intention to commit the crime arises earlier, as part of the interaction of the drinking-group. Again, however, the intention does not pre-exist the drinking-situation.

He and a friend had been drinking during the night in an all-night bar and early in the morning, about 7 a.m., they were riding around and decided to stick up some people. . . . it was not planned but was decided that night when both were drunk . . . . (Conklin, 1972b)

[He and three friends] had been drinking in a bar when someone suggested they get some money. . . . With an unloaded tear gas container and an unloaded pistol with the firing pin missing [they] held up a hotel. . . . He knew where the hotel was, but said the decision to rob it was a spur of the moment decision arrived at by the 4 of them. . . . (Ibid.)

Thus it is clear that the intention to commit the crime is generated in the group drinking-situation. Is the *motive* behind the intention to commit the crime also an outgrowth of the situation, as proposed in schema B? To answer this question, the nature of the motive must be ascertained. It would appear that the purpose of robbery is to obtain money, and certainly this is usually part of the reason for these crimes. But the fact that respondents fairly often mention that the money was not important to one or all of the participants suggests that other motives also play a role. The lack of centrality of the money motive is obvious in the following quotations:

The victim happened to be the first cab driver to come along and they were looking for a cab home. His friend began the holdup and he pulled his knife after the friend grabbed the driver. He had not seen the victim before. The robbery was not planned and the victim was not chosen in any particular way. . . . He robbed because his partner started to. He and his friend had no particular need for the money, as they both had some with them at the time. . . . He says the money was unimportant to him. (Conklin, 1972b)

I thought that maybe he could be of help to me in alleviating my condition. I used to go over to his home or go to the tavern with him and his wife. I felt more at ease around him and his wife. There was never any reference to the past. I went out with him on a robbery while I continued to work. I didn't need my portion of the take. (Finestone, 1967, p. 580)

If money is not the sole motive, or even perhaps the dominant motive, for these crimes, where can the other motives be found? Since we are concerned with group crime, it is instructive to follow the lead of the juvenile-gang literature and examine the possibility that the motive of the crime is related to the group context in which it occurs. This is a productive approach because it is clear that peer pressure influences some people to participate in crime. As the following quotations illustrate, some are motivated to accommodate their companions and are thus convinced to participate despite reservations about the crime itself:

> The respondent and his partner were drinking; they picked up a third person who "was drunk and wanted money". This person "suggested that they do robberies to get some money as he was broke. L. and his partner offered him money, as they had a bigger job planned for the next day. However, the third person wanted to rob that night. L. said that "he hadn't wanted to rob because he already had some money ... he expected little money in these robberies; since he had a big job planned for the next day, he didn't want to do them, but did to shut the third guy up". (Conklin, 1972b)

> G. L. and R. were drinking and were "half crocked". S. said he knew about a car [which they could steal] which somebody wanted so they could get rid of it. G. had doubts because he didn't want to violate his parole. But he went along anyway and that's how he ended up [in prison]. (Cordilia, 1983)

At other times, the influence of peers is more immediate. One partner may without previous discussion start committing a crime, giving the other the choice of helping him or refusing to co-operate. In the situation described below, the respondent began to co-operate with his companion once the crime had already been initiated. He did this despite his recognition of the high risk involved, since the robbery occurred a few blocks from his home.

> [He and his partner] had been up for 4 days on pills and liquor and were drunk at the time. ... [They] entered a liquor store to get a jug of wine. ... His friend asked for a jug of wine; the clerk refused, saying he was too drunk to buy it. His partner said that in that case, he would take the wine. ... He then pushed the other man into the back room and told his partner that since he was taking the wine, it was armed robbery anyway and that they might as well take the money. (Conklin, 1972b)

We can state therefore that, for at least some participants in this pattern of crime, schema B holds in the sense that the motive (co-operation with companions) is generated in the situation immediately preceding the crime. However, while the criminal action of the followers arises out of the group situation, the act of suggesting or initiating the crime has not been explained by situational factors. In the juvenile-gang literature, initiation of crime has been attributed to the need for status in the group or for increasing the cohesion of the group (Short and Strodtbeck, 1974; Jansyn, 1966; Gordon, 1967). While there is no evidence here that initiation of the crime is related to status concerns, there is some indication that the need to maintain the group is relevant. In one very straightforward example of this, some respondents stole to obtain money to continue drinking together, which was the sole purpose and activity of the group:

> He and a friend, both undisguised, held up a cab driver for $7. . . . They were both drunk at the time. . . . His friend suggested the holdup to get drinking money, picking up a bottle and breaking it for a weapon. . . . He himself was very amused by his friend's antics and was laughing throughout the robbery but [was] very drunk. . . . They had no expectations about how much money they might get but wanted to get money for drinking as they had run out. The next day was St. Patrick's Day and they wanted to drink until the parade . . . . (Conklin, 1972b)

> D. claims that when he stole, he always did it with someone, with people he drank with. . . . When D. and his partner got drunk together, D.'s partner often wanted more money "to have a good time". D. would go along with him as he cruised the streets looking for a house where the lights were out. "We would break into the house and take what looked valuable at the time. Most of the time, it was junk." (Cordilia, 1983b)

The crime may also serve a maintenance function in the group in less obvious ways. In writing about juvenile gangs Gordon states,

> if a group lacked a task, purpose, or mission as a result of not being integrated into a demanding external system – as may in fact be the case for streetcorner gangs with respect to conventional society – then it would fail to generate a major part of the rewards and sentiments that its members might expect to gain from it. . . . One solution would be to adopt or contrive tasks that justify dependence between members and call for co-operation in a common enterprise. (1967, p. 58)

One such task, suggests Gordon, is a criminal venture. Like juvenile gangs, the drinking-groups described here tend to be divorced from any external system; they are limited to the activity of drinking together. While it would be difficult to obtain direct evidence that crime is used as a means of strengthening ties among group-members, such an explanation is at least consistent with the lack of concern with money as a motive and with the sense of play or group adventure that pervades many such crimes. More direct evidence of the ovrriding importance of maintaining the group is provided by the fact that the crimes are committed by the whole drinking-group. No one is excluded for being incompetent or too intoxicated. That maintaining the group is a central goal for initiators as well as for followers and is *more* important than carrying off a successful robbery makes sense of the sequence of events described below, in which a man is included in robberies by his more sober companions despite the fact that they know he is incapacitated to a degree that might prove a danger to them.

> They handcuffed me and on the way down to 11th and State they asked me questions about the holdups. I said I didn't know, I didn't believe that I had been there on the stickups. I had been drunk and had been at a dozen or more taverns. I asked my rap partners later and they said that I had been there. They said I was in both places. I asked them if I had a gun and they said no. They wouldn't let me have a gun in the condition I was in for I might have shot somebody. Even the people who fingered me said that I didn't have a gun. (Finestone, 1967, p. 580)

Thus, situational factors related to group process may play a role both in the initiation of the crime as well as in the participation of group members. The crime may be initiated in order to obtain money to continue drinking, the activity which binds the group together. The crime may also serve as a way of solidifying the group by providing it with a common enterprise that calls for co-operation between members. The participation of followers may also be explained by situational factors operating in the group; though they may not be motivated to commit the crime for its own sake, they are motivated to co-operate with their drinking-companions.

The next question to be examined is the role of alcohol. Alcohol serves as a catalyst in the process we have been describing in that it renders the drinker more responsive to situational influences. Criminologists often attribute intoxicated behavior to the "disinhibiting" effects of alcohol. Students of alcohol use have contended, however, that disinhibition is too general a concept to be useful in explaining why a particular type of behavior, such as robbery in a group, occurs rather than other behaviors which might normally also be inhibited, such as assaulting other members of the group or becoming sexually provocative (Pernanen, 1976).

The position taken here is that heavy alcohol consumption lowers conceptual and abstracting ability so that the person is focused on "behavior cues in the immediate situation" (Pernanen, 1976, p. 413). Thus, the types of cue to which a person responds when drinking are in a much narrower range and much more tied to the immediate context (in this case, the group situation) than if the person were sober. With attention centered on the present, the issue of maintaining the group comes to the fore of consciousness while the risks involved fade into the background. Thus, in an intoxicated state, the person is more vulnerable to influences in the immediate situation. However, when sobriety rearranges the individual's priorities, these perceptions and the actions to which they led may be incomprehehsible. In the words of one respondent, "After we sobered up at the police station, we said, 'Holy Christ: What did we do that for?'" (Finestone, 1967, p. 580).

The final question is to consider briefly the role which historical factors play in the process leading to crime.[4] In the sequence illustrated by schema B, historical factors lead to participation in the criminogenic situation. Since the pattern described in this chapter is similar to a pattern found among juvenile delinquents, it is instructive to examine the historical factors which have been singled out in the literature on juvenile-gang crime. Relationships with family and peers have been cited as a critical variable explaining juvenile ganging-behavior. Their lack of close social ties and low level of interpersonal skills lead them to be dependent on the gang; however, the relationships in the gang do not satisfy their interpersonal needs. This high level of need and low level of satisfaction gives rise to situations in which crimes arise as means of strengthening their position in the group or strengthening the group itself (Short and Strodtbeck, 1974; Gordon, 1967; Jansyn, 1966).

The literature on casual criminals and on drinking-groups reveals that the former share certain traits with juvenile delinquents and that the latter have similarities to delinquent gangs. Casual criminals tend to be isolated people with loose or non-existent ties to family and with lives disrupted by prison terms (Roebuck and Johnson, 1962). They have few social ties, and have few means of meeting people.[5] Bars are settings which offer easy sociability, and, since people tend to feel comfortable in bars populated by others like themselves, these men who have been in trouble with the law tend to frequent establishments where trouble is common (Clinnard, 1962; Prus, 1983). Once in a bar, they find that drinking helps create the feeling of closeness with others which they seek.[6] The relationships which are formed in bars are, however, tenuous, and are tied to the drinking-situation.[7] Though these interactions may be intense over a short period of time, reports of having been deserted in dangerous situations or betrayed to the police by members of the drinking-group are common. As the following quotation illustrates, men in a situation of isolation can quickly become highly involved with people whom they meet in a drinking-context. The relationships, however, are not deep; they can end as quickly as they start, and loyalty to drinking-partners is not necessarily maintained outside the drinking-situation.

> One day I went home early feeling sick, and I found my wife making it with another guy. I slapped her around some, and left feeling mad. I went to a bar and started pouring down the booze – this was the first time in nearly three months. This other guy and I sat getting drunk and talking about how shitty life was. Then we went outside and stopped a cab and got in. After the cab started up, I grabbed the driver by the neck and told him to drive out of town. After he did that we made him get out and I beat him up and the other guy took his wallet. . . . We went back to [the other guy's] place and I stayed a week. I didn't go back to work, so I guess I was fired by that time. . . . I'd almost

> forgotten about the cab job, but three months later the cops came to the house and arrested me. My buddy had ratted on me when the cops grabbed him for something else. (Petersilia et al., 1977, pp. 104–5)

Thus, these men are in the same situation as isolated juveniles who rely on their tenuous ties with gang-members. Owing to their lack of other social ties, they are motivated to enhance their links with the drinking-group. The weakness of the drinking-group itself leads them to engage in activity to breathe life into it whether that is stealing money to continue drinking together, submitting to their companions' pressure to commit crime, or initiating a criminal venture in order to increase the cohesiveness of the group.

CONCLUSION

Criminologists have neglected situational factors in explanations of adult crime. This chapter has provided a schema for conceptualizing the role of situational factors in causing crime and has described how a group drinking-situation gives rise to casual robbery. In addition, two points are made which suggest new directions for research on adult crime. First, a link is establishd between juvenile and adult crime. There is an artificial boundary in the literature between juvenile and adult criminality. Evidence presented here, however, suggests that there is some continuity between the two. While it is true that some juvenile delinquents grow up to lead conventional lives and that others mature into professional criminal careers, a third group continues involvement in occasional, unskilled, unplanned crimes.[8] These casual criminals also continue the juvenile pattern of social isolation and, though not involved in a gang, may participate in drinking-groups which serve some of the same functions. This chapter has shown how the group process among drinking-companions gives rise to crime in a pattern mirroring that of juvenile gangs. It is likely that other aspects of the juvenile-delinquency literature can help explain aspects of casual adult crime.

A second issue involves the role of alcohol in situational explanations of crime. Although a substantial proportion of prison inmates (ranging from 30 to 60 per cent) claim that they were drinking at the time of the crime for which they were imprisoned (US Department of Justice, 1983; Greenberg, 1981), criminologists have paid insufficient attention to the role of alcohol in crime. Alcohol has the property of focusing the attention of the drinker on the immediate situation. This chapter has described how alcohol plays a role in the process leading to crime by causing the drinker to concentrate on the short-run situational rewards of crime and mentally distance himself from the long-range consequences. This suggests that alcohol magnifies the significance of situational factors and thus that it is specially important to examine the role of these factors in crimes where alcohol has played a part.

NOTES

1 Detailed criminal and drinking histories of 32 male inmates of a medium and a maximum security prison in a north-eastern state were collected for a study of the effects of imprisonment which I published under the title *The Making of an Inmate: prison as a way of life* (1983). At the time the subjects were being screened for eligibility for a pre-release counseling-program, owing to the fact that they had been classified as having an "alcohol problem". An inmate was so classified if he was known to have had any difficulties in his life which could be attributed to alcohol and, especially, if such difficulties entailed contact with the legal system. Using this very inclusive definition, about 80 per cent of inmates in the institutions studied here were considered to have an alcohol problem.

Of the 32 inmates interviewed, 25 had committed some form of property crime (though this was not necessarily the crime for which they were imprisoned). Of these 25, four had committed at least one robbery or burglary in a group drinking-situation. In addition, one inmate's criminal history consisted entirely of such crimes.

Research was carried out by means of structured one-and-a-half-hour interviews during imprisonment and over a one-year period after release. The purpose of the interviews was to gather data on inmate response to imprisonment and the effects of this response on post-release behavior. A portion of the interview schedule involved collecting detailed data on criminal and drinking histories.

2 Sixty-seven men imprisoned for robbery in Massachusetts were interviewed for a study of robbery by John E. Conklin under the auspices of the Center for Criminal Justice at Harvard Law School. The results of the study were reported in Conklin (1972). The subjects were a random sample of male inmates serving time for robberies committed in Boston between 1 January 1968 and 30 June 1970. The interview data included a description of the events leading up to the robbery, the way in which the robbery was carried out, the motivation of the robber, the role of crime partners, and the use of alcohol and drugs.

3 Case materials found in scholarly works on casual property crime were used as data. Major sources were Finestone (1967), Petersilia et al. (1977), Roebuck and Johnson (1962) and Irwin (1970). The criminological theory found in these works is also referred to in this chapter; however, this is distinct from the direct use of their case material as data.

4 As for the historical factor of pro-criminal norms, it is likely, as suggested earlier in this chapter, that casual criminals neither feel positively about theft as a way of life, as does the career criminal, nor consider robbery and burglary to be totally unsuitable behavior. Thus, like the juvenile delinquents described by Matza (1964), their behavior is not tightly constrained by norms; rather they are free to be influenced by circumstances.

5 Finestone's description (1967) of recidivism among Polish–American parolees was extremely useful to this study and highlighted several of the factors which are part of the pattern described here. Finestone's parolees tended to be isolated, to seek companionship in bars, and to commit unplanned crime arising out of group drinking-situations.

6 According to Mowrer, "The custom of drinking together to symbolize common feeling and unity is almost universal in present-day culture" (1942, p. 263).

7 Short and Strodtbeck make the analogy between the drinking-group and the gang. They also note the limited nature of relationships formed in bars: "a benign search for 'companionship' with habitués of bars and pool halls may be moderately rewarding, but the relationships are specific to the bar and they are likely to be tenuous" (1974, p. 277).

8 Irwin (1970), Roebuck and Johnson (1962) and Glaser (1972) note that casual criminals tend to be former juvenile delinquents.

REFERENCES

Clinard, M. 1962: The public drinking house and society. In D. Pittman and C. Snyder (eds), *Society, Culture and Drinking Patterns*, New York: Wiley.

Conklin, J. E. 1972: *Robbery and the Criminal Justice System*. Philadelphia: Lippincott.

—— 1972b: [Study of Robbery]. Unpublished interview data.

Cordilia, A. T. 1983: *The Making of an Inmate: prison as a way of life*. Cambridge, Mass.: Schenkman.

—— 1983b: [Study of Drinking and Criminal Histories]. Unpublished interview data.

—— 1985: Alcohol and property crime: exploring the causal nexus. *Journal of Studies in Alcohol*, 46, 161–71.

Cressey, D. R. 1953: *Other People's Money*. New York: Free Press.

Finestone H. 1967: Reformation and recidivism among Italian and Polish criminal offenders. *American Journal of Sociology*, 72, 575–88.

Gibbons, D. C. 1971: Observations on the study of crime causation. *American Journal of Sociology*, 77, 262–78.

—— 1983: Mundane crime. *Crime and Delinquency*, 29, 213–27.

Glaser, D. 1969: *The Effectiveness of a Prison and Parole System*. Indianapolis: Bobbs-Merrill.

—— 1972: *Adult Crime and Social Policy*. Englewood Cliffs, NJ: Prentice-Hall.

Gordon, R. 1967: Social level, social disability and gang interaction. *American Journal of Sociology*, 73, 42–62.

Greenberg, S. 1981: Alcohol and crime: a methodological critique of the literature. In J. J. Collins (ed.), *Drinking and Crime*, New York: Guilford.

Hirschi, T. 1969: *Causes of Delinquency*. Berkeley, Calif.: University of California Press.

Irwin, J. 1970: *The Felon*. Englewood Cliffs, NJ: Prentice-Hall.

Jansyn, L. 1966: Solidarity and delinquency in a street corner group. *American Sociological Review*, 31, 600–14.

Lemert, E. 1951: *Social Pathology*. New York: McGraw-Hill.

—— 1953: An isolation and closure theory of naïve check forgery. *Journal of Criminal Law, Criminology and Police Science*, 44, 296–307.

Letkeman, P. 1973: *Crime as Work*. Englewood Cliffs, NJ: Prentice-Hall.

Matza, D. 1964: *Delinquency and Drift*. New York: Wiley.

Miller, G. 1978: *Odd Jobs: the world of deviant work*. Englewood Cliffs, NJ: Prentice-Hall.

Mowrer, E. 1942: *Disorganization: personal and social*. Philadelphia: Lippincott.

Pernanen, K. 1976: Alcohol and crimes of violence. In B. Kissin and H. Begleiter (eds), *The Biology of Alcoholism*, New York: Plenum.

Petersilia, J., Greenwood, P. and Lavin, M. 1977: *Criminal Careers of Habitual Felons*. Santa Monica, Calif.: Rand.

Prus, R. 1983: Drinking as activity: an interactionist analysis. *Journal of Studies in Alcohol*, 44, 460–75.

Roebuck, J. and Johnson, R. 1962: The jack-of-all-trades offender. *Crime and Delinquency*, 8, 172–81.

Roebuck, J., Johnson, R. and Windham, G. 1983: Professional theft. In G. Waldo (ed.), *Career Criminals*, Beverly Hills, Calif.: Sage.

Rothstein, E. 1962: Attributes related to high social stature: a comparison of the perceptions of delinquent and non-delinquent boys. *Social Problems*, 10, 75–83.

Short J. 1967: Social structure and group processes in gang delinquency. In M. Clinard and R. Quinney (eds), *Criminal Behavior Systems*, New York: Holt, Rinehart and Winston.

Short, J. and Strodtbeck, F. 1974: *Group Process and Gang Delinquency*. Chicago: University of Chicago Press.

Sutherland, E. and Cressey, D. 1970: *Principles of Criminology*. Philadelphia: Lippincott.

Thrasher, F. 1963: *The Gang*. Chicago: University of Chicago Press.

US Department of Justice 1983: *Prisoners and Alcohol*. Bureau of Justice statistics bulletin.

Wade, A. 1967: Social processes in the act of juvenile vandalism. In M. Clinard and R. Quinney (eds), *Criminal Behavior Systems*, New York: Holt, Rinehart and Winston.

Washburne, C. 1956: Alcohol, self and the group. *Quarterly Journal of Studies in Alcohol*, 17, 108–23.

Yablonsky, L. 1959: The delinquent gang as a near group. *Social Problems*, 7, 108–17.

12

Institutions and the Promotion of Violence

Robert Johnson

INTRODUCTION

Some institutions are in the business of violence. Others are served by violence. Violence is a product of institutional arrangements and is in some sense useful to these institutions. This violence is properly called *institutional* violence so that it may be distinguished, in terms of its origin, character and purpose, from *personal* violence.

In its most blatant form, institutional violence involves the intentional use of overt violence by agents of an institution in pursuit of institutional goals. At its worst, this violence is typified by the death-camp slaughter of innocents, and, at its best, by the military fighting a just war. These situations are quite different morally, of course, but in each instance violence is produced and orchestrated by the institution to achieve its ends.

Violence on the scale of a holocaust or a war is the result of systematic efforts by institutions to structure situations and to generate dispositions and perceptions which, together, yield "contingent consistency" (see Toch, in chapter 3 above). Generally speaking, institutional arrangements exploit the fact that "we must react to situations as we perceive and interpret them in line with the dispositions we bring to them" (ibid.). More specifically, institutional arrangements capitalize on the normal tendency for people to minimize or deny responsibility for their violence; and actively to look for ways to mollify their conscience and to make their violence, particularly when it is directed against debased groups, a justified and even laudable activity (Bandura, 1979). So far as is practical and necessary, the links among situations, dispositions and perceptions – especially exonerating perceptions – are prearranged by the institution and rehearsed by its personnel to promote predictable and guilt-free uses of violence.

Institutional violence is not limited to the work of death-camp guards or

I wish to thank the editors as well as my colleagues Sandra Baxter, Richard R. Bennett, James J. Fyfe and Hans Toch for their helpful comments and suggestions.

men at arms. This violence can be more subtle and indirect. Perhaps a better word would be insidious, as when employers let workers suffer – and sometimes slowly die – as a result of occupational hazards. When these hazards can be minimized or even eliminated, as is commonly the case, employers are culpable for them. The injuries, diseases and deaths that result cannot be blamed on impersonal forces; they are not the outcome of natural disasters or random accidents but rather are products of human design. These workers have been abandoned by their employers and, as a result, laid open to an *assault* by their work environments. Their employers might just as well have attacked them with weapons. As Friedrich Engels observed over a century ago,

> If one individual inflicts bodily injury upon another which leads to the death of the person attacked we call it manslaughter; on the other hand, if the attacker knows beforehand that the blow will be fatal we call it murder. Murder has also been committed if society places workers in such a position that they inevitably come to premature and unnatural ends. Their death is as violent as if they had been stabbed or shot. . . . Murder has been committed if society knows perfectly well that thousands of workers cannot avoid being sacrificed so long as these conditions are allowed to continue. Murder of this sort is just as culpable as the murder committed by an individual. (Quoted in Reiman, 1984, p. 34)

Courts have only recently begun to examine occupational injury and disease in light of this reasoning, and have considered only egregious cases (see *Newsweek*, 8 July 1985, p. 57). Nevertheless, the logic which tells us that some workers are victims of institutional violence is unimpeachable.

Institutional violence, then, may occur by act or omission. In each instance, this violence originates in organizational roles and activities. Thus institutional violence has comparatively little to do with the passions, predilections and peculiarities of personality, or even personality–situation interaction, that account for most personal violence. Though it is true, as Toch states in chapter 3, "that individual personalities and the situations people encounter are not wholly divisible", the focus of institutional violence is quite explicitly on "violence-relevant situational features". Institutional violence conforms to Allport's observation, brought to our attention by Toch, that "situational determinants are most important where duties and roles, where tasks and functions, are heavily prescribed. Personality determinants are most important where the task is more free and open and unstructured". There is indeed an interplay of situation and personality in the production of institutional violence, but situational factors predominate. Indeed, situational factors are often intentionally organized so as to mute the expression of personality factors. This is seen most clearly in selection and socialization procedures designed to transform personnel from unique and therefore variable *individuals* in the institution's employ into standard and hence interchangeable *agents* of that institution.

Emphasis is placed on situational factors – on the "duties and roles . . . tasks and functions" to which Allport refers – in part because they are more readily subject to control and manipulation in the institutional context than are personality factors. Perhaps more to the point, common personal motives for violence such as jealousy or insecurity, which typically reflect personality dispositions, are weak, absent or irrelevant in the case of institutional violence. (When standard personal motives are present, they often contaminate the institutional agenda. When, for instance, an officer of the law is chronically unsure of himself and bullies suspects to cement his authority, the resulting violence is not so much institutional violence as it is personal violence carried out under the cover of an institutional role.) Generally, the agent of institutional violence holds no grudge against his victim; at least he has no animus against the victim as an individual, though the victim's social group is often viewed in stereotypical and even contemptuous ways. The pesonal identity, character and sometimes even the conduct of the victim may be irrelevant. In its pure form, the agent of institutional violence is a servant of organizational goals; his violence is situation-specific and focused upon appropriate "targets" of his institution.

To date, our understanding of the dynamics of institutional violence has been unduly influenced by extreme cases, most notably Nazi death camps and military massacres (see Kelman, 1973). That focus has produced a number of important insights, to which I have alluded, but is needlessly narrow. Institutional violence is of many types, serves many aims and impinges upon diverse audiences. An adequate account of institutional violence must consider a range of situations in which institutions directly or indirectly promote violence that affects their inhabitants, their clients or the larger population.

In this chapter I propose a general framework for understanding institutional violence. This framework is derived from content analysis of a variety of institutional situations featuring violence. They include the *military* at war, during massacres, as occasional proprietors of prisoner-of-war and death camps, and as a source of torturers (usually in the context of military dictatorships); *police* and *prisons* in the routine use or threat of physical force and in the regular though less common use of deadly force (note here as well that police and prison personnel are sometimes drafted during politically turbulent times to fill the ranks of torturers); and, finally, a range of hazardous *industrial work environments* marked by situations that breed high rates of injury, disease and death. These work-settings are essentially of the lineage condemned by Engels. Included are factories, coal mines, steel mills, cotton mills, asbestos plants and chemical plants.

The rationale for inclusion of the military, the police and prisons as sources of violent institutional situations is almost self-evident. These institutions have virtually cornered the market in the use of direct and overt institutional violence. A general model of institutional violence could not be developed without considering them. The selection of industrial work situations for inclusion in the sample is less easily defended, but the rationale is similar. Industrial work-settings are often prototypes of hazardous work environments. The harms produced in some of these settings feature gross physical injury and debilitating disease, which serve as tangible evidence of bodily violence that can be traced directly to the conditions of work. Some other work environments, including both blue-collar and white-collar environ ments, produce injury and disease and can be said to do violence to workers (see Reasons et al., 1981). This violence is mediated by psychological stress, however and hence does not reflect directly the effect of some external environmental assault. And the harms involved, such as ulcers and other psychosomatic ailments, are less intuitively indicative of violence. Nevertheless, the work situations that produce these harms follow the dynamics of institutional violence in the workplace (see Reasons et al., 1981), and also exhibit the general characteristics of institutional violence which are the subject matter of this chapter. I have excluded them from my sample, however, because of the indirect and ostensibly "non-violent" harms at issue, which may distract some readers from the dynamics of institutional violence at work in these instances.

Returning to my sample, we can see that violence in the military and criminal-justice contexts is a stipulated means to goal achievement. In hazardous industrial work environments, violence is an unintended, often unacknowledged, yet tolerated corollary of goal achievement. My aim in this chapter is to identify the institutional arrangements that operate across this sample to structure situations and, to a lesser extent, develop dispositions and perceptions that (1) neutralize normal moral restraints against violence and (2) supply the motives and mechanisms necessary to carry out violence, or to permit violence to occur, on a regular basis.

INSTITUTIONAL VIOLENCE

The primary condition of institutional violence is some form of authorization to harm others by acts of commission or omission. These authorizations take hold in institutions that are organized in the form of bureaucracies which are isolated from mainstream moral values or at least shielded from regular review and judgment in light of those values. These organizations, moreover, socialize their personnel so as to insulate them from awareness or appreciation of the moral dimensions of their behavior. Together, authorization, bureaucracy, isolation and insulation foster dehumanization. Dehumanization, in turn, is the key condition required to engage in or to permit violence "without moral restraint" (Kelman, 1973; see also Arendt, 1963; Lifton, 1973 and Milgram, 1975).

Dehumanization makes both the agents and the victims of violence little more than pawns of the institution. As a result, dehumanization neutralizes the normal human sentiments of sympathy or guilt that might interfere with the use of violence. One cannot feel sympathy or guilt over objects, particularly if in one's role one becomes an object as well. Moreover, by freeing people from the constraints of conscience, which after all apply most compellingly among fellow human beings, dehumanization in effect *creates* motives for violence. In other words, seeing another person as sub-human not only weakens restraints against violence but also may actively promote violence. As Bandura has noted,

> People strongly disapprove of cruel behavior and rarely excuse its use when they interact with humanized individuals. By contrast, people seldom condemn punitive conduct and *generate self-disinhibiting justifications for [violence]* when they direct their behavior toward individuals divested of humanness. (1979, p. 228, emphasis added)

We commonly believe that debased people are "insensitive to maltreatment and influenceable only through the more primitive methods" (Bandura, et al., 1975, p. 255). The only language such persons "really" understand, we tell ourselves, is violence. In the institutional context, people are most likely to direct violence toward others when they, as well as their victims, play dehumanized roles. Hence institutional violence, whether carried out in a manner that is cold and impersonal or tinged with contempt, involves dehumanized or object–object relations. Normal human morality is suspended, and violence becomes a more or less salient personal motive that is incorporated into the routine operation of the institution.

Situational constraints

Authorizations to harm are of two types: transcendent and mundane (Kelman, 1973). Transcendent authorizations define people as expendable means to such desired ends as military victory, social control, or accumulation of profit.[1] Transcendent authorizations are often vague prescriptions or slogans that can be endorsed without full awareness of the violence they entail. The call for military victory appeals to patriotism but does not draw attention to the death and destruction inherent in war. In the slogan "Victory at any price", for example, the operative word is "victory", not "price". Such laudable goals as justice or law and order are equally general and fail to mention the violence they require for their achievement. (Note that justice often demands a "war on crime".) Nor does the general mandate to maximize profit in industrial production highlight the injury and disease that are often associated with increased production quotas and decreased attention to safety. Even Hitler's grotesque "final solution" to the "Jewish problem" was initially so vague in its formulation as to be almost innocuous; ostracism, immigration or at worst deportation would seem to have qualified, though of course the term "solution" proved to be a euphemism for genocide.

Equally vague and elusive are the human targets of these slogans. Enemies, pariahs, criminals and even assembly-line workers are readily seen as sub-human creatures or lifeless abstractions. The violence they suffer is unreal and easily minimized or ignored. To the extent that this violence is recognized at all, it may be seen as deserved. This is most apparent in the case of enemies for "only the enemy is seen as *really* violent", and this violence is apt to be depicted as "innate, incurable and irrational" (Shulman, 1971, pp. 222, 224). The putative ferocity of the enemy "defines him as subhuman and our own acts, however brutal, as justified" (p. 222). More generally, violence can be justified by reference to the disreputable character and conduct of the victim. When one is dealing with purportedly shiftless or lazy or promiscuous folk, for instance, otherwise "reprehensible acts" against them can appear "trifling or even benevolent" (Bandura, 1979, p. 227).

Examples abound of institutional violence masquerading as a "trifling or even benevolent" enterprise. SS commandant Himmler reportedly gave pep talks to concentration-camp guards that applauded them for their involvement "in something historic, grandiose, unique . . . a great task that occurs once in two thousand years" (Kelman, 1973, p. 45). Dr Mengele, the Auschwitz "Angel of Death", infamous for, among other concentration-camp atrocities, his medical experiments with twins, quite explicitly saw the camps as an opportunity to Nazify science and hence "to deepen and extend the Nazi racial vision" and ultimately to purify the Aryan race (Lifton, 1985, p. 22). In his words, "it would be a sin, a crime . . . and irresponsible not to utilize the possibilities that Auschwitz had for twin research. . . . there would never be another chance like it" (p. 23). The misery that concentration camps would produce, even if justified in some perverse way by Nazi ideology, was never mentioned in Himmler's talks; nor did the victims' plight figure in Mengele's calculations of the merits of medical experimentation. Jews were presumed to have polluted Aryan genes and culture; for a crime so monstrous, they were deemed fit for systematic annihilation. At bottom, they were not accorded the status as fellow human beings which would have given meaning to their suffering and would, moreover, have precluded the preposterous anti-Semitic beliefs that undergirded Nazi ideology.

There are a host of other situations which are of a piece with the logic of the death camps but are of a less extreme and virulent nature. Soldiers, for instance, are enjoined to fight for the glory of their flag, their country and their way of life. The notion that one must slaughter the enemy, including women and children, is either overlooked entirely or implicitly justified by classifying the enemy as less than fully human (Kelman, 1973; see generally Goldman and Segal, 1976). Police are asked to risk their lives to man the the "thin blue line" that separates civilized society from the predations of those who would rend the body social. The violence this requires is transmuted to the more sanitized notion of force applied to citizens whose humanity is discounted – they are enemies, "assholes", or animals we must control (Westley, 1953, 1970; Bittner, 1975; Van Maanen, 1978). Prison officials cage our worst offenders; when the prisoners rebel or escape, they become nameless "cons" who are the legitimate targets of official violence (Lombardo, 1982). Prison officials who carry out executions protect society from criminals so corrupt as to be beyond correction, redemption or even simple punitive confinement (Johnson, 1981). (Note that the perennial "war story", as told time and again by soldiers, police and prison personnel, grossly exaggerates the dangers posed by one's opponents and thus serves to minimize and justify one's own violence.) Industrial managers, finally, are urged to worship production and to exploit fully the machinery that powers a productive enterprise. Too often, workers are seen and treated as cogs in the very machines they run; in the foreman's rendition of the "war story", workers are ungrateful and lazy cogs at that. When the workers are injured or diseased, a fate their marred characters seem to invite, they may be discarded like so many worn out or defective machine parts (Reasons et al., 1981; Reiman, 1984).

Mundane authorizations are more specific than transcendent authorizations. They spell out how stipulated ends will be achieved. This involves, for example, killing soldiers in battle or upon surrender, killing civilians in and around war zones, killing concentration-camp inmates or condemned prisoners, killing criminals in the process of apprehending them, killing rioting or escaping prisoners in the process of restraining or reclaiming them, or ignoring pervasive workplace dangers that comprise an often lethal assault on the health of workers as well as, in the case of some asbestos and chemical plants, their families and neighbors.

Mundane authorizations typically are issued in the form of orders or directives that shape the routine of one's work. These orders may be direct and unambiguous ("shoot to kill"), purposely euphemistic ("shower the barracks" when the showers emit lethal gas; "carry out the will of the court" when that will calls for killing a fellow human being), or hazy and hard to interpret ("prisoners must be fed from your own rations"; "we have no accommodations for prisoners of war"). There may be no specific orders at all, but only a social climate that condones violence ("production comes first"; "we're in business to make money, not friends"; or, as the Mayor of Detroit recently proclaimed, "our cops are the toughest gang in town").

In times of crisis, mundane authorizations may be exploited to meet personal needs. Military massacres, for example, frequently occur after the troops have sustained losses and particularly after a popular soldier or officer has been killed. Incensed soldiers then stretch their authority to include shooting anything that moves and might therefore be construed, however implausibly, to pose a danger (Lifton, 1973; see also Kelman, 1973). Before entering the Vietnamese village of My Lai, for example, soldiers heard a "funeral oration" for "a popular and much respected noncommissioned officer, Sergeant George Cox", who had died the preceding day, the most recent of a host of casualities (Lifton, 1973, p. 38). The message conveyed by Captain Medina, who had delivered the oration, was reportedly that "nothing would be walking, growing, or crawling" after the assault on My Lai. "Referring to the pained emotions the men felt about Cox's and others' deaths, Medina was said to have told the men to 'let it out, let it go'. Which they did" (ibid.).

Less dramatic examples of crises and the manipulation of mundane authorizations occur in other contexts. Some industrial foremen, for example, faced with unrealistic production quotas, push workers beyond their limits. Rest breaks are shortened or cancelled, and machines and work areas poorly maintained; workers thus confront unusually exhausting and dangerous work conditions (Reasons et al., 1981; Reiman, 1984). Similarly, chemicals and other hazardous wastes may be dumped illegally to save time and money, particularly when the economy is poor and business is precarious (Reiman, 1984). Those who have to "make production" thus make decisions that cut corners and save money, but also jeopardize the health and well-being of workers and in some cases even citizens in the surrounding communities (Reiman, 1984; Reasons et al., 1981). For a few individuals, crises become a routine feature of their institutional role. For example, police officers and prison guards with fragile egos have "a starting capital of insecurity or egocentricity available for investment in violence-promoting premises" (Toch, 1980, p. 189). Too often, they find compensatory violence to be recurring if illegitimate facts of their work lives.

Moral restraints against violence become an issue when mundane authorizations must be acted upon. At this juncture, the disembodied or stereotyped targets of violence are engaged as individuals: specific soldiers or civilians must be killed; individual condemned prisoners put to death; a worker with a face, a name and a family allowed to sustain injuries or to die from an occupational disease. Recognition of the humanity of the victim is stressful and might well undermine one's willingness to act (or fail to act) in accordance with the dictates of the institution. Dehumanization of both the front-line organizational personnel and those who are harmed by them protects against this possibility. Prominent among the sources of dehumanization are (1) a bureaucratic organizational format, (2) the isolation of the organization, and (3) the insulation of the workers or agents of the institution.

The bureaucracy as an organizational form necessarily entails dehumanization. This type of organization, to quote Weber, "compares with other organizations exactly as does the machine with nonmechanical modes of production" (quoted in Gerth and Mills, 1946, p. 214). The ideal bureaucrat is possessed of complementary virtues. To quote Weber once again, he "conducts his office . . . [in] a spirit of formalistic impersonality, 'Sine ira et studio', without hatred or passion, and hence without affection or enthusiasm" (Weber, 1947, p. 340). Of course, bureaucracies have another face – a more informal, sub-cultural side to them (Page, 1946; Blau, 1969). Nevertheless, institutional violence tends to draw upon the formal side of the organization; under pressure to act violently or to ignore the violence around them, people take shelter, as it were, behind their official roles (Milgram, 1975; Kelman, 1973). One becomes, in essence, an anonymous member of the institution's "collective instrumentality" (Bandura et al., 1975, p. 268). Under these conditions, one may feel little or no personal responsibility for one's actions (Milgram, 1975). Alternatively, one may feel personally responsible for one's conduct but view any guilt or anxiety as a cost of maintaining one's honorable commitments to the institution; such painful emotions may even serve as badges of courage and validations of one's integrity as a member of the institution's "troops" (see Mantell and Panzarella, 1976). In either case, like one's colleagues, one comes to understand the situation as it is defined by the formal organization. The formal side of the bureaucracy can be accentuated, and indeed can become a self-contained world, when the organization and its personnel are sufficiently isolated from the larger society.

Isolation may be achieved in varying ways and degrees. The most obvious and effective sources of isolation involve physical means: barriers may be erected, for example, or activities may be conducted in distant, desolate or dangerous places. Isolation under these conditions can be quite extreme, even total; stone walls encircling remote prisons effectively corral inmates and exclude the viewing public.[2] Symbolic means may sometimes be enough; signs that ban unauthorized personnel, and usually indicate a danger or hazard to the uninitiated, are often effective deterrents (Goffman, 1961). Cultural patterns that exclude outsiders and shroud actions behind a veil of ignorance can also be potent sources of isolation, as seen in the police emphasis on solidarity and secrecy that effectively sets them apart from the citizens they serve (Westley, 1956; Skolnick, 1966).

The extent to which an institution is isolated from the larger society will vary in response to external factors that shape institutional adaptation. The military during peacetime, as well as the prison and police force under routine conditions, may be comparatively open or permeable institutions; they may permit considerable variation in how their inhabitants live and work (Karsten, 1978; Toch, 1977a; Wilson, 1968). These institutions become more isolated, and hence more total and constraining, under conditions of stress. For the army, the stress of impending combat converts a "Sad Sack" platoon to a "fighting machine" (Stouffer et al., 1949, esp. vol. I). The prison becomes more monolithic and oppressive, with guards and inmates locked into stereotypical roles, under conditions of crowding (which breeds tension and violence) or where crises such as escapes or riots take place (Lombardo, 1982). Police close ranks when confronted with a hostile community; abuses of power featuring violence become disturbingly common (Chevigny, 1969; Stark, 1972). Impending executions transform death rows from storage areas or repositories to more abusive and combative settings (Jackson and Christian, 1980; Johnson, 1981), and the same holds for a regular policy of executions. A similar change occurred in some Nazi death camps as well. There is evidence that the pre-holocaust concentration camps were less oppressive than when genocide became standard operating-procedure in the camps, and that the slave-labor camps were less oppressive than the death camps (Bettleheim, 1960; Des Pres, 1977).

Isolation protects the institution and its personnel from observation and judgment by the larger society, and conveys the illusion that the institution comprises a separate and unaccountable world with its own moral order. The organization becomes, as it were, a situation unto itself; the official view of the world becomes a compelling "reality". The larger society is excluded from the world of the institution, and the institution is therefore free to develop its own closed world and to pursue its interests with unrestrained efficiency. In its most bald form, the ethical imperative is, "What works is right."

Isolation of the organization is complemented by insulation of workers or agents. Insulation protects individuals from recognizing the moral implications of their actions. When such implications are considered – when people come to suspect or believe that what they are doing is either wrong or at least morally problematic – one's personal morality is deemed secondary to institutional loyalty: that is, to the imperative to maintain one's commitments to proper authorities. In either event, removed from the sobering gaze of society and shielded from the normal dictates of one's personal conscience, violence is changed from the morally objectionable, or at least morally suspect, to the mundane. Violence may even seem quite noble, as when one conceives of one's institution as engaged in a fight against one evil or another. Violence becomes, at bottom, a part of one's job. And, though violence may be a difficult part of one's job, it is no longer a morally blameworthy event.

The process that results in the perception of violence as normal and even desirable, as well as the disposition to inflict violence or to permit it to occur, involves the socialization of individuals to fit the organizational enterprise. This process begins with recruitment and training, and is complete when the person sees himself as an agent of an institution that is essentially beyond human control and accountability. At this juncture, the person is insulated from any meaningful awareness of the moral dimensions of his behavior.

Situational socialization

Recruitment and selection focus on people who are likely to conform to the institutional regime and accept the "pejorative stereotyping and indoctrination" (Bandura, 1979, p. 229) essential to carrying out violence, or permitting it to occur, on a more or less regular basis. In varying degrees, what might be termed a "situational self" is cultivated. This situational self is meant to supersede one's regular self when one plays an institutional role. Lifton (1985) refers to this phenomenon as "doubling", to indicate that two selves cohere within the same person. These selves do not normally come into conflict or even competition, however, because they are selectively mobilized by situational forces.

Indices of susceptibility to institutional socialization, and hence the development of situational selves, include the tender age of most recruits, their conservative views of authority, or even their explicit allegiance to a particular ideology or policy. Thus army and police recruits, particularly those subsequently conscripted for duty as torturers or as members of other violent elites, tend to be young and politically conservative (Karsten, 1978; Bennett, 1984; Amnesty International, 1975); concentration-camp guards were usually sworn Nazis (Moore, 1978); and death-row guards are often avid supporters of punishment (Turnbull, 1978). Foremen are typically "company men" (Reasons et al., 1981). These men (and sometimes women) often commence their institutional service with authoritarian leanings (see Adorno et al., 1950). Over time, some of them develop monothematically authoritarian, and sometimes even fanatical, personalities and roles. Dr Mengele is a compelling example. As a young man, Mengele was a Nazi ideologue and, later, a member of the SS; he reached the full bloom of his fanaticism in the arid moral milieu of the death camps (Lifton, 1985).

Training, whether in formal classes or on the job, is meant to mold recruits into institutional role incumbents. Generally, a "gradual desensitization process" is at work (Bandura, 1979, p. 229); one's role is taken up in small increments and hence comes to seem quite normal. As training unfolds, the dangers or uncertainties of the job, and the security that can be found in conformity and a show of unity, are emphasized. Hence soldiers, police and guards emerge from training with (1) a concern for survival in the face of danger, (2) a respect for rules and regulations that give shape to the job, and (3) a clearer sense of their roles and mutual obligations to protect and support one another (Faris, 1976; Bennett, 1984; Johnson and Weiner, 1981). Foremen, similarly, are trained and otherwise encouraged to think of themselves as part of a "management team" that must somehow "extract" productivity from reluctant and potentially disruptive workers.[3]

Training aims to produce a sense of agency (Milgram, 1975). As a formal role incumbent in the organization, the person has been encouraged, if not directly instructed, to see himself as an instrument of authority who follows directives in the form of orders, procedures or "the law". Discretion in interpreting instructions may be narrow or wide, but a belief that what one does is either permitted or required reduces sharply one's feelings of personal responsibility (Milgram, 1975). Alternatively, a sense of agency may promote feelings of responsibility which are directed to the goal of loyally playing one's role, however personally reprehensive one's role-generated conduct may be (see Mantell and Panzarella, 1976). Even the policeman who is regularly embroiled with citizens and, in the extreme case, is really only a street brawler in uniform can see himself as responding to attacks upon the institution of the law which happen to be visited upon him personally (Westley, 1953, 1970; Toch, 1965). This violence and counter violence is his (situational) cross to bear, and he tries to do so, as he sees things, with dignity if not decorum. In the final analysis, the moral justification is "I was simply doing my job", whether this job is done in a passive and obedient way or in an active and loyal way.

Bureaucratic institutions emphasize regularity of procedure, if not discipline and order, so that little which is unusual or remarkable ever occurs. Routines discourage personal introspection and criticism of oneself or one's institution; the fact that one's collegues adhere to these same routines adds to the impression that institutional activities are normal (Kelman, 1973; Milgram, 1975). Moreover, the real nature of one's behavior and its consequences is often disguised by a euphemistic language or jargon. Violence is described in morally neutral terms, as so many "operations" or "encounters" or simply "events" that make up the institution's routine (Kelman, 1973; Milgram, 1975). Violence may even be described in perversely congenial terms, as though it were a pleasant or pleasurable activity. Thus it is that some torturers refer to brutal interrogations as "social gatherings" or "tea parties", and describe themselves as though they were members of devil-may-care fraternaties (Amnesty International, 1975). At most, institutional language admits to "accidents" or even "tragedies" for which, of coure, no one can fairly be held responsible (Reasons et al., 1981, Reiman, 1984).

The person who follows "standard operating-procedure" and talks the "lingo" of the institution in effect operates in the moral equivalent of automatic gear. (He may be more or less aware of this contrived arrangement, depending on whether his role is marked by passive and hence blind obedience or by active and hence more informed commitment to the institution.) When violence is common (as in combat) or ritualized (as in executions), it follows procedures that readily exonerate institutional actors. When violent acts are rare and unscheduled events, as in police use of deadly force or the prison guard's killing of a rioting inmate, they are more spontaneous and hence problematic, because they seem to involve the person more than the role. Violent acts of this sort are restructured and made routine through (1) institutional forms and hearings that make them bureaucratic events, (2) sub-cultural support for violence as a regrettable but unavoidable part of the job, and (3) rituals and euphemisms that shroud the act in secrecy or understatement (Van Maanen, 1980; Lombardo, 1982). Though occupational injury and disease are disturbingly prevalent in many industrial work-settings, these disabilities are not daily occurrences; they are handled in a way similar to that of police or prison-guard use of deadly force. They, too, are restructured to become normal and hence non-culpable events. Thus it is that institutional negligence is obscured by a system that makes disabilities appear as (1) compensable or non-compensable items in a "no-fault" insurance system, (2) instances of the tragic but inexorable dangers of working for a living, and (3) invitations to lazy workers to "malinger" and otherwise "milk" their employers (Reasons et al., 1981). In varying ways, then, violence becomes an event, its victim a statistic or case, and both are subsumed within organizational routine.

Bureaucratic routines foster a narrowing of moral concern to that of a job well done; they discourage basic questions about the morality of the institution's activities or invoke the morality of obedience or loyalty to duly constituted authority (Milgram, 1975; Mantell and Panzarella, 1976). The good worker is the efficient and dependable worker, the reliable technician. Technicians do not disrupt institutional routines by faltering in their duties or by asking questions, even if they harbor private doubts about the undertaking. The good combat soldier remains steady under fire, regardless of the chaos and death that surround him; he follows orders and gets the job done (Stouffer et al., 1949). The ideal Nazi guard kept inmates under control and herded them, more or less perfunctorily, to their deaths (Dicks, 1972). The model death-row guard treats his charges dispassionately, delivering them to the executioner in a timely and controlled manner (Turnbull, 1978; Johnson, 1984). The ideal cop is both productive of arrests and forceful in his demeanor; as a matter of course, he dispenses "justice without trial" (Skolnick, 1966). The ideal industrial foreman "makes quota" and gets ahead; in effect, his workers are left to fend for themselves (Reasons et al., 1981).

The division of labor in bureaucracies is such that no one takes full responsibility for violence (Milgram, 1975). Policy-makers make policy, managers manage, front-line workers act. Each can – and does – wash his hands of the other; each does his job. Hence, standard bureaucratic division of labor further divorces workers from the moral significance of institutional policy. Even Auschwitz's Mengele, who had considerable autonomy and showed much individual initiative in his macabre labors, exhibited a marked "obedience to the received order" as manifested in the Nazi hierarchy (Lifton, 1985, p. 23). He was an instrument, however privileged and indeed elevated, of the Nazi regime and its historic destiny.

At a more mundane level, bureaucratic excuses proliferate among the masses who fill out the ranks of the institution. After all, soldiers don't start wars, and concentration-camp guards didn't design the "final solution". Death-row guards don't sentence the condemned, and many do not participate directly in executions. Police don't write laws or create the social or psychological conditions that drive some men to crime. Foremen don't set quotas for production. One acts only on a segment of the larger reality, and comes to see this reality in fragmented and ultimately dehumanized terms. The statement of a prison warden about his obligation to execute condemned prisoners is quite telling in this regard: "I look at the criminal justice system as a sewer pipe. I'm just at the end of the sewer pipe. The police did their job, the courts did their job, now I have to do my job" (Johnson, 1984, p. 1). The warden sees his job, we must infer, as disposing of the human waste the courts have condemned to die.

A bureaucratic institution, with its closed world and limited roles, can readily be seen as having an impersonal and unalterable momentum of its own (Milgram, 1975). (It would surely be an Augean task to clean or dismantle the criminal-justice sewer system our warden reluctantly serves, and one can hardly criticize him for simply shovelling the muck that comes his way.) It is no longer a human institution, subject to control and change. Instead, "the book" must be followed, not changed, whether this is the official rule book or the unofficial (sub-cultural) rule book (Westley, 1953, 1970; Weiner and Johnson, 1981). Authority must be honored at all costs. The person is a good worker or technician and a loyal employee; it is the job that is bad (Hughes, 1958).

Dehumanization and violence

Simply playing one's role in a bureaucracy means relinquishing some autonomy, and hence being less fully human, at least while one is under orders or otherwise doing one's job. Where one's activities appear to be morally neutral, little more than this level of dehumanization may be necessary to carry out acts that produce harm.

Industrial foremen, for example, simply oversee a work process that inflicts harms which in some cases take decades to materialize. When these harms finally become apparent – when, for example, a cotton-mill worker of long tenure comes down with brown lung from inhaling cotton dust on the job – foremen and their superiors can readily blame the workers themselves. They may claim, for example, that the worker's personal habits (such as smoking) or congenital deficiencies ("weak lungs") account for the illness (Johnson, 1982). When the link between occupational conditions and harm is obvious, as when stepped-up production quotas produce an increase in accidents, blame can still be placed on careless, stupid or dishonest employees

(Reasons et al., 1981; Reiman, 1984). Even when the connection between occupational conditions and diseases such as brown lung is established (see Bouhuys, 1979), the facts can be discountd because, after all, they apply to those same careless or stupid or dishonest workers whose personal deficiencies amassed those spurious accident statistics. In any event, the foreman simply does his job. He is neither reformer nor villain, but simply an instrument. He means no harm and often sees no harm. If there is responsibility to assign, it lies with the organization.

Dehumanization in this instance is situation-specific and purely perceptual; the industrial foreman and his supervisors are agents of the institution only when they are on the job, at which time they see themselves and their workers in object terms. A situation-specific set of dehumanized perceptions of oneself and others may also permit violence of a more direct nature. The bomber pilot can wipe out distant, anonymous masses of humanity by simply pushing a button; he can readily see himself as a military technician with a job to do, his victims so many statistics or sectors of a map.[4] Even soldiers in the field of battle can adopt this fiction. Though combat soldiers typically engage in violence that is more direct and visible than that of the bomber pilot, they may have only fleeting contact with their victims (lumped together as an anonymous enemy), and may come to see their violence in neutral terms, as a matter of "body counts", "land gains" and "campaigns" (Kelman, 1973; Lifton, 1973). In each of these instances, as well as in laboratory simulations, "dehumanization is especially conducive to aggression [because] people have a reduced sense of responsibility for the consequences of their actions" (Bandura et al., 1975, p. 266).

Violence of a direct, intimate and face-to-face nature, however, is painfully obvious in its implications. To carry out such violence may require dehumanization of a different order, a dehumanization that entails an actual and not just symbolic loss of humanity. There is little doubt, for instance, that Mengele ultimately saw himself in superhuman (and hence dehumanized) terms, as a sacred instrument of Nazism and not a mere mortal. "It was an axiom", one of the Auschwitz twins told Lifton "that Mengele is God" (1985, p. 24). This alone is unremarkable. What is striking, however, is that, over time, Mengele actually came to incorporate within his Auschwitz self the evil by which he lived and which vividly revealed itself in his " 'dead eyes' – eyes that showed no emotion, that avoided looking into the eyes of others" (ibid.).

Yet Mengele did retain a non-Auschwitz self, even if its existential importance diminished as his work in the camps came progressively to take over his psychic life. Correspondingly, Mengele's victims suffered a dual fate. Some of them he seemed to like; according to the record, one is even tempted to say that Mengele loved some of "his" twins. He treated some of the twins with great kindness and apparent affection, but only when relating to them with his non-Auschwitz self. Even his favorites, however, amounted to so many bodies to be dissected and studied when he dealt with them in the context of his formal role as an agent of the death camps. To settle a question of medical science of presumed relevance to the master race, Mengele unhesitatingly killed his favorite twins. As objects of science and props for Nazi ideology, these and other victims could be killed with brutal efficiency and even dissected "while they were still warm" (Lifton, 1985, p. 22). Here we have object–object relations in their literal – and most repugnant – form.

Mengele's violence is chilling at least in part because he approached his work with enthusiasm and commitment; he appeared to thrive on brutality, even as his Auschwitz self grew and he became numb to his own feelings. The violence of the death-camp guards was more prosaic, but also more difficult to carry out and more damaging to them personally. They were drawn from the non-descript masses of the Nazi party. Like Mengele, they had a mission to perform in the service of the Nazi cause, and this no doubt kept many of them going. But, unlike Mengele's, theirs was a lowly mission which was, moreover, badly tarnished by the tragedies that were daily facts of life in the camps. Mengele's schizoid personality and sense of omnipotent purpose greatly facilitated the development of his impenetrable Auschwitz self (Lifton, 1985, p. 24). He adapted well in the camps, if such a thing is possible, and went on to live an apparently normal – and, by all accounts, guilt-free – life in exile. By contrast, the death-camp officers could not easily distance themselves psychologically from their victims. Their Auschwitz selves were less well formed. One day guarding and the next day killing men, women and children – including infants – came hard to them; heavy drinking and even suicide were common among the rank-and-file guards (Dicks, 1972). Though there is no evidence bearing directly on this point, it is probable that the experience left psychological scars.

To make the death-camp guards' situation tolerable, they had to go to great lengths to mute their own feelings of empathy and guilt, feelings which were apparently strong even after their socialization to their institutional role. It is for this reason, no doubt, that many of them drank heavily both on and off the job. Moreover, their victims could not be seen and treated as people; to recognize their humanity would be unbearable, because it would mobilize the very feelings of empathy and guilt the officers fought to suppress. Hence the prisoners could not be treated with the kindness "Uncle Pepi" – as some of Mengele's younger subjects called him, referring unknowingly to his non-Auschwitz self – sometimes bestowed on his prospective victims. For, in the final analysis, only the literal dehumanization of the prisoners, brought on by the death-camp regime, made it possible for the guards to play their role in the holocaust. This dehumanization, in Des Pres's words,

> made it easier for the SS [guards] to do their job. It made mass murder less terrible to the murderers. . . . Inhibited by pity and guilt, the act of murder becomes harder to perform and results in greater psychic damage to the killer himself. If, on the other hand, the victim exhibits self-disgust; if he cannot lift his eyes for humiliation, or if lifted they show only emptiness – then his death may be administered with ease or even with the conviction that so much rotten tissue has been removed from life's body. (Des Pres, 1977, p. 68)

A less extreme but essentially similar process is at work in the execution of condemned prisoners. Prison officials, and particularly death-row guards, participate in premeditated and indeed elaborately planned killings. Their victims, however guilty they may be of serious crimes, are utterly helpless and hence harmless at the time of their execution. The guards have almost certainly come to know the prisoners over their years of confinement on death row; the violence they or their fellow officers inflict is near at hand and readily visible in its impact. From a psychological viewpoint, this is an exceedingly grisly job that should activate moral restraints against killing fellow human beings. To overcome these restraints, the guards must (1) embrace their organizational role as agents of the death penalty – that is, develop situational selves that allow them to become dehumanized in their work; and (2) oversee a regime of confinement that dulls or even kills off the humanity of the condemned.

Perceptual tricks or illusions may work for bomber pilots but they are not enough to permit death-row guards to convince themselves that they are not personally involved in killings or that their victims are not human. Nor is there any overarching purpose or ideology which discounts the humanity of the victims, as was the case for a Mengele. (And presumably we have few schizoid megalomaniacs like Mengele among the ranks of the death-row officers.) However, like their death-camp counterparts, death-row guards can disengage from the violence of execution if the condemned prisoners are in fact sub-human and are revealed as such in their daily existence on death row. By most accounts, this type of dehumanization is often achieved on death row. The prisoners are warehoused for death; they deteriorate as human beings and their keepers become increasingly numb to this human tragedy (Camus, 1969; Johnson, 1981). Thus there is, among the condemned and their guards, a parallel development of dehumanized situational selves and impersonal relationships appropriate to the carrying out of executions. (Personal relationships based on non-death-row selves no doubt also occur, though such relationships are uncommon and, moreover, become less viable as execution dates draw near.) Ultimately, both the guards and the inmates become less than fully human in the death-row context, and hence more able to play their roles in the executions that culminate death-row confinement.

Execution of captive criminals, then, is a contemporary phenomenon that shows in relief the dynamics of institutional violence in general and dehumanization in particular. To get the job of execution done, the authorization to kill is unambiguously grounded in statutes, prison policies, court decisions and, finally, the governor's acquiescence by failing to invoke clemency. The ritual of killing is carefully delineated and faithfully followed. (Even the condemned man's last meal, a potentially touching encounter, is made into an impersonal ritual.) The various official participants in the process cling tightly to their organizational roles and thus come to hold dehumanized views of themselves and the condemned; often they must actively, and even abusively, distance themselves from the prisoners nominally under their care. In the end, these dehumanized perceptions disguise, and in varying degrees also reduce and even destroy, both their own humanity and that of the prisoners. In this manner, killings *of* and *by* human beings are transformed into impersonal executions carried out by "instruments of authority acting within stipulated routines on condemned prisoners rendered as objects to be . . . dispatched in the execution chamber" (Johnson, 1981, p. 130).

A REFORM AGENDA

It is easy to be smug about institutional violence. Much of the literature on this subject deals with unambiguous and indefensible abuses of our fellow men. Who but a permanent resident on the lunatic fringe applauds the concentration camp or the torture chamber? Who yearns to participate in a military massacre? What man (or woman) champions occupational illness and disease in the name of profit? The institutional processes that shape these injustices would seem to be inherently evil (see Sanford and Comstock, 1973). By noting the correspondence of such processes across a range of institutional situations, as I have done in this chapter, it would seem to follow that all such institutions and activities are evil. This is incorrect, though it is true that, even where defensible, institutional violence can be carried out more humanely than is presently the case. At the risk of sounding glib, we must reach a more congenial accommodation with some forms of institutional violence. Let me explain.

Police, prison and the military are necessary evils in an imperfect and often ugly world.[5] It would be nice to dispense with them, but short of the Millenium that would not be a wise social policy. Of this group of institutions, the most explicitly violent is the military. I submit that efficient use of military violence can be humane. In doing this, I hope to establish, by inference, that the police and prisons, which are less violence-promotive organizations, can also merge efficiency and humaneness. Finally, I wish to close this chapter by suggesting that efficiency in the use of institutional violence can be obtained without resort to dehumanization when the objective of that violence is just, and, moreover, that efficiency so obtained reduces the likelihood that injustices will be produced by our institutions.

More than any other institution examined in this chapter, the legitimate business of the military is violence. The goals of the military are twofold: (1) to deter potential aggressors, and (2) to achieve victory in combat with those aggressors who are undeterred. These goals are best achieved when the military is capable of institutional violence that is predictable, controlled and effective – in a word, disciplined. To put the matter bluntly, "in war, the army that proves most successful in making its raw recruits into killers possesses an immeasurable advantage" (Hastings, 1985, p. 4). The capacity for disciplined killing is both awe-inspiring and potent; the image which comes to mind is that a relentless machine of destruction. Both the prospect and the reality of such violence serve the military's goals.

Paradoxically, efficient or disciplined violence on the part of the military can, in principle if not always in practice, serve also the goal of humaneness. Disciplined institutional violence permits wars to be carried out with a minimum of damage inflicted upon one's enemy; targets can be chosen tactically, and hence judiciously, in contrast with the indiscriminant savaging of people and environments that is the hallmark of an unrestrained war. Disciplined institutional violence also inflicts less psychic damage upon one's own personnel than does undisciplined violence, which allows for the operation of personal motives and concerns. Though soldiers are dehumanized by their role and by their work, and this is a harm, they presumably would be traumatized or brutalized by their own violence were it not securely subsumed within their obligations as agents of the military who follow orders and perform jobs rather than simply vent personal passions.

The fusion of efficiency and humaneness in the use of institutional violence is of paramount importance in a democratic society. By its very nature, a democratic society places a high value on life and liberty. Ideally, a democratic society seeks to resolve conflicts, including not only military conflicts but also those civil conflicts mediated by the police and the prisons, in the least destructive way possible (Phillips, 1984; Toch, 1977b). It is for this reason that indiscriminant retaliatory strikes – whether against civilian populations during wars, or against political terrorists or domestic criminals during peace – are impermissible as a matter of policy in most democratic societies, but are standard operating-procedure in totalitarian countries.[6]

The search for minimally destructive ways of resolving conflicts is a continuing one. Though some uses of institutional violence serve appropriate social ends and can be defended even as they are presently constituted, it is essential that we explore alternative strategies for the generation of this violence. The military, the police and prisons have each developed their own strategies of management following a conception of human nature which holds that most men and women are basically lazy and perhaps even stupid.[7] No one can entrust people of such low caliber with jobs that call for initiative or responsibility. As a result, institutional personnel are converted into passively obedient, or at best actively loyal, agents of an omniscient regime. Nobody in the organization gets hurt much in the process, at least during routine times, but neither is there much personal growth or fulfillment. There is also the risk that excessive violence, which inflicts gratuitous harm on both the agents of institutional violence and its victims, will be undertaken during times of crisis. These difficulties can be avoided by better management.

Contemporary management perspectives call for tapping an innate human desire to be effective and competent in one's work; to make things happen rather than to be a pawn (even a loyal pawn) in a process that is beyond one's comprehension or control (Toch and Grant, 1982). These management strategies are participatory and, ideally, democratic in approach. They give workers an active role in shaping policy. And, while machine-like consensus is rare in such organizations, these regimes are not undisciplined in their operation or their products. Indeed, under certain conditions, the self-imposed discipline born of participatory management may be a more reliable task-master that the externally imposed discipline that marks traditional autocratic management.[8] With participatory management there is personal growth and a sense of fulfillment, as well as commitment to the organization that meets these basic human needs (Toch and Grant, 1982).

Participatory management would involve front-line staff in the establishment of rules for the use of violence. Conscious and explicit moral justifications for violence would, as a result, be developed among the personnel most likely to use violence. Thinking matters through and acting on principles other than obedience or loyalty would no doubt be difficult – it is certainly easier simply to follow orders – but these are altogether proper activities. We *should* grapple with moral dilemmas, and indeed should even agonize over them when violence is at issue. Just uses of institutional violence can occur with the participation of persons who, as autonomous human beings, understand and assent to institutional roles and activities they have had a hand in shaping. Institutions such as the military, police and prisons can and should generate "violence *with* moral restraint" carried out by personnel who are fully aware of the moral terrain on which they operate. This violence, ideally, would be deployed only when the larger moral purposes of *protecting life* and *keeping the peace* cannot be achieved by using less extreme measures (Toch, 1977b). Participatory management of violence in pursuit of these ends would place our legitimately violence-promotive institutions squarely in the mainstream of the society they serve.

Participatory management of violence would also reduce the likelihood that abusive policies will be instituted or, if instituted, followed. Participatory-management approaches preclude the blind obdience and uncompromising loyalty to authority upon which unjust policies depend. They would keep institutional personnel in touch with their own humanity and, by way of empathy, the humanity of others. This point is crucial. Social-learning theory, field observation and controlled empirical research all confirm the general notion that "it is difficult for people to behave cruelly towards others when they are characterized in ways that personalize and humanize them" (Bandura, 1979, p. 228; see also Bandura et al., 1975).

Feelings of isolation from society and of insulation from one's own values would also be reduced by participatory management. There would be no pawns of violence here – in other words, no object–object relations that defy and defile our shared humanity and spawn the needless violence that is all too common under present policies. Nor would dehumanzed roles be missed. Today's soldiers, police and guards are drawn from a society that is increasingly interested in enriched and meaningful work roles that serve worthy human ends. Violence is, regrettably, an avenue to some legitimate ends, but it can be deployed sparingly and with humaneness as a primary consideration. Participatory management would breed the proper sensibilities among *our* agents of violence, and may prove both useful and liberating to them and the society they serve.

NOTES

1 Another transcendent authorization is science. Much harm has been done in the name of science, particularly when science is conscripted into the service of profit or social control. The most notable instance is hazardous medical experimentation, whether undertaken to develop new drugs or to purify the species. I have excluded this topic from my study because such experiments are rare, though by no means non-existent (see Jones, 1981), outside prisons and concentration camps. Following the logic of this analysis, these experiments occur when the laboratory becomes a closed world; they are less prevalent and extreme outside prisons and concentration camps because the host institutions usually universities or research centers, do not become as total and controlling.

I have also excluded from analysis the whole range of profit-inspired violence associated with such harmful medical practices as unnecessary surgery and drug prescription. Though these activities claim many lives every year, they tend to occur when medical personnel work as entrepreneurs rather than as institutional agents (see Reiman, 1984). This behavior is not, in other words, a clear case of institutional violence.

2 Factories and other industrial plants are often similarly enclosed and marked off-limits to outsiders, with workers processed within the confines of the plant in a manner akin to prisoners (Reasons et al., 1981; Johnson, 1982). It is not merely an accident of history that prisons and factories are similar in their architectural

design and administrative format. The sixteenth-century English Bridewell and Houses of Correction were the early models of both the penitentiary and the factory (see Dobash, 1984).

3 This is a product of "Theory *X*" thinking, which views workers as lazy and recalcitrant (McGregor, 1960). This view is still quite prevalent in management circles (Toch and Grant, 1982).

4 This attitude was given perhaps its quintessential expression by Paul Tibbets, pilot of the *Enola Gay*, the 'plane that dropped the atomic bomb on Hiroshima: "I feel no guilt, no second thoughts. The bomb did what it was supposed to do. It ended the war" (*Washington Post*, 31 July 1985, p. D1).

5 Some *methods* used by these institutions are not necessary evils. We need prisons, for example, but the death penalty – which is carried out in prisons – is a punishment we can live without. Even the most heinous offender can be sentenced to life imprisonment – a "civil death", if you will, that serves as a "practical moral alternative to the death penalty" (Johnson, 1984, p. 578). We can also live without prison-guard or police brutality of all stripes; guards and police can maintain order without promiscuous violence. The same point holds for the military; one can fight an effective yet restrained war.

6 It goes without saying, in the context of this chapter, that policies prohibiting indiscriminate retaliatory strikes are sometimes contravened, and indeed may even be violated systematically under certain conditions. Such breaches of policy (and sometimes law) follow the dynamics of institutional violence I have examined in this chapter. The point is that, when such violations of policy occur in democratic societies, officials can be, and sometimes are, held accountable for them. Such moral niceties are absent in totalitarian societies. Totalitarian societies, as the name implies, have in effect become total institutions (Goffman, 1961; Reiman, 1976). There is, as a result, a pervasive lack of moral restraint in the use of violence. This makes totalitarian societies formidable enemies of democratic societies (Revel, 1983).

7 See note 3, above.

8 Toch and Grant tell us that participatory management has been used to structure work roles in a variety of institutions including some police forces and maximum-security prisons. While Toch and Grant did not specifically extend their analysis to the military, there are striking parallels between some correctional and law-enforcement roles and the roles of such military personnel as the military policeman and the drill sergeant (see Faris, 1976). The general point is that expanded roles and responsibilities can both reflect and enhance self-discipline in a range of institutional contexts.

REFERENCES

Adorno, T. W., Frenkel-Brunswik, E., Levinson, D. J. and Sanford, N. 1950: *The Authoritarian Personality*. New York: Harper and Row.

Amnesty International 1975: *Amnesty International Report on Torture*. New York: Farrar, Straus and Giroux.

Arendt, H. 1963: *Eichmann in Jerusalem*. New York: Viking.

Bandura, A. 1979: The social learning perspective: mechanisms of aggression. In H. Toch (ed.), *Psychology of Crime and Criminal Justice*, New York: Holt, Rinehart and Winston.

Bandura, A., Underwood, B. and Fromson, M. E. 1975: Disinhibition of aggression through diffusion of responsibility and dehumanization of victims. *Journal of Research in Personality*, 9, 253–69.

Bennett, R. R. 1984: Becoming blue: a longitudinal study of police recruit occupatioal socialization. *Journal of Police Science and Administration*, 12, 47–58.

Bettleheim, B. 1960: *The Informed Heart: autonomy in a mass age*. New York: Free Press.

Bittner, E. 1975: *The Functions of the Police in Modern Society*. New York: Jason Aronson.

Blau, P. M. 1969: *Bureaucracy in Modern Society*. New York: Random House.

Bouhuys, A. 1979: Cotton dust and lung disease: presumptive criteria for disability compensation. Unpublished paper developed under contract no. B-9-M-8-4694, Office of the Assistant Secretary of Labor for Policy, Evaluation and Research, Washington, DC.

Camus, A. 1969: Reflections on the guillotine. In *Resistance, Rebellion and Death*, New York: Knopf.

Chevigny, P. 1969: *Police Power: police abuses in New York City*. New York: Vintage Books.

Des Pres, T. 1977: *The Survivor: an anatomy of life in the death camps*. New York: Pocket Books.

Dicks, H. V. 1972: *Licensed Mass Murder*. New York: Basic Books.

Dobash, R. R. 1983: Labour and discipline in Scottish and English prisons: moral correction, punishment and useful toil. *Sociology*, 17, 1–25.

Faris, J. H. 1976: The impact of basic combat training: the role of the drill sergeant. In N. L. Goldman and D. R. Segal (eds), *The Social Psychology of Military Service*, Beverly Hills, Calif.: Sage.

Gerth H. H. and Mills, W. C. (trs) 1946: *From Max Weber: essays in sociology*. Oxford: Oxford University Press.

Goffman, E. 1961: *Asylums: essays on the social situation of mental patients and other inmates*. New York: Anchor Books.

Goldman, N. L. and Segal, D. R. (eds) 1976: *The Social Psychology of Military Service*. Beverly Hills, Calif.: Sage.

Hastings, M. 1985: Their Wehrmacht was better than our army. *Washington Post*, 5 May, pp. C1 and C4.

Hughes, E. C. 1958: *Men and their Work*. New York: Free Press.

Jackson, B. and Christian, D. 1980: *Death Row*. Boston, Mass.: Beacon Press.

Janowitz, M. (ed.), *The New Military: changing patterns of organization*. New York: Russell Sage Foundation.

Johnson, E. 1984: Some states prepare for first executions in 20 years or more. *Wall Street Journal*, 6 November, pp. 1 and 21.

Johnson, R. 1981: *Condemned to Die: life under sentence of death*. New York: Elsevier.

—— 1982: Labored breathing: living with brown lung. Paper presented at the Annual Meeting of the American Society of Criminology, Toronto.

—— 1984: A life for a life? *Justice Quarterly*, 1, 569–80.

—— 1985: "Make way, dead man coming": an essay on the condemned and their executioners. Unpublished manuscript, American University.

Johnson, R. and Weiner, R. I. 1981: Organization and environment: the case of correctional personnel training programs. *Journal of Criminal Justice*, 9, 441–50.
Jones, J. H. 1981: *Bad Blood: the Tuskegee syphilis experiment*. New York: Free Press.
Karsten, P. 1978: *Soldiers and Society*. Westport: Greenwood Press.
Kelman, H. 1973: Violence without moral restraint: reflections on the dehumanization of victims and victimizers. *Journal of Social Issues*, 29, 25–61.
Lifton, R. J. 1973: Existential evil. In N. Sanford and C. Comstock, *Sanctions for Evil: sources of social destructiveness*, San Francisco: Jossey-Bass.
—— 1985: Mengele. What made this man? *New York Times Magazine*, 21 July 1985.
Lombardo, L. X. 1982: Stress, change, and collective violence in prison. In R. Johnson and H. Toch, *The Pains of Imprisonment*, Beverly Hills, Calif.: Sage.
Mantell, D. M. and Panzarella, R. 1976: Obedience and responsibility. *British Journal of Social and Clinical Psychology*, 15, 239–45.
McGregor, D. 1960: *The Human Side of Enterprise*. New York: McGraw-Hill.
Milgrim, S. 1975: *Obedience to Authority*. New York: Harper and Row.
Moore, B., Jr 1978: *Injustice: the social bases of obedience and revolt*. White Plains, NY: Sharpe.
Page, C. H. 1946: Bureaucracy's other face. *Social Forces*, 25, 88–94.
Phillips, R. L. 1984: *War and Justice*. Norman, Okla.: University of Oklahoma Press.
Reasons, C. E., Ross, L. L. and Paterson, C. 1981: *Assault on the Worker: occupational health and safety in Canada*. Toronto: Butterworth.
Reiman, J. H. 1976: Privacy, intimacy and personhood. *Philosophy and Public Affairs*, 6, 26–44.
—— 1984: *The Rich Get Richer and the Poor Get Prison: ideology, class and criminal justice*. New York: Wiley.
Revel, J. F. 1983: *How Democracies Perish*. New York: Doubleday.
Sanford, N. and Comstock, C. 1973: *Sanctions for Evil: sources of social destructiveness*. San Francisco: Jossey-Bass.
Shulman, R. 1971: Parkman's Indians and American violence. *Massachusetts Review*, 12, 221–39.
Skolnick, J. H. 1966: *Justice without Trial: law enforcement in a democratic society*. New York: Wiley.
Stark, R. 1972: *Police Riots*. Belmont, Mass.: Wadsworth.
Stouffer, S. A., DeVinney, L. C., Star, S. A. and Williams, R. M. 1949: *The American Soldier*, vol. I: *Adjustment during Army Life*. Princeton, NJ: Princeton University Press.
Stouffer, S. A., Lumsdaine, A. A., Lumsdaine, M. H., Williams, R. M., Smith, M. B., Janis, I. L., Star, S. A. and Cotrell, L. S. 1949: *The American Soldier*, vol. II: *Combat and its Aftermath*. Princeton, NJ: Princeton University Press.
Toch, H. 1965: Psychological consequences of the police role. *Police*, September–October, pp. 22–5.
—— 1977a: *Living in Prison: the ecology of survival*. New York: Free Press.
—— 1977b: *Police, Prisons and the Problem of Violence*. Crime and Delinquency Issues monograph, publ. no. (ADM; 76–364.
—— 1980: *Violent Men: an inquiry into the psychology of violence*. Cambridge, Mass.: Schenkman.
Toch, H. and Grant, J. D. 1982: *Reforming Human Services: change through participation*. Beverly Hills, Calif.: Sage.

Turnbull, C. 1978: Death by decree: an anthropological approach to capital punishment. *Natural History*, 87, 51–67.

Van Maanen, J. 1978: The asshole. In P. K. Manning and J. Van Maanen (eds), *Policing: a view from the street*, New York: Goodyear.

—— 1980: Beyond account: the personal impact of police shootings. *Annals of the American Academy of Political and Social Science*, 452, 145–56.

Weber, M. 1947: *The Theory of Social and Economic Organization*, tr. A. M. Henderson and T. Parsons. Oxford: Oxford University Press.

Westley, W. A. 1953: Violence and the Police. *American Journal of Sociology*, 59, 34–41.

—— 1956: Secrecy and the police. *Social Forces*, 34, 254–7.

—— 1970: *Violence and the Police*. Cambridge, Mass.: MIT Press.

Wilson, J. Q. 1968: *Varieties of Police Behavior: the management of law and order in eight communities*. Cambridge, Mass.: Harvard University Press.

13

The Split-Second Syndrome and Other Determinants of Police Violence

James J. Fyfe

Discussions of police violence are often blurred by the failure to distinguish between violence that is clearly extralegal and abusive and violence that is simply the unnecessary result of police incompetence. This distinction is important because the causes of these two types of violence, and the motivations of the officers involved, vary greatly. Extralegal violence involves the willful and wrongful use of force by officers who knowingly exceed the bounds of their office. Unnecessary violence occurs when well-meaning officers prove incapable of dealing with the situations they encounter without needless or too hasty resort to force.[1]

EXTRALEGAL POLICE VIOLENCE

It is tempting but probably simplistic, to conclude that extralegal police violence results exclusively from the aberrations or prejudices of individual officers or their commanders. If this kind of violence were totally – or even primarily – attributable to officers who regard their badges as licenses to vent hostile and anti-social drives, we should be well advised to try to eliminate it by selecting and monitoring officers with greater care.

Certainly, these personnel processes are important, but it is probably useless to rely almost exclusively on them as the strategy for reducing extralegal police violence. First, our skill at predicting human behavior is not highly developed. Except in obviously extreme cases,[2] it is nearly impossible for personnel administrators to determine which police candidates of officers will eventually engage in extralegal violence. Second, as investigators of police corruption have suggested (City of New York, 1972), it is likely that characteristics of police work and police organizations, rather than characteristics of police officers, are the major determinants of police misconduct.[3]

Klockars (1980) makes such an argument in his formulation of a police "Dirty Harry Problem". He argues that some police perceive the procedural limitations under which they work as arbitrary barriers to achievement of one of their most important goals: the protection of good folk through the apprehension and conviction of criminals. Such officers operate on a presumption of suspects' guilt, and become frustrated when legal processes result in acquittals of people who have, in fact, committed the crimes of which they have been accused. Subsequently, to serve what they (and much of the public) see as justice, these officers resort to "dirty means" – fabrication of evidence, intimidation and even torture – to circumvent such perceived barriers to justice as judical exclusion of illegally obtained evidence, and to make sure that their suspects ultimately receive in court what the officers regard as their just due. Even though the actions of such officers may reflect a widely held view that there should be little distinction between factual guilt and legal guilt (Packer, 1968), they involve, Klockars asserts, wrongful moral choices by the officers themselves. The best way, according to Klockars, of preventing such wrongful choices is to punish the individual officers and the police agencies who make and tolerate them.

As Klockars acknowledges, however, his approach to this kind of violence is not entirely satisfactory. To penalize individual officers who have been trained and socialized by their employers to believe that policing cannot be done by the book and that abuse and misconduct are the most effective means of accomplishing police goals is probably unfair and would almost certainly be ineffective. Extralegal police violence is probably more closely attributable to politically expedient, but morally wrong, definitions of appropriate police conduct at the highest levels of police agencies than to the deviance of street-level officers. Thus, a better way to reduce such violence is to alter the organizational expectations and norms to which the officers who commit abuses conform.

For that reason, Klockars is much more persuasive in his suggestion that police *agencies* bear penalties for extralegal violence than in his qualified advocacy of individual punishment. Certainly, officers who apply wrongful definitions to their work may *deserve* to be punished. But such wrongful definitions are likely to survive them and to dictate the behavior of other officers unless their superiors – and the citizens whose taxes ultimately pay for disciplinary measures against the police – learn that the costs of encouraging or tolerating the use of dirty means to achieve good ends are intolerable.

Thus, as the United States Supreme Court indicated in *Monell* vs *New York City Department of Social Services*,[4] one way to correct high-level tolerance or encouragement of public officials' misconduct is to make citizens liable for their employees' misdeeds. Implicit in this approach is the theory that concerned citizens will then demand that officials behave in a manner that is more consistent with both law and their financial interests. But, because the citizenry usually does not comport with this neat theory, this approach is not totally satisfactory either.

Citizens are often apathetic rather than concerned about the operations of their officials, including the police. Many of them simply expect officials to be there when needed, and become concerned only when officials have failed to meet this responsibility, or when they have personally experienced or witnessed what they regard as a grave injustice at the hands of officials. Further, many of the most concerned citizens regard with great distaste and little empathy the people against whom the police employ extralegal violence. The citizens who have the time to devote to civic affairs belong to the middle and upper classes, who rarely are the victims of police abuse; but it is they who sit on the juries that determine whether police have exceeded the bounds of their authority and, if so, whether the citizens – themselves included – should compensate the victims.

There is probably no better way to reform the wrongful behavior of police officers than to hit in the pocket the citizens to whom they are accountable. But this tactic often fails because those same citizens determine whether and how hard their pockets should be hit, and because they often do not regard as peers the victims of police abuse. Consequently, reality demands that more operationally practicable means of reducing extralegal police violence be found.

One such method is simple but rare: the engagement of leaders willing to disabuse the citizenry of their unrealistic expectations of the police. In a democracy, rates of crime, levels of disorder and the safety of "good people" are more closely associated with social conditions than with the number of police or the willingness of the police to employ dirty means to achieve the good ends of order and public safety. Few elected officials or police chiefs, however, are willing to run the risk of appearing to be soft on crime by announcing to apathetic citizens that crime and disorder are *their* problems rather than police problems and that, unless they are willing to give up many of their freedoms, no level of police presence or toughness is likely to improve matters.[5]

Were more mayors and police chiefs willing and courageous enough to do so, the pressures upon them and their personnel to achieve ends that lie beyond their means would dissipate, as would the temptation to bend the rules in attempts to achieve the impossible.[6] Until we grow a new breed of elected executives and police chiefs who are somehow able to change unrealistic public expectations of the police, however, we will not remove the major source of extralegal police violence, but must expect it to continue, however dissipated by other, less direct, approaches.

INCOMPETENCE AND UNNECESSARY POLICE VIOLENCE

While extralegal police violence is egregious, it probably occurs far less frequently – and probably less frequently injures sympathetic and factually innocent victims – than does police violence emanating from simple incompetence. Such violence occurs when police lack the eloquence to persuade temporarily disturbed persons to give up their weapons, but shoot them instead. It occurs when, instead of pausing to consider and apply less drastic and dramatic alternatives, officers blindly confront armed criminals in the midst of groups of innocent people. It occurs when officers called to quell noisy but non-violent disputes act in a way that provokes disputants to violence to which the police must respond in kind. In short, it occurs when well-meaning police officers lack – or fail to apply – the expertise required to resolve as bloodlessly as possible the problems their work requires them to confront.

Much unnecessary violence occurs because many of us, including many police, have not adequately analysed the role of the police or the problems they confront. Thus, we have not devised adequate solutions to these problems, and have instead settled for a standard of performance from the police that is far below what we should tolerate from other groups.

THE ROLE OF THE POLICE

A common conceptualization is that the police, along with the courts and correctional agencies, are a component of the criminal-justice system. This observation is true but, for two major reasons, it may lead to shallow analysis of the police and their problems. First, the courts (excluding civil courts) and correctional agencies devote their efforts exclusively to crime-related matters, but police officers do not. The clients of court personnel are those who have been charged with or victimized by crime; without exception, they are alleged criminals and their presumed victims. The people with whom the officials of correctional agencies interact most directly are those who are awaiting trial on criminal charges, or those who have been convicted of crime; without exception they are alleged or convicted criminals. But, in addition to bringing the alleged perpetrators and victims of crime to the attention of the courts, police regularly interact with people in circumstances in which criminal behavior is doubtful or clearly absent. The clientele of the police includes participants in minor disputes and traffic accidents, those who are lost and in need of travel directions, those who suffer sudden illness or injury, and many others whose problems have nothing whatever to do with crime, criminal law or criminal justice.

In addition, in many cases in which it is clear that some violation of criminal law has occurred, police possess greater discretion to devise informal and unrecorded dispositions of offenders than is true of any other criminal-justice officials. The police officer who sends a disorderly group of teenagers on their way on the grounds that it is more just – or more convenient – than arresting them may do so in the knowledge that no official record of his encounter with them will appear anywhere. What he does and says in such a case disappears into the ozone and, unlike a court or correctional-agency decision to release, cannot be objectively reconstructed by reference to any transcript or detailed official document.

In large measure, the police officer decides which of the people with whom he interacts shall come to the attention of the courts. He exercises a degree of discretion that is usually unrestricted by the prior decisions of any public official.[7] He cannot sentence offenders or impose harsh correctional conditions upon them, but he often has the power to choose between letting them go free and initiating a process likely to result in the imposition of penalties by other officials. He also has great power to impose upon his clientele penalties that do not require court agreement with his actions. Should he decide to arrest rather than to release, nothing a prosecutor, judge, defense attorney or correctional-agency official can do is likely to erase that arrest from the police record. Even when he recognizes that conviction is unlikely, the police officer knows that arrest will result in substantial inconvenience and cost.

But, as has been made clear in several attempts to define the police role, the police cannot be comprehensively discussed or understood in terms of their responsibilities to apprehend criminals or to enforce laws. Their job, Wilson (1968) suggests, includes the duty to see that popular conceptions of order are maintained. The police serve to prevent "behavior that either disturbs or threatens to disturb the public peace or that involves face-to-face conflict among two or more persons" (p. 16).

Goldstein (1978) concurs in part, arguing that law enforcement does not describe the role of the police, but instead defines only one of many methods that they may apply to achieve this goal. Bittner (1970) points out another method employed by police to maintain order: the use or threatened use of legitimate force (that is, as approved by both the government and most of the people served by the police) to coerce individuals to behave in accordance with society's expectations.

Still, the functions of the police are so complex that they are not adequately captured by even the broad "order-maintenance" descriptor. Just as many police tasks have little to do with crime or law, many have little to do with threats to public order, and many involve no coercion or threat or use of force. The police are on duty 24 hours a day, seven days a week, Sundays and holidays included, in order to tackle a variety of problems and crises. These range from tree-bound cats, through lost children and persons locked out of their homes, to people who have been horribly mangled in automobile accidents. In none of these cases is the quality of police response less critical for those concerned – the mother of a lost child, or the man whose femoral artery has been severed in a car crash – than in cases where the police are required to exercise their law-enforcement and order-maintenance responsibilities.

The breadth of police work is what makes Goldstein's definition of the role of the police the most comprehensive and satisfactory. He observes that

> The police function, if viewed in its broadest context, consists of making a diagnostic decision of sorts as to which alternative might be most appropriate in a given case. In this respect the total role of the police differs little from their role in administering first aid to sick and injured persons. (1977, p. 41)

Goldstein is correct. Police officers, like doctors, lawyers, psychologists and marriage counselors, are human-service workers. Like these others, police are paid to diagnose problems that befuddle the rest of us, to treat those within their competence, and to refer to more specialized agencies and officials those problems that they themselves cannot solve. Just as we call upon the doctor to investigate and treat internal complaints not responsive to our own treatment efforts, so we call upon the police to investigate and treat complaints deriving from certain external conditions that we cannot otherwise ameliorate – noisy neighbors, assault or robbery, the injury of a loved one by a hit-and-run driver.

Police officers, however, treat their clients and professional problems under conditions that do not affect most other human-service workers, and that greatly increase the potential for violence. Police–client interactions are uniquely *urgent, involuntary* and *public.* Unless we and the police fully appreciate the causal relations between these three conditions and violence, we inadequately diagnose police problems. The result is that we witness and experience violence that need not have occurred.

Urgency of police–citizen encounters

Police are generally unable to select the times at which they will perform their services. They are expected to respond to and resolve our problems *now,* while we routinely agree to wait until two weeks from Thursday to obtain help for our medical and legal dilemmas. In Bittner's terms, the police task consists of resolving problems "*that-ought-not-to-be-happening-now-and-about-which-somebody-had-better-do-something-now*" (1974, p. 30). As a consequence, police usually encounter their clients in circumstances analogous to those faced by hospital emergency-room personnel: they deal with people immediately after their problems have come to light, and must treat not only the substance of these problems, but also the shock that accompanies their clients' discoveries that suddenly all is not well.

Involuntariness of police–citizen encounters

The constraint of time usually denies police officers the luxury of picking and choosing their clientele from among those deemed in need of police attention, and places great limits on their ability to refer clients and problems to more highly qualified specialists. When we do get to see our family doctor, he may diagnose but decline to treat a problem that he views as most amenable to resolution by a more specialized colleague. But a police officer summoned to a late-night domestic dispute cannot withdraw with a referral to a better trained and more competent officer who does not come on duty until the morning. Regardless of his ineptness, and because his clientele includes the neighbors who cannot sleep because of the noise, he is duty-bound to establish at least temporary peace before he leaves, even if he has to coerce some of his clients to accept his prescriptions.

Therein lies another unique characteristic of police work: many of those who come to police attention do not seek it, but become unwilling clients through the intervention of third parties or of officers themselves. When this happens, just as officers cannot usually decline clients who come to their attention, so their clients cannot withdraw from treatment no matter how distasteful they find it. Given the choice, very few of the clients arrested or brought to book by the police would consent to this form of treatment.

Public setting of police–citizen encounters

Unlike even emergency-room personnel, police officers are unable to choose the places in which they perform their services. The work of police patrol officers occurs not in private offices, but in public settings or other locations in which the problems of their clientele have come to light. As a result, police officers suffer the disadvantage of performing in places in which clients' behavior is not constrained by the formality and decorum of a professional setting and the realization that one is on another's territory. The clientele of the police are governed only by the behavioral rules of the street.

Another consequence of the public setting of police work is that officers must be attentive not only to the immediate problems of the clients they have been summoned to treat, but also to third-party reactions to their efforts. If they are to avoid criticism and even interference from bystanders, police officers summoned to restrain emotionally disturbed or drug-crazed persons on the street must do so in a way that is demonstrably proper and humane.

The police officers' concern with the *appearance* of propriety and humaneness is not shared by mental-health professionals who work in residential facilities, or who administer shock therapy to patients in the privacy of their clinics. Nor is it shared by others who must render their services in public places. Ambulance personnel, for example, often perform their work in public, but it rarely involves resolution of disputes or other competing interests, so they need not concern themselves with their audiences' perceptions of their fairness. In addition the work of ambulance personnel usually involves more distastefully gory and less intriguing and public problems than those of the police, so that bystanders watch the proceedings less closely. It is much easier, less nauseating and more interesting to watch the police subdue a street drunk than it is to watch a team of emergency medical technicians treat a man whose leg has been severed in an automobile accident. Finally, the techniques used by ambulance personnel are far more arcane than are those of the police: few bystanders have any experience or expertise in stanching the flow of blood or treating shock, but nearly everybody has attempted to resolve a dispute, calm an unreasonable or unruly person, and seen the ways in which television police subdue suspects. Consequently, few bystanders feel competent to judge or protest the work of ambulance personnel, but many view themselves as qualified to assess the work of the police. As can be seen from cases where riots have been precipitated by bystanders' dissatisfaction with police actions, some are even willing to demonstrate their disagreement violently and immediately.

Police officers must also be acutely aware that the presence of an audience of bystanders may affect their clients' behavior. In some cases, the embarrassment of having one's problems aired in public may cause – or increase – irrational behavior on the part of the client. In others – the crowd encouraging the young man poised to jump from a high roof comes to mind – bystanders may become direct actors in police encounters. In still others, as Muir observes, police respond to street disputes that are "played out on two levels – in the relationship between the two antagonists, and in the relationship of the crowd to the disputants. Police officers have to perceive both levels" (1977, p. 102). Muir describes a situation in which police arrived at a crowded recreation center and found a bat-wielding young man confronting an aide. This case, which superficially appeared to be an attack by an inner-city youth upon an older authority figure could be satisfactorily resolved only if the police took time to learn the antagonists' motivations and the importance of the crowd. Here, the young man suspected that the aide had raped his 13-year-old sister, so that

> From the point of view of the brother of the victim of the alleged rape, he was retaliating not only from a desire for retribution but to deter future marauders. . . . The brother was establishing face in the neighborhood, a reputation for dogged revenge; in thrashing his sister's rapist, he was making a harsh example for all the crowd to see. . . . He was publishing his message for those persons that really counted, those who might think they could push his

> family around. In the brutish neighborhood he and his family inhabitated, the brother was making himself "a man of respect" . . . .
>
> In the relationship between the crowd and the brother, the crowd's definition of honorable conduct became crucial. Depending on its expectations of him, his attack on the aide would have different meanings. . . . Anyone who had the talent to influence the crowd's philosophy in this matter could make a great deal of difference to what the brother felt he had to do to establish face. (pp. 102–3)

To summarize, then, a proper analysis of the police role requires acknowledgement of many unique characteristics of the work of street-level officers. Policing is a form of human-service work that requires officers to diagnose the problems they confront, and to decide which of several means of solving them – invoking the law, threatening to invoke the law, employing force or, as in Muir's example, attempting to persuade – is most likely to be successful. The broader discretion available to police officers than to other criminal-justice officials, however, is limited by several constraints unique to policing. There is an urgency about police work that does not affect court or correctional-agency officials or most others whose work involves diagnosis and treatment of human ills. The police cannot select the times or places at which they treat their clientele. They often must do so at odd hours and in very public places. Consequently, if they are to avoid criticism or adverse response by third parties, they must be greatly concerned not only with *doing* the right thing, but also with *appearing* to do the right thing. This compounds the difficulties of police work, because the people they treat are often adversaries rather than individuals who have come to the police for help. The people at the core of police problems often do not agree with police diagnoses of those problems or even that any problem exists. They do not see the police as individuals who have come to help them. Once the police have come, however, neither they nor the police may withdraw until the problem at hand is at least temporarily remedied.

The urgent, involuntary and public relationship between police officer and client creates a high potential for violence. To avert it, police must often apply considerable diagnostic skills, and must learn to manipulate these causal variables in ways that diminish the likelihood that violence will result. If urgency and time constraints sometimes lead to violence, it follows that police should slow the pace of their encounters with citizens so that cooled tempers and the restoration of reason may eventually lead to non-violent outcomes. If involuntariness sometimes leads to violence, it follows that police should attempt to diminish their clients' feelings that something is being done *to* them, by trying to win their confidence and devising problem solutions that at least appear to be collaborative rather than exclusively coercive. If the public settings of police–citizen encounters sometimes lead to violence, it follows that police should inject as much privacy as possible into these encounters.

There is evidence that attempts by police to manipulate time and involuntariness, and to make more private highly volatile encounters between police and citizens, do reduce violence. Recent police efforts to diagnose and plan for hostage situations and situations involving armed and barricaded persons have led to a high rate of bloodless resolution of these situations. The time-manipulative techniques employed in these situations include avoidance and delay of armed confrontation unless it is clear that lives are in imminent danger. Involuntariness is manipulated by trained negotiators who attempt to determine the motives and win the confidence of their subjects, and to convince them that surrender is in their own best interests. Privacy is introduced into these situations by carefully controlling media access to hostage-takers and *vice versa*, and by clearing the public from the immediate areas. These privacy techniques serve the multiple purposes of protecting uninvolved citizens, eliminating the audiences to whom hostage-takers may wish to play, reducing hostage-takers' loss of face at the time of surrender, and eliminating the possibility that the attention of bystanders or the media will encourage hostage-takers or barricaded persons to further rash actions (see, for instance, Schlossberg and Freeman, 1974).

Despite the apparent success of such defusing-techniques, many of us – and many police leaders – often encourage officers to think of themselves as rough and ready men and women of action whose prime function it is to show up quickly at emergencies and to make their diagnoses on the spot. Unless we more strongly encourage officers to develop the requisite diagnostic skills to deal with certain types of situation when they occur, we are likely to witness many more hasty and inaccurate diagnoses and many unnecessarily violent attempts to treat police problems.

POLICE DIAGNOSTIC EXPERTISE

As too many experiences have demonstrated, police often do not attempt diagnosis until they are in the midst of treating critical problems. The 1965 Watts riot began when, despite the violent reaction of a large and growing crowd drawn by the protests of the suspect's mother, two police officers persisted in their attempts to arrest a drunken driver whom they had already identified and could presumably retake later under quieter circumstances. The 1971 Attica prison riot resulted in the deaths of 39 inmates and hostages when New York State police officers, who usually work alone or in small groups in rural areas, were armed with shotguns and armor-piercing rifles and directed to storm and retake the tear-gas-filled, heavily-walled yard of a maximum-security prison inhabitated largely by inner-city convicts. A block in Philadelphia burned down in 1985 when, in an attempt to evict a radical group, a police helicopter dropped onto the roof of an adjoining wooden house an incendiary device that had apparently never before been used by police in any field situation.

Looking back, it is easy to say that these decisions should not have been made. It would probably have been wiser for the police in Watts to have retreated, and to have returned to make their arrest in quieter and less public circumstances. In Attica and Philadelphia, continued negotiation or less drastic tactics probably would have better served the fundamental police responsibility to protect life than did the hastily devised tactics that were employed.

THE SPLIT-SECOND SYNDROME

It is difficult to define the factors that led well-meaning officials to make the bad decisions just reviewed, but it appears that they are reflections of what might be called a "split-second syndrome" that affects police decision-making in crises. This syndrome serves both to inhibit the development of greater police diagnostic expertise and to provide after-the-fact justification for unnecessary police violence. It also serves as a guide to many of the equally unfortunate low-visibility decisions made by individual police officers every day.

The split-second syndrome is based on several assumptions. First, it assumes that, since no two police problems are precisely alike, there are no principles that may be applied to the diagnosis of specific situations. Thus, no more can be asked of officers than that they respond as quickly as possible to problems, devising the best solutions they can on the spur of the moment. This, of course, places an extraordinary burden upon officers, who must make life-or-death decisions under the most stressful and time-constrained conditions.

Second, because of these stresses and time constraints, a high percentage of inappropriate decisions should be expected, but any subsequent criticism of officers' decisions – especially by those outside the police, who can have no real appreciation of the burdens upon officers – is an unwarranted attempt to be wise after the event. Thus, if we are to maintain a police service whose members are decisive in the crises to which we summon them, we had best learn to live with the consequences of the decisions we ask them to make. If we do not, we risk damaging police morale and generating a police service whose members are reluctant to intervene on our behalf.

Finally, the split-second syndrome holds that assessments of the justifiability of police conduct are most appropriately made on the exclusive basis of the perceived exigencies of the moment when a decision had to be taken. So long as a citizen has, intentionally or otherwise, provoked the police at that instant, he, rather than the police, should be viewed as the cause of any resulting injuries or damage, no matter how excessive the police reaction and no matter how directly police decisions molded the situation that caused those injuries or damages.

Thus, should police receive a report of an armed robbery in a crowded supermarket, they should be granted great leeway in their manner of response, because no two armed-robbery calls are precisely alike. If, in the course of responding, they decide that, to prevent the robber from escaping, the best course of action is to confront him immediately in the midst of a crowd of shoppers, they should not be told they should have acted otherwise. When they do challenge the alleged robber and he suddenly reacts to their calls from behind by turning on them with a shiny object in his hand, the only issue to be decided by those who subsequently review police actions is whether, at that instant, the suspect's actions were sufficiently provocative to justify their shooting him. That is so regardless of how the prior actions of the police may have contributed to their peril; regardless of how predictable it was that the suspect would be alarmed and would turn toward the police when they shouted to him; regardless of how many innocent bystanders were hit by bullets; and regardless of whether the reported armed robber was in fact an unhappy customer who, with pen in hand to complete a check for his purchase, had been engaged in a loud argument with a clerk during which he had said that the store's prices were "robbery".

The underpinning of the split-second syndrome, in short, is the assumption that the sole basis on which any use of force by the police needs to be justified is the officers' perceptions of the circumstances prevailing at the instant when they decide to apply force. The officers involved in the incident described above did, of course, possess much information that would lead them to believe that the subject of their call was a robber. When he turned on them, they were entitled, in the heat of the moment, to believe that their lives were in imminent danger. When they made the split-second decision to pull the trigger, they were also entitled to believe that no less drastic action would adequately protect their lives, so they were fully justified in shooting. Under the split-second syndrome, this shooting was a legitimate use of force under provocation.

But such an analysis lends approval to unnecessary violence, and to failure of the police to meet their highest obligation: the protection of life. Split-second analysis of police action focuses attention on diagnoses and decisions made by the police during one frame of an incident that began when the police became aware that they were likely to confront a violent person or situation. It ignores what went before. As the successful application of hostage techniques illustrates, it also ignores the fact that there are general principles that may be applied by officers to a variety of highly predictable, potentially violent situations.

It requires no great diagnostic ability to determine that the officers involved made a significant contribution to the bloody finale of the incident described above. Officers who respond to reports of robberies by charging through the front door and confronting suspects from exposed positions are almost certain to find themselves in great danger, real or perceived, and to face split-second decisions involving their lives, the lives of suspects and the lives of bystanders. Thus, instead of asking whether an officer ultimately had to shoot or fight his way out of perilous circumstances, we are better advised to ask whether it was not possible for him to have approached the situation in a way that reduced the risk of bloodshed and increased the chances of a successful and non-violent conclusion.

AVOIDING SPLIT-SECOND DECISIONS

Even though most potentially violent situations encountered by the police are not as clear-cut as the one described in the previous section, opportunities usually do exist for officers to attempt to prevent the potential for violence from being realized. Police are usually assigned to the same geographic areas for long periods, but in my experience they are rarely encouraged to leave their patrol cars when there is little happening and to survey the places in which they might someday be asked to confront potentially violent situations. Were they to do so, they would be able to formulate tentative advance plans for dealing with reported supermarket robberies, warehouse burglaries and the like. Most often, police are directed by radio to scenes of potential violence (Reiss, 1971) and so are usually not on the spot at the time. Thus, even in the few minutes it takes them to get there, they have some opportunity to avoid split-second decisions by analysing available information and planning their responses in advance of arrival. If they do not, and if they fail to structure their confrontations in a manner that is most likely to avert bloodshed, almost any violence that results is unnecessary, and should be condemned rather than rewarded with headlines, honors and medals.

Two principles, tactical knowledge and concealment, may be useful diagnostic tools in deciding how to deal with potentially violent people and situations.[8] Tactical knowledge includes prior knowledge of the setting and actors involved. Most often, police officers summoned to potentially violent situations have far less tactical knowledge than is desirable. While they usually know only what they have been told over the radio, any potential adversaries know precisely what is happening, where it is happening and who is involved. Since this places officers at a great disadvantage, it is important that they employ techniques for enhancing their tactical knowledge before committing themselves beyond the point of no return. If they fail to do this, they may easily fall prey to the more knowledgeable violent subjects of their calls, or may misinterpret the actions of innocent persons – such as the outraged shopper with a pen – in a way that may create violence where none exists. Like the military, they must be expected to learn as much as possible about the settings in which they may have to intervene.

Concealment includes disguising one's intent or identity, as well as employing actual physical cover or shelter. Officers – especially those in uniform – are usually at a disadvantage where this factor is concerned. When they respond to scenes of potential violence (for instance, armed robberies in progress), they are readily identifiable, while the subjects of their calls (the robbers) usually are not. Consequently, officers should employ all possible means of concealing themselves or their presence until the moment of least hazard. Doing so generally involves confronting from positions of concealment subjects who are temporarily without concealment. In the example of the reported supermarket robbery, this might mean that responding officers should avoid losing concealment by actually entering the supermarket, and should instead surreptiously take up positions of concealment outside it (for instance, behind parked cars) and wait for their suspect to come to them. The military knows that the safest way to confront potential adversaries is to wait for the appropriate moment to ambush them from positions of concealment, but police are often encouraged to charge up hills.

The use of concealment not only minimizes the risk of officers, bystanders and suspects, but may also prevent tragic mistakes. I can recount several occasions in which officers responding to such calls have neglected to seek concealment, have encountered armed individuals from positions of total exposure, have – with some justification – perceived imminent danger to themselves, and have shot persons later found to be plain-clothes police officers or crime victims who had armed themselves to pursue the actual perpetrators. Many of these tragedies might have been avoided if the officers involved had instead confronted these individuals from positions of physical cover. From such positions, officers make themselves near impossible targets, and are able to give their perceived adversaries opportunities to identify themselves or to drop their weapons without placing themselves in jeopardy.

Application of these principles requires that officers diagnose the most critical problems they face – those that may require the use of extreme force – *before* they occur, and that they attempt to apply to their resolution techniques of tactical knowledge and concealment. We demand that from the military and from the fire service, both of which spend considerable time diagnosing and planning for exigencies that we are someday likely to ask them to resolve. We do not tolerate it when their actions in emergency situations demonstrate that they have been taken by surprise and forced to react on the basis of instinct rather of careful advance diagnosis and planning. But, when police resort to forcible means to resolve readily foreseeable problems that could have been peacefully resolved with advance diagnosis and planning, we not only tolerate but also often reward their behavior. The police officer who shoots and kills an armed robber is often rewarded for his efforts with a medal. Should he instead kill a shopper with a pen, he is likely to be viewed as the unfortunate victim of a shared tragedy who, under the circumstances, had no choice but to take the action he did.

We should pay less attention to the outcomes of potentially violent situations than to questions of whether officers respond to them in ways likely to reduce the potential for violence. If we do not, we fail to legitimize genuinely unavoidable provoked force, and we reward and encourage an operating-style that eschews advance diagnosis, planning and training, and relies on officers' ability to make the most critical decisions under the worst possible conditions. That operating-style can only lead to frequent bad decisions by officers, who in the heat of the moment cannot reasonably be expected to devise solutions of equal quality to those that could be reached through careful advance planning. These results are grossly unfair to the public and to street-level police officers.

Thus, to reduce unnecessary police violence, we must define the police as diagnosticians, and we must demand that they learn that role thoroughly long before they actually confront someone who they have reason to believe is armed and dangerous. As we have done where hostage situations are concerned, we must define as successful those encounters where the police have done everything reasonably possible to avoid violence, and we must cease rewarding easily avoided split-second violence.

NOTES

1 As Bittner suggests, it is also necessary to distinguish between all types of violence and "the exercise of provoked force required to meet illegitimate acts" (1970, p. 36). There is little doubt that the police must be granted considerable license to employ such force, and, in our condemnation of what Bittner calls "provocative violence" by officials, we should be careful to avoid retracting the legitimacy of police authority to employ necessary provoked force. The police simply cannot function without this authority. We should take care too to distinguish between legitimate provoked force and incompetence-related violence. The former is that *required* to put down threats against officers or other challenges to official authority. The latter is unecessary, and occurs only because officers lack the expertise to employ readily available and less drastic means of putting down such threats and challenges.

2 As a result of bureaucratic procedures or administrative apathy, guns and law-enforcement powers have sometimes been granted to, or not withdrawn from, officer candidates or in-service officers whom personnel investigations have shown to possess gross psychological instability or character flaws. I have reviewed police personnel folders that disclose that officers accused of misconduct had been

hired by officials who knew that they had previously been excluded or dismissed from police service in other agencies because of congenital brain defects, extensive criminal records, long histories of drug abuse, assaults on supervisors and co-workers, or giving false sworn statements at previous official investigations of allegations that they had committed extralegal violence.

3 Friedrich reports that the data he analysed did "not support the notion that police use of force depends very much on the individual characteristics of the police" (1980, p. 89). Sherman's extensive survey (1980) of studies of police behavior found virtually no empirical support for assertions that individual officer characteristics are measurably related to any type of performance in office.

4 The major import of the judgment in this case is that public agencies are liable when plaintiffs can demonstrate in court that they have suffered constitutional deprivations at the hands of public officials, and that the unconstitutional acts of these officials were directly caused by agency custom and practice. Thus, if an individual were able to demonstrate that he had been unconstitutionally beaten and arrested by a police officer, and that the police department involved had a history of encouraging or tolerating such misconduct, he would presumably be entitled to money damages from both the officer and the government agency that employed him.

5 In addition, elected officials, who serve as intermediaries between citizens and police, may often be tempted to react defensively to judgments against police, regardless of whether such defensiveness is in the citizens' best interests. Consequently, citizens' ire may be redirected at what may be portrayed by elected officials as the arbitrariness of the courts, rather than at the police misconduct that gave rise to judgments against the taxpayers. For an elected mayor to acknowledge that his police department has operated unconstitutionally is not easy. It requires him to admit that the person he appointed as police chief (or who was otherwise determined to have been best qualified for that position) has performed his duties in a manner that violates the fundamental law of the land.

6 See Manning (1977), who argues that the police have assumed – or been given – the "impossible mandate" of responsibility for crime control and order maintenance, and that most police are unwilling to admit that they cannot accomplish it.

7 This is not to suggest that police currently operate with no *a priori* restrictions. As Goldstein (1977) points out, police operations are greatly influenced by legislators, and by the decisions made by prosecutors and judges in prior *similar* matters. My point is that police make decisions about specific individuals and situations before they have come to the attention of other officials.

8 These principles were first articulated in a training-program I developed in 1976 while on the staff of the New York City Police Academy.

REFERENCES

Bittner, E. 1974: Florence Nightingale in pursuit of Willie Sutton: a theory of the police. In H. Jacob (ed.), *The Potential for Reform of Criminal Justice,* Beverly Hills, Calif.: Sage.

—— 1970: *The Functions of the Police in Modern Society.* Rockville, Md: National Institute of Mental Health.

City of New York Commission to Investigate Allegations of Police Corruption and the City's Anti-Corruption Procedures 1973: *Commission Report.* New York: George Braziller.

Friedrich, R. J. 1980: Police use of force: individuals, situations and organizations. *Annals of the American Academy of Social and Political Sciences*, 452, 82.

Goldstein, H. 1977: *Policing a Free Society.* Cambridge, Mass.: Ballinger.

Klockars, C. 1980: The Dirty Harry Problem. *Annals of the American Academy of Political and Social Science*, 452, 33.

Manning, P. 1977: *Police Work*, Cambridge, Mass.: MIT Press.

Monell vs New York City Department of Social Services 1978: 436 US 658.

Muir, W. K. 1977: *Police: streetcorner politicians.* Chicago: University of Chicago Press.

New York State Commission on Attica 1972: *Attica.* New York: Bantam Books.

Packer, H. L. 1968: *The Limits of the Criminal Sanction.* Stanford, Calif.: Stanford University Press.

Reiss, A. J., Jr 1971: *The Police and the Public.* New Haven, Con.: Yale University Press.

Schlossberg, H. and Freeman, L. 1974: *Psychologist with a Gun.* New York: Coward, McCann and Geohagan.

Sherman, L. W. 1980: Causes of police behavior: the current state of quantitative research. *Journal of Research in Crime and Delinquency*, 17, 69.

Wilson, J. Q. 1968: *Varieties of Police Behavior: the management of law and order.* Cambridge, Mass.: Harvard University Press.

14

Aggression and Violence in the Family

Robert J. Powers

Aggression in the family is often a perplexing and disturbing phenomenon. At times, aggression may have constructive, positive effects; but at other times it may be highly destructive to family-functioning. On the negative side, aggression has been considered responsible for high rates of homicide (Wolfgang, 1958), spouse-battering (Straus et al., 1981), child abuse (Gil, 1970) and numerous other dysfunctional patterns of family interaction (Roy, 1982). On the positive side, aggression has been considered important in such functions as self-protection (Bowlby, 1984), increasing the intensity and directness of intimate contact (Bach and Wyden, 1968), and enhancing personal development through discarding or breaking through restraints, such as restrictive role assignments (May, 1972).

A primary purpose of this chapter is to increase understanding of the full situation or context of family aggression through identifying the varied forms and functions of aggressive behaviors. A further purpose is to describe causes or determinants of family aggression as an aid to controlling maladaptive forms and to discovering constructive alternatives. Finally, suggestions will be made for managing family aggression, with particular emphasis on the most severe or violent forms.

AGGRESSION DEFINED

Aggression is very difficult to isolate as a phenomenon and define, in that it is so central to individuals' struggles to survive and expand their influence. Aggressive behaviors have had vital survival value for the human species during the course of its evolution. Aggressive behaviors have enabled humankind to defend itself, to dominate other life forms, and greatly to reorder its environment. Aggression, however, is not an instinct (Freud, 1915/1957) or drive (Dollard et al., 1939), but rather represents a capacity or behavior potential (Rotter, 1954). As Kohut (1977). Winnicott (1975), Bandura (1973) and others observe, the infant is not innately aggressive, but develops aggressive behaviors in response or reaction to distressing events. The aggressive behaviors are greatly shaped by multiple social and environmental influences, and in that sense are learned.

Aggression has been commonly defined in terms of its destructive or negative effects. Buss (1961) describes aggression as any behavior that harms or injures others. Feshbach (1970), Kaplan (1972) and Berkowitz (1974) add the concept of aggression as intention to harm others. Baron (1977) further adds the concept that targets of aggression must be motivated to avoid the harm. According to Baron, "Agression is any form of behavior directed toward the goal of harming or injuring another living being who is motivated to avoid such treatment" (p. 7). Baron's definition has been well received and is very influential. The definition may be useful for certain purposes; however, it does not recognize constructive forms or functions of aggressive behaviors.

A great deal of aggression both in and outside the family has the primary aim of advancing the instrumental interests of the aggressor, and only secondarily, if at all, has the aim of harming or injuring others. For example, an individual may desire greater power and control in a relationship and may become verbally insulting or physically abusive in an effort to gain greater influence. The primary intention would be to enhance his/her control through intimidating or diminishing the other person. Efforts to harm the other may be only a secondary aim or a means to the goal of greater influence. There are, of course, many cases of family aggression where the primary motive does appear to be to do harm for its own sake – in a desire for revenge or retaliation for instance. However, even in instances of a primary intention to do harm, the pursuit of personal advantages or self-interests is often an important element.

In order to bring attention to the frequent self-enhancing or instrumental aims of aggression, as well as the aims of harming or injuring, aggression is defined here as *behavior which is directed toward advancing self-interests or the interests of others, but which is intended to harm another person (where that person is motivated to avoid the harm) or to damage property*.

This definition neither approves nor disapproves of aggression or violence. It is merely descriptive. It highlights the mixture of motives that usually – if not always – accompanies behavior that is directed at harming others or property. Aggressive behavior is defined in terms of its motives or intentions, not in terms of whether those motives or intentions are realized. In very many instances, the ultimate results of aggression are very different from the original aims. An individual may hit a spouse with the intention of coercing greater obedience, but instead may trigger retaliatory aggression, with even greater disobedience and loss of control. Further aggression may lead to escalating or "runaway" aggression, which is typical of many battered-spouse and battered-child syndromes (Feldman, 1979).

FUNCTIONS OF FAMILY AGGRESSION

Aggression may have many functions in family relationships, with differences both in the motives or aims of the aggression and in its effects. Researchers and clinicians have identified a great many common functions of family aggression. In the list of functions below, it is clear that at times the primary function of family aggression may be to advance self-interests, while the secondary function is to harm or injure others. At other times, the reverse may be true. The functions listed are not discrete. Each function may share certain elements or partial purposes with other functions.

1. Get attention or signal that needs are not being met (Tavris, 1982).
2. Coerce or manipulate to have needs met (Patterson, 1976).
3. Gain control of decisions and "rule-setting" in the family (Haley, 1963).
4. Experience increased power and self-esteem through inducing helplessness (Walker, 1977).
5. Increase intensity and directness of intimacy (Bach and Goldberg, 1974).
6. Avoid risks and vulnerability in intimacy (Feldman, 1979).
7. Dominate rivals for family love and approval (Freud, 1930).
8. Break through or discard restrictive role assignments (May, 1972).
9. Protect self from attack or harm (Bowlby, 1984).
10. Seek revenge for being harmed (Symonds, 1979).
11. Harm others for the inherent excitement or pleasure (Zimbardo, 1969).
12. Disrupt or change unrewarding balances in family relationships (Okun and Rappaport, 1980).
13. Manage impressions one makes upon others (Berkowitz, 1983).
14. Conform to cultural norms or expectancies (Dobash and Dobash, 1979).

An aggressive family action may have multiple or mixed functions. Through an aggressive act, such as a slap, a family member may desire not only to get attention and signal displeasure, but also to gain greater control over some decision, to change or break through a restrictive pattern of interaction, or to retaliate for recent wrongs. Further, aggressive functions may very well change over the course of an aggressive episode or an aggressive sequence of actions and counter-actions. Initially the primary function for a slap may be to get attention and indicate displeasure. If the target of aggression responds with emotional or physical aggression, the dominant function may become that of increasing or maintaining power in the relationship, through further slaps or hits. With further mutual aggressive transactions, the dominant function may well become that of harming or injuring.

Little attention has been given to the mixture of functions in aggressive family transactions. Identifying the varying functions is important for two particular reasons. First, an understanding of the functions of family aggression may help identify needs of family-members that, if met, would preclude further aggression or other dysfunctional behaviors, such as depression, that occur when needs are not met. Identifying the functions of aggression offers a useful intervention point for clinicians, family therapists and other agents of change. Second, charting changing functions over the course of aggressive exchanges may well clarify the process of escalation or "runaway" aggression, which often has such destructive consequences. Clinical evidence suggests that in escalating aggression there is very often a shift from primary functions of self-enhancement to primary functions of harming or injuring (Feldman, 1979). Yet, even when the function of injuring is dominant, there may still be important secondary functions such as removing a distressing or frustrating obstacle.

An important step in determining the varied functions of family aggression is identifying the many types or forms which aggression may take. Very often, the study of family aggression is restricted to examination of physical violence. As may be seen below, there are many other forms of family aggression, many of which may precipitate or otherwise contribute to extreme forms of aggression, such as violence.

FORMS OF FAMILY AGGRESSION

Aggression in the family may be viewed as a single act, such as a slap or verbal insult, or as a pattern or set of acts which have cumulative impact. There is value in identifying specific acts, especially the more extreme forms of physical aggression or violence. However, attention must also be paid to the pattern of aggressive acts of which the single act may be a part. The cumulative effect of the pattern of acts is often far greater than any single action.

Buss (1961) classified forms of aggression along three dimensions: physical and verbal, active and passive, direct and indirect. These categories may be usefully adapted to family aggression.

Physical and emotional aggression. Physical aggression in the family has generally received greater media attention than emotional aggression. Physical aggression is usually more readily identified and often appears to have greater negative impact. Straus and his colleagues (1981) classified common types of physical aggression in their Conflict Tactics Scale: slaps and pushes, hitting with fists or feet, hitting with blunt objects, sexual assault, use of a weapon. The same researchers distinguish between mild forms of physical aggression, such as slaps and pushes, and severe forms, such as hitting with blunt objects.

Emotional aggression includes a wide range of verbal behaviors, such as insults, as well as non-verbal behaviors, such as facial or bodily signs of rejection. Emotional aggression, such as withdrawal of approval and affection and attacks on self-esteem, may be more damaging psychologically than many forms of physical aggression (Symonds, 1979). Emotional aggression is implicit in physical aggression. A slap, for example, may serve as a non-verbal expression of disapproval. The reverse, however, is not true. In emotional aggression, by itself, there is no physical injury.

Active and passive aggression. Active aggression involves some effort on the part of the aggressor to harm another. Passive aggression entails intentional lack of effort (conscious or unconscious) which hinders others in having needs met or in attaining goals. Just as physical aggression has usually received more attention than emotional aggression, so active forms have usually obtained greater consideration than passive. In family relationships, however, passive aggression may play an important role in initiating or maintaining other forms of aggression.

Direct and indirect aggression. In direct aggression, the aggressor causes harm to the other through their own efforts or lack of effort. In indirect aggression, the harm is conveyed through others efforts or lack of effort. Insulting a spouse is an example of direct aggression, while talking negatively about the spouse to a child, who in turn rejects or disaproves of the spouse, is an example of indirect aggression.

Patterns or sets of acts which are aggressive are difficult to classify. The variety of such patterns is enormous. Walker (1977) describes a sequence of coercive behaviors in spouse abuse whose ultimate result is to induce a sense of powerlessness or helplessness. The sequence may include specific acts of violence, but the sense of helplessness is brought about by the full combination of aggressive actions, rather than any single event. Certain acts, such as a severe beating, may have greater relative impact than others. But even that one event, by itself, would not account for the profound sense of intimidation and helplessness.

Bach and Goldberg (1974) describe a number of patterns or styles or aggressive behaviors, many of which involve "hidden" or covert aggression. They describe patterns of moral criticism, for example, in which the overt motive is to correct misguided behaviors, but which is covertly aimed both at promoting a sense of self-superiority and at demeaning and undermining others. A single moral criticism may have small aggressive impact. But the aggressive effects of a continuing series of criticisms could be considerable. Bach and Goldberg also describe aggressive patterns involving abusive use of sickness, intellectualizations, non-rewarding, doubting and feigned helplessness.

Eric Berne (1964) applied the term "games" to patterns of interpersonal aggression. According to Berne, games have a socially acceptable façade and an aggressive ulterior aim of manipulating, exploiting, weakening or in varied ways "doing in" (that is, defeating) others. In the game "If it weren't for you", for example, a person may marry for the safety of certain restrictions by the partner, but then aggressively induce guilt by protesting about the restrictions. In the game of "Corner", a family-member is asked to take on various responsibilities, and then is attacked as incompetent. In "Schlemiel", a family-member may gain a reputation for clumsiness which allows him or her to break things and in other ways act aggressively. Berne lists a number of other games which represent forms of family aggression – for instance, "Threadbare", "Lunch bag" and "Uproar".

Gregory Bateson (1968) used the term "double bind" to describe patterns of aggressive family maneuvers in which one injunction is contradicted by another. When the pattern is repeated and the target is unable to escape from the interpersonal field, severe psychological disturbance, including schizophrenia, may result. Okun and Rappaport provide an illustration of the principle elements in the double bind:

> A family consists of a young girl and her mother and father. . . . The girl is constantly given the message that she does not "show enough consideration" for her parents. . . . When she "approaches" them to "show consideration", she is told, "You are crowding us; don't interrupt our privacy!" . . . When she "retreats" to show consideration for their "privacy", she is told, "You don't care about us; stop ignoring us!" . . . She is ten years old and does not have the permission to leave the family system. (1980, p. 42)

Although progress has been made in identifying varied forms of family aggression, much work remains to be done. It is quite apparent, however, that there are a great many forms of family aggression beside direct physical aggression. In determining the full context or situation of the more extreme forms of aggression and violence, it may well be crucial to take into account the many other forms.

DETERMINANTS OF FAMILY AGGRESSION

Aggression in the family has many forms, and there are multiple factors which influence the nature of those forms. Person and situation variables can both greatly influence the onset and character of aggressive family behaviors. In personality research, there has been considerable controversy about the relative influence of person and situation variables on behavior (Pervin,

1985). Trait theorists have tended to emphasize the importance of person factors, while many behaviorists and social psychologists have tended to emphasize situation factors. Mischel (1977) observes that person and situation variables are always both important and that their relative impact may vary according to the individuals and conditions studied.

Three primary models have been used to account for the effects of person and situation factors on family aggression: the unidirectional model, the bidirectional model, and the transactional or reciprocal model. The unidirectional or "mechanistic" model represents the traditional antecedent–consequence approach (Endler, 1983; Lazarus and Folkman, 1984). Causal effects are considered in one direction from independent or antecedent variables to dependent or consequent variables. The great advantage of the unidirectional model is in identifying single powerful determinants of behavior, when they exist. Much of the research on family aggression – especially family violence – has taken this approach (Gelles, 1980; Newberger and Bourne, 1985). The bidirectional model is a process model which takes into account responses of other persons and effects in the environment over time in shaping the forms of aggressive family behaviors. Causal effects are considered to be bidirectional or two-way (Bandura, 1977). The transactional or reciprocal model is also a process model. Persons and situations are considered to be mutually interdependent over time and are viewed as forming a dynamic or organismic system. Changes in one component of the system may create corresponding changes in other components (Bandura, 1978; Framo, 1970).

Unidirectional model

In the unidirectional model, person and situation variables can be considered separately in their influence on family aggression, or may be considered together as combining or adding their effects in an interactive manner. *Person factors* include both physiological and psycho-social variables. Physical disorders such as brain lesions and hormonal imbalances have been associated with increased family aggression (Barnhill, 1980). Age also has been associated with family aggression, with persons under the age of 30 showing the greatest frequency and severity of violence (Straus et al., 1981).

Sex differences, as person factors, show both physiological and psycho-social influences. Maccoby and Jacklin (1974) offer the following evidence that males are generally more aggressive: (1) males are more aggressive than females in all major societies; (2) sex differences in aggression are found early in life; (3) sex differences are found for man and sub-human primates; (4) aggression is related to sex hormones – the male hormone testosterone having been repeatedly shown to alter aggression levels in sub-human animals. In research on the family, there is considerable controversy about whether males or females are more aggressive. Males evidently have a higher incidence of physical aggression and violence, while females have a higher incidence of verbal/emotional aggression (Martin, 1976; Gelles and Cornell, 1985). However, homicide rates for women killing men are approximately the same as for men killing women – 48 and 52 per cent, respectively, of all murders where the killer and victim are of different sexes (Wolfgang, 1958). Further, Steinmetz (1978) reports a high incidence of wives battering husbands. Further research is needed for definitive evidence on the role of sex differences.

Premorbid personality has frequently been identified as a primary element in family aggresion. Psychodynamic theorists have emphasized the importance of such factors as unresolved childhood fixations and conflicts (Freud, 1940), ego deficits (Hartmann, 1939), maladaptive "internalized objects" (Kernberg, 1976), and arrested development of the elf (Kohut, 1977) in generating increased aggression within the family, as well as in society generally. Behavioral theorists have stressed the importance of classical conditioning in "cueing" aggression with certain family members (Berkowitz, 1983). Social-learning theorists have emphasized the impact of observational learning and modeling of aggression, especially during formative childhood years (Patterson, 1976). Considerable evidence has been found for intergenerational transmission of aggression (Kalmuss, 1984). Individuals exposed to severe family aggression and violence as children are more likely than others to be violent in their own families as adults. It is not clear whether this tendency is primarily due to psychodynamic conflicts or to behavioral conditioning and observational learning. In all likelihood, both influences frequently are of major importance.

A wide range of personality traits have been associated with increased family aggression, including low self-esteem (Martin, 1976), inexpressiveness (Ponzetti, 1982) and possessiveness (Star, 1980). Individuals with particularly aggressive dispositions have been identified – for instance, people with anti-social and intermittently explosive temperaments (Hanks and Rosenbaum, 1977). But persons with withdrawing and passive-aggressive tendencies have also been noted (Rosenbaum and O'Leary, 1981), as have highly controlled individuals (Megargee, 1966) and highly impulsive and uncontrolled persons. In addition, an assortment of other mental disorders have been associated with heightened family aggression: for example, schizophrenia, affective disorders and borderline personality organization (Barnhill, 1980; Gayford, 1975). Identification of personality traits may contribute to the prediction of family aggression, but probably in a relatively small way: it may be more important to consider situational factors.

Situations may have a powerful effect in either preceipitating and maintaining family aggression or in diminishing or eliminating it. In general, highly structured family situations such as attendance at a church service or a parent–teacher association meeting reduce the probability of aggression, while less structured situations in the home increase it (Mischel, 1977). Through classical conditioning, originally neutral stimuli in family situations may acquire increased potential as elicitors of aggression. Berkowitz (1983) describes the associative processes by which the presence of a weapon increases the probability of aggression. He further describes how family-members may become associated with aversive stimuli, and in turn act as elicitors of aggression. Children, for example, who are the result of an unwanted pregnancy, physically unattractive or sickly may become aversive stimuli and tend to evoke relatively strong aggressive reactions from their parents, particularly in periods of stress. Similarly, the wife or husband may become an aversive reminder of unpleasant events – financial problems, say – and thereby tend to elicit increased aggressive responses. The strength of the associative conditioning to the aversive stimuli depends on many factors, such as personal values and expectancies, emotional and material resources, and counteractive positive experiences and associations with the other person(s).

In addition, Berkowitz describes a form of "involuntary" family aggression in which one's own aggression serves as a cue or stimulus to further aggression. He points out that, just as the sight of people fighting in a movie can stimulate aggressive tendencies in viewers, "persons embroiled in violent conflict can be stimulated to attack their opponents ever more strongly by the sight of their own and their antagonists' aggressive actions" (1983, p. 178). Berkowitz cites an illustration of escalating aggression and violence in a mother's interactions with her child: "And I grabbed her and I looked at her. . . . She looked at me like I was poison. And I whupped Julia and I whupped her and I whupped her and it looked like the more I whupped her, the more I wanted to whup her. I couldn't whup her enough" (from Kadushin and Martin, 1981, p. 196).

Reinforcements for aggressive behaviors in family situations increase the likelihood that the aggression will be repeated, while punishment or lack of reinforcement decreases that likelihood (Bandura, 1977). Gelles (1983) advances a "costs–gains" view of family aggression in which aggression is maintained when rewards or gains outweigh the costs. According to Gelles, family-members may act aggressively toward other family-members for a wide variety of internal and external reasons, such as desire to live up to sub-cultural images of a "real man", and reactions to social and economic stress, such as unemployment. Family-members continue to act aggressively "because they can" (p. 161). The rewards of their aggression/violence in the family interactions outweigh the costs. The recipients of the aggression may lack the skills or resources to increase the costs of the violence to the aggressor – for instance, through communicating clearly one's boundaries, "cancelling the hitting-license" or involving the police. The individual then faces the often difficult question of whether the costs of remaining in the relationship outweigh the perceived emotional and economic costs of leaving. Gelles summarizes his "exchange" view of aggressive family interactions in the following three propositions:

1 Family members are more likely to use violence in the home when they expect that the costs of being violent are less than the rewards.
2 The absence of effective social controls over family relations decreases the costs of one family member being violent toward another.
3 Certain social and family structures serve to reduce social control in family relations and therefore reduce the costs and/or increase the rewards of being violent (p. 158).

A number of factors producing situational stress have been found to play a role in family aggression. Physical conditions of crowding (Booth and Edwards, 1976), poor housing-facilities (Gelles and Cornell, 1985) and change in residence (Straus et al., 1980) have been related to increased family aggression and violence, as have social conditions of unemployment (Fitch and Papantonio, 1983), unwanted pregnancy (Weitzel and Ross, 1983) and unequal social status between partners (Hornung et al., 1981). It should be noted that the correlations with aggression are low in the above studies. There are many instances of similar physical and social conditions with no increase in aggression, and even a decrease.

Interaction effects may be highly important in family aggression. Persons and situations are interactive when they combine to create effects not found for the factors separately – i.e. with other persons or situations. A concern for interaction effects in family aggression represents a search for specificity in aggressive events. Investigators have long recognized that certain individuals will act aggressively in certain situations but not in others. Also, certain situations have tended to engender aggressive responses from individuals, while other situations have not. As Steele (1978) observes, in many cases of partner abuse the aggressor never acts violently with persons other than his/her spouse or children. Also, many such individuals confine their violence to the home and appear as models of self-control and restraint in public.

Pathological intoxication is a particularly good example of interaction effects in family aggression. In pathological intoxication, a person variable, hypersensitivity to alcohol, combines with a situation variable, presence and use of alcohol, to create episodes of sudden and wild aggression and violence which may affect family-members (Bach-y-Rita et al., 1970). The aggression and violence occur immediately after the ingestion of a small amount of alcohol. Without the special reactivity to alcohol the aggression or violence would not occur; nor would it occur if alcohol were unavailable.

Alcohol and drug use often represent important interaction effects in family aggression. According to a great number of research studies, there is a very frequent association of substance abuse and violence among family-members. Appleton (1980) surveyed 30 battered women in a hospital emergency room and found that 87 per cent reported more-than-moderate drinking by their partners prior to battery, while 13 per cent identified more-than-moderate drug use. In a project for battered women, Carlson (1977) interviewed 101 women, most of whom reported that their partners abused alcohol (60 per cent) or drugs (21 per cent). 10 per cent of the women acknowledged abusing alcohol themselves, while 5 per cent admitted abusing drugs. Roy (1977) reviewed 150 cases randomly selected from over 1000 cases at AWAIC (Abused Women's Aid in Crisis). Approximately 85 per cent of the violent partners had an alcohol and/or drug problem. In numerous other surveys of partner abuse, high percentages of alcohol or drug use have been found (Bayles, 1978; Gayford, 1975; Walker, 1979).

Powers and Kutash (1982) found that alcohol and drug abuse contribute to aggression in the family through complex interactions of drug type with premorbid personality and setting. Of the four primary classes of psychoactive substances, depressants and stimulants were found to have the greatest influence on family aggression, with alcohol being particularly influential. Narcotics were noted to have many indirect influences through withdrawal effects and the frequent emotional and financial strain of maintaining a drug habit. Hallucinogens were found to have the least affect on family aggression, with marijuana, in particular, appearing to be more a calming-agent than a factor in increased aggression.

Bidirectional and transactional models

Unidirectional models provide valuable insights into the causes and nature of family aggression. Bidirectional and transactional models add to those insights by considering family aggression as a process over time. The *bidirectional model* emphasizes both an aggressor's impact upon other persons and situations, and the reactive impact of the persons and situations upon the aggressor. Causal influences are viewed as a sequence of actions and counter-actions over time. A person, for example, may change his/her environment by moving to a smaller home, but then may be affected by loss of privacy, crowding and so on. Similarly, the person may affect other persons in that home through aggressive acts, such as verbal insults, and then be affected by a variety of aggressive responses, such as emotional withdrawal or intentional inefficiency.

The *transactional model* emphasizes interdependency. An aggressor, other persons and situations are considered a system, and changes in any one component may effect changes in the other components. Ludwig von Bertalanfly (1968) used the analogy of a biological organism to describe the interdependence of varied elements in a system – for instance, heart, lungs, brain. Causal effects are considered gratuitous or irrelevant. Framo, for example, writes from a transactional, family-systems view that

> the concept of causation acquires a different meaning, in that specific causes are not sought for specific events; even the principle of multiple determination is not adequate. Some day scientists may not even have in their vocabulary the expression "What caused what?" . . . all events are considered as occurring within a configuration of transactional fields, fluid processing and concomitant variation. (1970, p. 22)

Bandura (1978) emphasizes a basically transactional viewpoint. He uses the term "reciprocal determinism" to designate transactional relationships, and contrasts a reciprocal model with unidirectional and bidirectional models. In descriptions of reciprocal determinism, Bandura, like Framo, appears to question the relevance of causal inference. Phillips and Orton (1983) present a cogent critique of Bandura's position. They assert that almost any example of reciprocal determinism can be shown to adhere to traditional causal principles, by being understood as a sequence of actions and counter-actions – or bidirectional effects – over time. They observe that in practice it may often be difficult or impossible to identify all the causal links in bidirectional interchanges among persons and situations. However, they justly conclude that "this is a practical deficiency, and it does not show the endeavor is misguided in principle" (p. 163).

In studies of family aggression, a combination of bidirectional and transactional perspectives is useful. The bidirectional view focuses on reciprocal causal influences, while the transactional view highlights the special nature of family interdependencies, as distinct from interactions with other individuals, groups and environments. The primary emphasis should be upon discovering the bidirectional influences, but the family context or mutual interdependencies should always be kept in mind. In *Gestalt* psychology terms, the bidirectional, causal influences would be the "figure" in the study of family aggression, and the underlying interdependency or transactions the "ground".

Aggression in the family is a highly complex process, often consisting of many different forms. At present, research methods are inadequate to determine all the bidirectional and transactional influences which shape the many forms (Endler, 1983; Coyne and Lazarus, 1980). Nevertheless, clinicians and researchers have identified a number of bidirectional and transactional relationships that determine in part the many different forms of aggression. Five examples of global bidirectional and/or transactional processes in family aggression are provided below.

1 *Family members often "select" situations of aggression.* Endler (1983) points out that persons not only react to situations, but also select or "shop for"

situations in which they are likely to have certain experiences. In relation to family aggression, Charny (1980) observes that individuals often seek clashes and contradictions in their original selection of each other. Men and women frequently select a mate who are particularly strong in an area in which they themselves are particularly weak. Numerous and varied forms of aggression may occur as individuals struggle to adopt some of the opposite characteristics and functions of the other, and thereby step outside their own "role assignments". According to Charny, "These clashes generate energy and resourcefulness, and through the clash of opposites with one's partner, each mate has an opportunity to get a new grip on the qualities he or she is most lacking" (p. 40). Charny further asserts that children often unconsciously select for their personalities qualities that are opposite to many of the prominent features in their parents' personalities. Erikson (1959) also observes that children often adopt roles complementary to their parents' and at odds with parents' conscious desires, though they may fulfill their unconscious wishes. The selection of these opposing characteristics and roles may well lead to numerous situations of aggression in which there is an attempt by one or more of the family-members either to control others or to step outside assigned roles. Frequently, as Charny (1980) suggests, the aggressive clashes may bring vitality and greater range in relationships. At times, however, the clashes may be destructive.

2 *Family members negotiate "rules" or norms to regulate aggression.* Communication theorists note that the negotiation of norms or rules for acceptable behaviors, including aggression, is a continuous process (Jackson, 1968). All behavior interactions are forms of communication and serve to define or redefine the acceptable character or behavioral norms of the relationship. Jay Haley describes the process well:

> When any two people meet for the first time and begin to establish a relationship, a wide range of behavior is potentially possible between them. They might exchange compliments or insults or sexual advances or statements that one is superior to the other, and so on. As the two people define their relationship with each other, they work out together what type of communicative behavior is to take place in this relationship. From all the possible messages they select certain kinds and reach agreement that these shall be included. This line they draw which separates what is and what is not to take place in this relationship can be called a mutual definition of the relationship. Every message they interchange by its very existence either reinforces this line or suggests a shift in it to include a new kind of message. In this way the relationship is mutually defind by the presence or absence of messages interchanged between the two people. . . . This agreement is never permanently worked out but is constantly in process as one or the other proposes a new kind of message or as the environmental situation changes and provokes changes in their behavior. (1963, pp. 6–7)

Many forms of aggression may be considered acceptable by family-members while others are not. In some families, passive forms of aggression may be accepted, while direct physical forms are not. Some families may condone certain forms of physical aggression, such as slapping, pushing and spanking, while other families disapprove of all such forms. In establishing rules for aggression and other behaviors, family-members may be greatly influenced by cultural and sub-cultural norms. Inevitably, however, each family develops features that are unique.

Conflicts arise when one family-member advocates or uses forms of aggression or other behaviors that are unacceptable to one or more of the other family-members. Struggle then ensues as to who sets the rules in the family and what penalties are meted out for violations of the rules (Hansen and L'Abate, 1982). Aggression is itself a mode of communication. Aggression or threat of aggression is one "power tactic" for establishing control or governorship over the rules of the relationship and for punishing violations of the rules (Haley, 1963). Physical forms of aggression may be the most dramatic types of power tactics, but other forms of aggression may be just as or even more effective. Symptoms of physical or emotional complaints may exert powerful controlling influences in relationships. Haley (1963) describes the aggressive and controlling effects of a wide range of symptoms, including those of schizophrenia, emphasizing that the symptoms emerge largely in reaction to aversive influences and serve as a means of counteracting or balancing them.

Weitzman and Dreen (1982) extend the work of Haley and other communications theorists in describing the characteristics of marriages in which wife-beating occurs. According to Weitzman and Dreen, battles for control in relationships tend to cluster around at least six major themes: (1) distance and intimacy, (2) jealousy and loyalty, (3) dependence and independence, (4) rejection and unconditional acceptance, (5) adequacy and inadequacy, and (6) power and powerlessness. In marriages where there is resort to wife-beating, rules for resolving conflicts over these issues are more rigid than in other marriages. Relationships tend toward unilateral control with little flexibility in the negotiation of rules. Violence functions to maintain the role structure and to thwart the change process.

Weitzman and Dreen point out that battles for control may occur over seemingly innocuous matters, such as dirty dishes and meal times, because they mask a deeper struggle for control in the relationship. The seemingly inexplicable behavior of a husband who becomes enraged and physically attacks his wife because she has burnt the toast becomes quite understandable as an attempt to maintain his "rules" and influences.

3 *Family members' aggression tends to elicit aggression.* Mischel (1977) noted that a person's own behavior largely determines others' reactions to him or her,

and that the best single predictor of what one person will do to another is what that other person did to him or her. In relation to aggression, Mischel states that "If A provokes B, B will reciprocate aggressively. In that sense, the person is generating his or her own conditions" (1977, p. 350). Although a person may tend to respond to one form of aggression with further aggression, he or she may very well choose a different form. For example, Margolin (1979) found that women often respond to physical aggression with verbal and emotional forms of counter-aggression, rather than corresponding physical assault.

Exchanges of aggression and counter-aggression are basic to two important forms of escalation of aggression. The first form, "runaway" aggression, consists of a series of aggressive and counter-aggressive actions which increase in severity until, perhaps, one or more of the family-members is greatly harmed physically or emotionally. Family arguments which escalate to assault or homicide are classic examples of this process. Again, the forms of aggression need not be the same for the different family members. The important factor is the reciprocal increase in intensity or severity of the aggression and counter-aggressive behaviors (Martin, 1976).

In certain instances, aggression may serve to terminate or decrease an escalating exchange, rather than increase it. Patterson (1976) found that, if one family-member suddenly increases the intensity of aversive behavior, the other may terminate his or her attack. Although the escalating aggression may be stopped for the present, high-amplitude aggression tends to be reinforced for the one family-member and a submissive stance reinforced for the other (Patterson, 1976). The consistently submissive stance may well have severe negative effects on feelings of self-esteem and self-efficacy, as Walker (1979) points out in her description of acquired helplessness. Further, the "submissive" partner may later employ other forms of coercive aggression and rekindle the escalatory process.

The second form of escalation, delayed or "explosive" aggression, consists of one family-member acting aggressively and one or more of the others responding non-aggressively but covertly harboring resentments and angry feelings. Escalation of aggressive intent may occur covertly within the initial target of aggression when ruminating about the pain or harm suffered. At times a single aggressive action can initiate such rumination, but more commonly a series of aggressive actions elicits and stimulates the process. Eventually, the initial target of aggression may "explode" in extreme forms of aggression with little or no immediate provocation. Blinder (1985), for example, describes the case of "Solly", who responded with silent anger for years to his wife's aggressive control of their relationship, especially the finances; but then one evening killed her while she was sleeping, Kalogerakis (1974) describes an adolescent who shot and killed his grandmother, who had been haranguing him for years with little or no provocation. The adolescent afterward reported great relief that she would never be able to nag him again.

4 *Perceptual distortions may increase family aggression.* Object-relations theorists, such as Fairbairn (1952), Framo (1970) and Gillman (1980), advance a process understanding of family aggression by describing the influences of introjection and projection. Individuals are viewed as internalizing or introjecting different features of parents and significant others and defending against "bad" or unacceptable elements of the introjections by "splitting them off" and projecting them onto others. Through the process of "projective identification" the individual may then act aggressively to control or persecute the recipient of the projections as bad (Gillman, 1980). A child, for example, may internalize a parental "object" who demands cleanliness, later split off renounced features or behaviors as unclean, project them onto a spouse and then persecute the partner as messy and unacceptable. Aggression thus arises from a distorted perception of the other. The object-relations view is helpful in understanding many aggressive family transactions where one individual persists in trying to control or punish another when there appears to be no objective or rational reason, or where the effort to control or punish appears to be greatly out of proportion to the degree of provocation or wrongdoing.

Dicks (1967) observes that in aggressive transactions family-members often have an unconscious commitment to protecting yet persecuting projected parts of themselves in other family members. He writes, "By protecting the image of the partner (for example as a 'drunk' or as 'sexually inadequate' or 'slovenly', and so forth) they are in the other secretly cherishing the rejected, bad libidinal ego with its resentments and demands while *within* the dyadic system they can persecute it in an interpersonal framework" (pp. 122–3).

5 *Families may develop transactional "structures" which promote aggression.* Family-systems theorists regard family aggression and violence as in themselves disturbed family interactions but also, and more importantly, as indicators of more general disturbances in the transactional structures of the relationships (Hansen and L'Abate, 1982). Systems theorists view family-members as an organization of interdependent individuals in mutual interaction. Family aggression is considered a product of the entire family organization, but particularly influenced by certain family sub-systems. Three primary sub-systems are spouse–spouse, parents–children, and siblings; but numerous other sub-systems may be influential, such as grandparent–grandchild and spouse–grandparent (Okun and Rappaport, 1980). Bowen (1978), for example, views aggression and violence as indicators of low levels of differentiation of the individual from other family-members. Aggression may well represent an attempt at self-preservation and differentiation in relation-

ships which are too close or "enmeshing". At times, however, the aggression may be disruptive to family-members, creating anxiety and stress and so bringing an even greater threat of fusion and enmeshment. A cycle of disintegrative aggressive family transactions may then become chronic, with negative impacts upon the family sub-systems as well as on future generations. Family-members unable to cope with aggressive transactions may seek to reduce mutual tension by focusing on or "triangulating" a third family-member. Usually the "triangulated" individual is the most vulnerable in the family system, such as a child. Displaced aggression may then be reflected in varied forms of emotional and physical abuse.

MANAGEMENT OF FAMILY AGGRESSION

Family aggression is managed by maintaining the forms and severity of aggression within limits acceptable to family-members and/or the larger social community. As noted above, the "rules" for family aggression are continuously defined and refined by family-members through the ongoing "communications" (Haley, 1963) of their many interactive behaviors. Family therapists and other mental-health workers may assist family-members in negotiating rules for aggressive behaviors acceptable to the whole family as well as the means whereby the rules may be maintained or enforced. In some cases, family-members may condone certain forms of aggression, such as severe corporal punishment of children, that are unacceptable to the wider community, which may regard such punishment as child abuse. The task of the community then is to help negotiate new rules with the families, as well as the means of maintaining the rules, through educational, psychotherapeutic or legal interventions.

In assisting families with problems of aggression, assessments of forms, determinants and functions of the aggression are highly important. Forms of aggression will help reveal *what* has happened; determinants will help show *why* it has happened; and functions will help clarify the *meaning* or significance of the events. In identifying forms of family aggression, attention should be paid to all forms of aggression and not just to those judged as unacceptable or as creating problems. In many instances, certain forms acceptable to family-members, such as harsh verbal criticism, may contribute greatly to precipitating or maintaining unacceptable forms, such as physical violence. Efforts also should be made to identify forms of aggression concealed in ostensibly helpful or innocuous behaviors. These "disguised" forms of aggression also may be important as precipitators and maintainers of other, unacceptable, aggressive behaviors.

Analyses of the determinants and functions of aggression provide important information for change. The determinants of family aggression provide targets for change. The targets may be person variables, situation variables, and/or their interactions. The targets may also include bidirectional and transactional processes over time. The functions of family aggression provide clues to needs of family-members which might be met through other forms of aggressive or non-aggressive behaviors. The functions also reflect the place or role of aggressive behaviors in the family system and provide clues as to how changes in the behaviors will affect the family system.

A great number of psycho-social and medical services are available to assist families in changing unacceptable patterns of aggression and establishing more constructive alternative behaviors. Edelman and Goldstein (1981) and Powers, Schlesinger and Benson (1983) describe educational programs; Barnhill (1980) discusses medical services, especially for substance-abuse problems; and Carlson (1977) and Nichols (1976) outline social-casework techniques. Marital and family therapists describe interventions for problems of aggression from behavioral (Marsh et al., 1976), psychodynamic (Gillman, 1980) and family-systems (Gurman and Kniskern, 1981) perspectives. Alexander and Parsons (1982) have developed a "functional family therapy" approach which has particular relevance for treating maladaptive forms of family aggression.

Severe forms of aggression and violence present special treatment problems. The first priority is to stop physical forms of violence. Gelles (1982) advocates "cancelling the hitting-license", through having aggressors accept responsibility for their abusive and violent behaviors and rejecting "excuses", such as loss of control and alcohol and drug use. Cook and Frantz-Cook (1984) advocate a systemic approach which includes agreements to be non-violent and the coaching of alternative behaviors. Saunders (1977) advocates (1) "self-cueing" techniques, which help individuals become aware of physiological cues just prior to violent episodes; (2) covert sensitization, which inhibits violent responses by pairing mental images of the response or its antecedents with an aversive event; and (3) changing the consequences of violence through such interventions as calling the police if violence occurs or immediately leaving the home for one or more nights. Fleming (1979), Walker (1979) and Roy (1977) describe the use of shelters and legal restraints as steps in preventing repeated violence.

Severe emotional abuse is also a target for special treatment interventions. Margolin (1979) views family abuse as a mutual problem, rather than the fault of any one family-member, and advocates specific contracts and plans for breaking up habitual patterns of conflict and discovering more successful ways of having needs met and resolving problems. Charny (1980) asserts that "it is not the ability to stay out of trouble, but to get out of trouble" which is critical in family life, and presents strategies for processing conflicts in a constructive manner. Weitzman and Dreen (1982) give special attention to locating the point at which escalating conflicts become unproductive and then helping family-members clarify themes in the escalation process and develop responses different from those which have increased the conflict.

In managing family aggression, the full context or situation of the behavior(s) must be taken into account. Each aggressive episode is multi-determined and has a particular role or meaning in the ongoing process of family interrelationships. One form of aggressive behavior may serve a variety of functions, and, conversely, very different forms of aggression may serve similar functions. Considering the complexity of family aggression, important progress has been made in recent years – especially since the early 1970s – in improving means of effectively managing aggressive behaviors. Nevertheless, as shown by media and research accounts of disabling partner and child abuse, considerable work remains to be done.

REFERENCES

Alexander, J. and Parsons, B. V. 1982: *Functional Family Therapy*. Monterey, Calif.: Brooks/Cole.

Appleton, W. 1980: The battered woman syndrome. *Annals of Emergency Medicine*, 9, 84–91.

Bach, G. R. and Goldberg, H. 1974: *Creative Aggression: the art of assertive living*. New York: Avon.

Bach, G. R. and Wyden, P. 1968: *The Intimate Enemy: how to fight fair in love and marriage*. New York: Avon.

Bach-y-Rita, G., Lion, J. R. and Ervin, R. R. 1970: Pathological intoxication: clinical and electroencephalographic studies. *American Journal of Psychiatry*, 127, 698–703.

Bandura, A. 1973: *Aggression: a social learning analysis*. Englewood Cliffs, NJ: Prentice-Hall.

—— 1977: *Social Learning Theory*. Englewood Cliffs, NJ: Prentice-Hall.

—— 1978: The self system in reciprocal determinism. *American Psychologist*, 33, 344–58.

Barnhill, L. R. 1980: Clinical assessment of intrafamilial violence. *Hospital and Community Psychiatry*, 31, 543–51.

Baron, R. A. 1977: *Human Aggression*. New York: Plenum.

Bateson, G. 1960: Minimal requirements for a theory of schizophrenia. *Archives of General Psychiatry*, 2, 477–91.

Bayles, J. A. 1978: Violence, alcohol problems and other problems in disintegrating families. *Journal of Studies on Alcohol*, 39, 551–3.

Berkowitz, L. 1974: Some determinants of impulsive aggression: the role of mediated associations with reinforcements for aggression. *Psychological Review*, 81, 165–76.

—— 1983: The goals of aggression. In D. Finkelhor, R. J. Gelles, G. T. Hotaling and M. A. Straus (eds), *The Dark Side of Families: current family violence research*, Beverly Hills, Calif.: Sage.

Berne, E. 1964: *Games People Play*. New York: Ballantine.

Blinder, M. 1985: *Lovers, Killers, Husbands and Wives*. New York: St Martin's Press.

Booth, R. T. and Edwards, L. J. 1976: Crowding and family relations. *American Sociological Review*, 41, 308–21.

Bowen, M. 1978: *Family Therapy in Clinical Practice*. New York: Jason Aronson.

Bowlby, J. 1984: Violence in the family as a disorder of the attachment and caregiving systems. *American Journal of Psychoanalysis*, 44, 9–27.

Buss, A. H. 1961: *The Psychology of Aggression*. New York: Wiley.

Carlson, B. E. 1977: Battered women and their assailants. *Social Work*, 22, 455–60.

Charny, I. W. 1980: Why are so many (if not all) people and families disturbed? *Journal of Marital and Family Therapy*, 6, 37–47.

Cook, D. R. and Frantz-Cook, A. 1984: A systemic treatment approach to wife battering. *Journal of Marital and Family Therapy*, 10, 83–93.

Coyne, J. C. and Lazarus, R. S. 1980: Cognitive style, stress perception and coping. In I. L. Kutash and L. B. Schlesinger (eds), *Handbook on Stress and Anxiety*, San Francisco: Jossey-Bass.

Dicks, H. 1967: *Marital Tensions*. New York: Basic Books.

Dobash, R. E. and R. 1979: *Violence against Wives: a case against patriarchy*. New York: Free Press.

Dollard, J., Miller, N., Doob, L., Mowrer, O. H. and Sears, R. R. 1939: *Frustration and Aggression*. New Haven, Conn.: Yale University Press.

Edelman, E. M. and Goldstein, A. P. 1981: Moral education. In A. P. Goldstein, E. G. Carr, W. S. Davidson and P. Wehr (eds), *In Response to Aggression: methods of control and prosocial alternatives*, New York: Pergamon.

Endler, N. S. 1983: Interactionism: a personality model, but not yet a theory. In M. M. Page (ed.), *Personality: current theory and research. Nebraska Symposium on Motivation, 1982*, Lincoln, Nebr.: University of Nebraska Press.

Erikson, E. H. 1959: Identity and the lifecycle, *Psychological Issues*, 1 (entire issue).

Fairbairn, W. R. 1952: *Psychoanalytic Studies of the Personality*. Boston, Mass.: Routledge and Kegan Paul.

Feldman, L. B. 1979: Marital conflict and marital intimacy: an integrative psychodynamic–behavioral–systemic model. *Family Process*, 18, 69–78.

Feshbach, S. 1970: Aggression. In P. H. Mussen (ed.), *Carmichael's Manual of Child Psychology*, New York: Wiley.

Fitch, F. J. and Papantonio, A. 1983: Men who batter: some pertinent characteristics. *Journal of Nervous and Mental Disease*, 171, 190–2.

Fleming, J. B. 1979: *Stopping Wife Abuse: a guide to the emotional, psychological and legal implications for the abused woman and those helping her*. Garden City, NY: Doubleday/Anchor.

Framo, J. L. 1970: Symptoms from a family transactional viewpoint. In N. W. Ackerman, J. Liev and J. K. Pearce (eds), *Family Therapy in Transition*. Boston, Mass.: Little, Brown.

Freud, S. 1957: Instincts and their vicissitudes [1915]. In *Standard Edition of the Complete Psychological Works of Sigmund Freud*, vol. XIV, London: Hogarth Press.

—— Civilization and its discontents [1930]. In *Standard Edition of the Complete Psychological Works of Sigmund Freud*, vol. XXI, London: Hogarth Press.

—— 1964: An outline of psycho-analysis [1940]. *Standard Edition of the Complete Psychological Works of Sigmund Freud*, vol. XXIII, London: Hogarth Press.

Fromkin, H. L., Goldstein, J. H. and Brock, P. C. 1977: The role of "irrelevance" derogation in vicarious aggression catharsis: a field experiment. *Journal of Experimental Social Psychology,* 13, 239–52.

Gayford, J. J. 1975: Wife battering: A preliminary survey of 100 cases. *British Medical Journal,* January, pp. 194–7.

Gelles, R. J. and Cornell, C. P. 1985: *Intimate Violence in Families.* Beverly Hills, Calif.: *of Marriage and the Family,* 42, 873–85.

—— 1982: Applying research on family violence to clinical practice. *Journal of Marriage and the Family,* 43, 9–20.

—— 1983: An exchange/social control theory. In D. Finkelhor, R. J. Gelles, G. T. Hotaling and M. A. Straus (eds), *The Dark Side of Families: current family violence research,* Beverly Hills, Calif.: Sage.

Gelles, R. J. and Cornell, C. P. 1985: *Intimate Violence in Families.* Beverly Hills, Calif.: Sage.

Gil, D. G. 1970: *Violence against Children: physical child abuse in the United States.* Cambridge, Mass.: Harvard University Press.

Gillman, I. S. 1980: An object-relations approach to the phenomenon and treatment of battered women. *Psychiatry,* 43, 347–58.

Gurman, A. S. and Kniskern, D. P. (eds), 1981: *Handbook of Family Therapy.* New York: Brunner/Mazel.

Haley, J. 1963: *Strategies of Psychotherapy.* New York: Grune and Stratton.

Hanks, S. E. and Rosenbaum, C. P. 1977: Battered women: a study of women who live with violent alcohol-abusing men. *American Journal of Orthopsychiatry,* 47, 291–306.

Hansen, J. C. and L'Abate, L. 1982: *Approaches to Family Therapy.* New York: Macmillan.

Hartman, H. 1939: *Ego Psychology and the Problem of Adaptation.* New York: International Universities Press, 1958.

Hornung, C. A., McCullough, B. C. and Sugimoto, T. 1981: Status relationships in marriage: risk factors in spouse abuse. *Journal of Marriage and the Family,* 43, 675–92.

Jackson, D. D. (ed.) 1968: *Therapy, Communication and Change,* Palo Alto, Calif.: Science and Behavior Books.

Kadushin, A. and Martin, J. 1981: *Child Abuse: an interactional event.* New York: Columbia University Press.

Kalmuss, D. 1984: The intergenerational transmission of marital aggression. *Journal of Marriage and the Family,* 46, 11–19.

Kalogerakis, M. G. 1974: The sources of individual violence. *Adolescent Psychiatry,* 3, 323–39.

Kaplan, H. B. 1972: Toward a general theory of psychosocial deviance: the case of aggressive behavior. *Social Science and Medicine,* 6, 593–617.

Kernberg, O. F. 1976: *Object-Relations Theory and Clinical Psychoanalysis.* New York: Jason Aronson.

Kohut, H. 1977: *The Restoration of the Self.* New York: International Universities Press.

Lazarus, R. S. and Folkman, S. 1984: *Stress, Appraisal and Coping.* New York: Springer.

Maccoby, E. E. and Jacklin. C. N. 1974: *The Psychology of Sex Differences.* Stanford, Calif.: Stanford University Press.

Margolin, G. 1979: Conjoint marital therapy to enhance anger management and reduce spouse abuse. *American Journal of Family Therapy*, 7, 13–23.

Mash, E. J., Hamerlynck, L. A. and Handy, L. C. (eds) 1976: *Behavior Modification and Families*. New York: Brunner/Mazel.

Martin, D. 1976: *Battered Wives*. New York: Simon and Schuster.

May, R. 1972: *Power and Innocence: a search for the sources of violence*. New York: Dell.

Megargee, E. I. 1966: Undercontrolled and overcontrolled personality types in extreme and social aggression. *Psychological Monographs*, 80 (entire issue).

Mischel, W. 1977: The interaction of person and situation. In D. Magnusson and N. S. Endler (eds), *Personality at the Crossroads: current issues in interactional psychology*, Hillsdale, NJ: Lawrence Erlbaum Associates.

Newberger, E. H. and Bourne, R. 1985: *Unhappy Families: clinical and research perspectives on family violence*. Littleton, Mass.: PSG.

Nichols, B. B. 1976: The abused wife problem. *Social Casework*, 57, 27–32.

Okun, B. R. and Rappaport, L. J. 1980: *Working with Families: an introduction to family therapy*. North Scituate, Mass.: Duxbury.

Patterson, G. R. 1976: The aggressive child: victim and architect of a coercive system. In E. J. Mash, L. A. Hammerlynck and L. C. Handy (eds), *Behavior Modification and Families*, New York: Brunner/Mazel.

Pervin, L. A. 1985: Personality: current controversies, issues and directions. *Annual Review of Psychology*, 36, 83–114.

Phillips, D. C. and Orton, R. 1983: The new causal principle of cognitive learning theory: perspectives on Bandura's "reciprocal determinism". *Psychological Review*, 90, 158–65.

Ponzetti, J. J., Cate, R. M. and Koval, J. E. 1982: Violence between couples: profiling the male abuser. *Personnel and Guidance Journal*, 61, 222–4.

Powers, R. J. and Kutash, I. L. 1982: Alcohol, drugs and partner abuse. In M. Roy (ed.), *The Abusive Partner: an analysis of domestic battering*, New York: Van Nostrand Reinhold.

Powers, R. J., Schlesinger, L. G. and Benson, M. 1983: Family violence: effects of a film program for alcohol dependent persons. *Journal of Drug Education*, 13, 153–60.

Rosenbaum, A. and O'Leary, K. D. 1981: Marital violence: characteristics of abusive couples. *Journal of Consulting and Clinical Psychology*, 49, 63–71.

Rotter, J. B. 1954: *Social Learning and Clinical Psychology*. Englewood Cliffs, NJ: Prentice-Hall.

Roy, M. 1977: *Battered Women: a psychosociological study of domestic violence*. New York: Van Nostrand Reinhold.

—— (ed.) 1982: *The Abusive Partner: an analysis of domestic battering*. New York: Van Nostrand Reinhold.

Saunders, D. G. 1977: Marital violence: dimensions of the problem and modes of intervention. *Journal of Marriage and Family Counseling*, 3, 43–9.

Star, B. 1980: Patterns of family violence. *Social Casework*, 61, 339–46.

Steele, B. F. 1978: The child abuser. In I. L. and S. B. Kutash and L. B. Schlesinger, *Violence: perspectives on murder and aggression*, San Francisco: Jossey-Bass.

Steinmetz, S. K. 1978: The battered husband syndrome. *Victimology*, 2, 499–509.

Straus, M. A., Gelles, R. J. and Steinmetz, S. K. 1981: *Behind Closed Doors: violence in the American family*. New York: Anchor.

Symonds, A. 1979: Violence against women – the myth of masochism. *American Journal of Psychotherapy*, 33, 161–73.

Tavris, C. 1982: *Anger: the misunderstood emotion*. New York: Simon and Schuster.

von Bertalanfly, L. 1968: *General System Theory*. New York: Braziller.

Walker, L. E. 1979: *The Battered Woman*. New York: Harper and Row.

Weitzman, J. and Dreen, K. 1982: Wife beating: a view of the marital dyad. *Social Casework*, 63, 259–65.

Wetzel. L. and Ross, M. A. 1983: Psychological and social ramifications of battering: observations leading to a counseling methodology for victims of domestic violence. *Personnel and Guidance Journal*, 61, 423–28.

Winnicott, D. W. 1975: *Through Paediatrics to Psycho-Analysis*. New York: Basic Books.

Wolfgang, M. E. 1958: *Patterns in Criminal Homicide*, Philadelphia: University of Pennsylvania Press.

Zimbardo, P. 1969: The human choice: individuation, reason and order versus deindividuation, impulse and chaos. In W. Arnold and D. Levine (eds), *Nebraska Symposium on Motivation*, Lincoln, Nebr.: University of Nebraska Press.

15

Sport and Aggression

Jeffrey H. Goldstein

The ways in which a society entertains itself are indicative of that society's values, beliefs and aspirations. Our leisure time is not so much time out from the workaday world as it is a means of teaching, strengthening and reiterating its credo. In this chapter we examine sports and its relationship to violence in Western society. The chapter divides into three parts: a discussion of the extent of sports-related violence; a review of theory and research on the effects of sports violence; and a review of measures to control or eliminate sports violence.

THE EXTENT OF VIOLENCE IN SPORTS

Since the late 1970s riot police have been called to quell disturbances among fans at the Super Bowl, a college all-star football game, New York Jets games, the 1971 World Series win in Pittsburgh, and the 1984 World Series in Detroit, as well as on many other occasions. Officials at football (i.e. American football) and soccer games have been pelted with rocks, beer bottles and metal darts, and, in at least two instances in Latin America, have been killed by indignant fans.

In recent years violence in sports has achieved official recognition as a "social problem". The fear of escalating violence among competitors and sports fans has led to government-sponsored commissions to investigate violence in boxing, ice hockey, football and soccer in the United States, Canada, Britain and West Germany.

It is widely assumed that there is more brutality in sports today than formerly. Yet it is by no means clear that this is so. In the not-too-distant past, violence committed while participating in sport was merely accepted without comment. Today, it is apt to lead to litigation. The violence that was

This chapter is based on a talk delivered at a meeting of the International Society for Research on Aggression, Mexico City, 1982, and a paper published in *National Forum* (Goldstein, 1982).

once seen as an inherent feature of many sports is now viewed within a larger socio-legal context (Mummendey and Mummendey, 1983; Smith, 1983). The development of this change is discussed below. The fact remains, however, that we do not know whether the incidence, prevalence or severity of sports violence has increased, decreased or remained constant (Goldstein, 1983; Guttmann, 1983). It is surprising that in an area that thrives on statistics (often carried out to the third decimal place), no record of sports violence is maintained. What is less debatable than temporal trends is that violence among both competitors and sports fans culminates in scores of deaths and thousands of serious injuries each year – to take just the tally for the United States.

Some investigators of aggression among British soccer "hooligans" have suggested that there is actually very little real violence among sports fans. Instead there is said to be a form of ritual display having status-enhancing and other social functions as its goal (Marsh et al., 1978; Taylor, 1971).

If sports violence has not increased, why does there now seem to be so much of it? There are at least two explanations for the increased public attention to, and awareness of, violence in sports. First, the general public's increased concern over sports-related aggression may stem not from any increase in such aggression, but from a lowered tolerance for violence of any sort. Indeed, the same argument may be made for family violence, once accepted as a routine part of domestic life and now increasingly intolerable. Child and spouse abuse are now widely regarded as problems of genuine social concern, whereas in the not-too-distant past they were considered private, family matters. In each case there appears to be an increase in the severity of the problem because we have only recently come to think of it *as* a problem. Violence at home and in play have gone from background to foreground.

Secondly, sports teams, particularly professional teams in North America, are increasingly viewed as business franchises, accountable to consumers (sports fans) in the same way as are other business organizations. Thus, legal and ethical codes once seen as irrelevant to sports have increasingly been applied to and used against them.

EFFECTS OF WITNESSING SPORTS VIOLENCE

There are reasons to believe that witnessing sports should be a healthy, non-aggressive pastime. That is certainly the popular wisdom. And there is some evidence to support the belief that sports can be, for both participants and observers, emotionally and intellectually satisfying (Goldstein, 1982; Zillman et al., 1979). However, we should also note that there is considerable evidence to suggest that witnessing violence in any form – whether it involves sportsmen and -women, television characters or one's parents – teaches aggression and can stimulate observers to violence. This evidence is reviewed below. It should be noted here, however, that there are both contradictory expectations about the effects of witnessing sports, particularly body-contact or "violent" sports, and contradictory findings in the research on the issue. It is the purpose of the following discussion to examine some of these expectations and the pertinent evidence.

Sports as catharsis

The prevailing view of body-contact sports among the lay public (and among a surprising number of social scientists) is that they serve as healthy outlets for pent-up hostility, frustration and aggression. The observer is thought to release in a vicarious way some unexpressed emotional or behavioral tension. Proctor and Eckard (1976) use the familiar psychoanalytic "hydraulic model" in arguing that spectator sports give the average fan a way to "lower his steam pressure by allowing him to spin his wheels and toot his whistle". Storr (1968) has stated that "rivalry between nations in sports can do nothing but good", presumably because it will siphon off aggression, thereby creating improved international relations. The list of psychologists, biologists and philosophers who have adhered to this cathartic position with respect to witnessing sports violence is impressive, and includes Robert Ardrey (1966), Sigmund Freud (1948) and Konrad Lorenz (1966). Of course, there is no reason why all these individuals cannot be wrong, but it may be noteworthy that many of them arrived at their positions through consideration of very different sorts of evidence.

This cathartic model of human aggressive motivation is both antiquated and untenable: it assumes a hydraulic system with a finite capacity for energy – a metaphor undoubtedly derived from the Industrial Revolution, during which it was formulated. (Today we know that a person is not a steam engine, but a computer.) Nevertheless, the very prevalence and endurance of this model in the public consciousness suggests that many people find it useful as a description of what happens, what they believe happens, or what they hope happens, to themselves and others as a result of witnessing sports.

The overwhelming majority of sports fans, of course, do not become noticeably more violent after watching a soccer, football or hockey game. So the catharsis view may, in fact, accurately describe the subjective experiences of most sports spectators. The very fact that sports fans become highly aroused and excited during such games and do *not* engage in overt aggression seems to suggest that such events may even teach self-control and aggression-management strategies (Goldstein, 1982).

There is not a great deal of evidence to support the contentions of adherents to the catharsis position. A study by Kingsmore (1970) reported a catharsis-like effect at professional wrestling-bouts. Nosanchuk (1981) found that devotees of martial arts who learn the philosophy that accompanies karate become less aggressive as their training increases. Generally, however, the empirical evidence has failed to find significant reductions in aggressiveness among either the spectators of body-contact sports or those who compete in them. Yet it would perhaps be a mistake to dismiss supporters of the catharsis model out of hand. We should note that nearly all the systematic research on the aggressive effects of sports has been conducted in Western countries since the late 1960s. This so limits the evidence as to time and place that general conclusions about the existence of catharsis effects at sports events probably cannot be based upon it.

Even so, in some research, such as studies by Berkowitz and Alioto (1973), Fromkin and others (1977) and Zillmann and his colleagues (1979), there are certain conditions under which the witnessing of violence does *not* lead to an "automatic" increase in aggressiveness among observers. This occurs particularly in situations where observers believe that the competitors harbor no animosity toward one another, and in those in which the observers themselves abhor violence in sport.

Sports and the stimulation of aggression

The empirical evidence on the effects of sports overwhelmingly indicates that witnessing violence on the playing-field increases proneness to aggression among observers. A growing body of literature about sports spectators suggests that they are more aggressive after watching a violent game than beforehand (see, for instance, Arms et al., 1979; Goldstein and Arms, 1971; Keefer et al., 1983; Leuck et al., 1979). Smith (1974) has noted that most fan violence follows soon after an act of aggression has occurred on the playing-field, thus lending support to a social-learning-theory position (Bandura, 1973).

Goldstein and Arms (1971) found that male spectators at a college football game were more hostile after the game than prior to it, even if their favored team won the game. This finding has been replicated at football, soccer, hockey and college wrestling matches in several countries. Despite the methodological weaknesses of the original study, recent systematic replications have invariably reported that fans at body-contact sports are more aggressive following a game then preceding it (in comparison with a control group of fans at non-violent sports events). For example, Arms and his colleagues (1979) replicated the Goldstein and Arms study using three different measures of aggression at two aggressive sports (hockey, wrestling) and one non-aggressive sport (swimming). As in previous research, increases in aggression were noted with all measures at the aggressive sports, but not at the non-aggressive sport. A study by Phillips and Hensley (1984) has even reported that on the third day after a heavyweight prize fight, the number of homicides in the United States rises significantly, by an average of 3.54.

While these studies are generally interpreted as supporting Bandura's social-learning theory, the evidence is open to additional interpretations, most notably deindividuation (Zimbardo, 1969), disinhibition (Goldstein et al., 1975), and the effects of autonomic arousal on aggressive behavior (Russell, 1981; Zillmann et al., 1979).

There are also some benign interpretations of spectator violence. Many instances of group violence at athletic events follow what is perceived to be some unfair or inequitable action on the field of play: a referee makes what is believed to be a bad decision, a player unnecessarily injures an opponent, or a winning horse is disqualified from the race. In such cases, fan violence may be seen as a response to injustice (Mark et al., 1983). On this interpretation, fan violence stems from a sense of fair play and not, as a disinhibition or deindividuation explanation would have it, from any base aggressive instincts that are otherwise held in check. Because sports fans have no or few acceptable channels for expressing their grievances and disapproval, violence becomes a means of communication. Furthermore, the catharsis-like feelings reported by some fans may result from the restoration of justice or equity following the demonstration of their disapproval.

Additional interpretations of fan violence have been proposed, and some may be necessary for a more complete understanding of the phenomenon. For example, why should fan violence occur at traditionally non-aggressive sports, such as baseball or tennis? If there is no violence being witnessed on the field, fans have no aggressive models to imitate. It takes a single act of witnessed or performed aggression, or conditions amenable to violence, for aggression to become disinhibited. If disinhibition is a cause of fan violence, how is the process initiated at non-violent games?

Williams and his colleagues (1984) have proposed an explanation of British soccer hooliganism in terms of a lower-class sub-culture that places a positive value on violence. Lower-class males are denied the traditional (middle-class) sources of identity and status: education and occupation. Because of segregation by age and sex among the British lower class, a status hierarchy emerges, based on drinking, sexual prowess and violence. While there is a tautology in this argument (it is the middle-class that sees and defines soccer hooliganism as a "problem"), the authors are correct in arguing for the role of values in fan violence.

As psychologists have long known, a person's perception of an event, rather than the objective event, is often the more important determinant of its effects. This is certainly true of sports, as demonstrated by Hastorf and Cantril (1954) in their classic study of perceptions of a college football game. It should come as no surprise, then, to learn that the attitudes of spectators determine not only how an event is perceived, but also what effects it has on their behavior (Mann, 1974). If spectators believe that opponents in a game despise one another, they tend to *enjoy* the game more, but also believe that the players' actions themselves are more hostile and competitive than if they believe the opponents are friends (Zillmann et al., 1979). If fans believe that boxers are deliberately trying to injure one another, rather than merely acting professionally and trying to win a bout, they are more aggressive when provoked afterwards (Berkowitz and Alioto, 1973). In this regard, a study by Harrell (1981) is most revealing. Active hockey fans who were tolerant of aggression (measured in response to the question, "In your opinion should fighting be allowed to go unpenalized because it is an important part of the game?" – to which about half the fans replied "Yes") were more hostile after the first and second periods of a professional hockey game than were fans who were intolerant of player aggression.

TOWARD SOLUTIONS

What of the many fans and competitors who argue that if it were not for their sport (whether a body-contact or non-contact sport) they would be more aggressive? Can't sports be used as an aggression-management technique? I think sports *can* be used as vehicles of self-regulation, but they seldom are.

Non-aggressive sports, and perhaps body-contact sports as well, can serve as anger- (and other forms of emotion-) regulating devices, provided that the competitor experiences anger prior to, rather than during, the match and that the match itself is both physically and mentally engrossing. If sports fans are able to identify closely enough with a competitor or team, then the requisite involvement may be present for spectators too.

Because humans are the supremely symbolic creatures they are, a remarkable ability exists to transform an emotion, such as might follow a mild insult, into a great wrong by rewriting history or reinterpreting the recent past. For example, a husband who feels slighted by his wife may reinterpret events of the past, which had hitherto not been interpreted as rejections, as subtle but intentional attempts to undermine his self-esteem. A slight anger may thus be transformed into a great one and it is this greater anger that is apt to be acted upon. If a person is sufficiently distracted from this task of revising history, the slight anger remains minor and, in fact, the arousal accompanying it may be reinterpreted or will dissipate with the passage of time. Sports that require fine motor skills and co-ordination are apt to be sufficiently involving to inhibit the intrusion of external events. By being distracting, sports may prevent a negative emotion from becoming more intense. They may also become associated, through classical conditioning, with the reduction of the negative emotion. This is true not only of sports but of nearly any physical activity requiring skill and concentration, from chess to computer games.

In view of the evidence cited that competitors' or spectators' attitudes toward competition and toward match violence are crucial determinants of subsequent aggression, reduction of fan violence will probably necessitate a change in the public's attitudes toward violence in sports. If, as noted at the beginning of this chapter, there is not necessarily more violence among sports fans than there used to be but greater concern with such violence, perhaps there is already a change under way in the public's view of sports violence. But given the spirit in which most modern sports are entered and witnessed, it is not surprising that competitors and fans become increasingly violent as a match or a playing-season progresses. Sports are often presented on television in a way that glorifies and rewards violent play. Cameras focus on the offender, rather than on his victim; announcers interpret violence as a sign of motivation and rarely denounce foul play. Indeed, they are more apt to fault an official for invoking a penalty than the offender for committing a foul.

If our analysis is correct, there is a variety of ways in which the undesirable effects of body-contact sports may be eliminated. The various recommendations made here and elsewhere (see, for instance, Goldstein, 1983; Yeager, 1979) fall into two categories. *Intrinsic measures* call for a change in emphasis and attitude as a way of reducing violence by fans and competitors. Competitors, managers, trainers, owners and fans must become less tolerant of match violence. It must not be tolerated by officials or management, who must make it clear that unnecessary violence detracts from the game. The recent heavy fines levelled against basketball-players Julius Erving of the Philadelphia 76ers and Larry Byrd of the Boston Celtics for fighting is a notable example. Sports broadcasters and reporters should begin to emphasize the important roles played by co-operation and aesthetics, and the pro-social aspects of sports (Goldstein and Bredemeier, 1977). If the pro-social aspects of sports were stressed to a greater extent than at present, one would expect an increase in positive social behavior among spectators. (See Berg, 1978, for the only study of helping-behavior in sports.)

Extrinsic measures tend to be more immediate. They emphasize control rather than reform. They include increased penalties against competitors and fans for violent behavior; stricter enforcement of anti-violence regulations; a reduction or elimination of the sale of alcoholic beverages at sporting-events (see Dewar, 1979); and post-game events to prevent fans from leaving *en masse,* which creates the conditions for exit panics (Mann, 1979).

None of this implies that sports *must* have a particular effect on the competitors' or fans' levels of aggression. It is probable that body-contact sports increase aggressiveness because of the spirit in which the games are played, viewed and promoted. When co-operative, non-aggressive elements of sports are made more salient, fans will be less apt to become aggressive themselves.

REFERENCES

Ardrey, R. 1966: *The Territorial Imperative*. New York: Atheneum.

Arms, R. L., Russell, G. W. and Sandilands, M. L. 1979: Effects on the hostility of spectators of viewing aggressive sports. *Social Psychology Quarterly*, 45, 275–79.

Bandura, A. 1973: *Aggression: a social learning analysis*. Englewood Cliffs, NJ: Prentice-Hall.

Berg, B. 1978: Helping behavior on the gridiron: it helps if you're winning. *Psychological Reports*, 42, 531–4.

Berkowitz, L. and Alioto, J. T. 1973: The meaning of an observed event as a determinant of its aggressive consequences. *Journal of Personality and Social Psychology*, 28, 206–17.

Dewar, C. K. 1979: Spectator fights at professional baseball games. *Review of Sport and Leisure*, 4, 12–25.

Freud, S. 1948: *Beyond the Pleasure Principle*. London: Hogarth.

Goldstein, J. H. 1982: Sports violence. *National Forum*, 62, 9–11.

—— (ed.) 1983: *Sports Violence*. New York: Springer.

Goldstein, J. H. and Arms, R. L. 1971: Effects of observing athletic contests on hostility. *Sociometry*, 34, 83–90.

Goldstein, J. H. and Bredemeier, B. J. 1977: Sport and socialization: some basic issues. *Journal of Communication*, 27, 154–9.

Goldstein, J. H., Davis, R. W. and Herman, D. 1975: Escalation of aggression: Experimental studies. *Journal of Personality and Social Psychology*, 31, 162–70.

Guttmann, A. 1983: Roman sports violence. In J. H. Goldstein (ed.), *Sports Violence*, New York: Springer.

Harrell, W. A. 1981: Verbal aggressiveness in spectators at professional hockey games: the effects of tolerance of violence and amount of exposure to hockey. *Human Relations*, 34, 643–55.

Hastorf, A. H. and Cantril, H. 1954: They saw a game: a case study. *Journal of Abnormal and Social Psychology*, 49, 129–34.

Keefer, R., Goldstein, J. H. and Kasiarz, D. 1983: Olympic Games participation and warfare. In J. H. Goldstein (ed.), *Sports Violence*, New York: Springer.

Kingsmore, J. M. 1970: The effect of a professional wrestling and a professional basketball contest upon the aggressive tendencies of spectators. In G. S. Kenyon (ed.), *Contemporary Psychology of Sport*, Chicago: Athletic Institute.

Leuck, M. R., Krahenbuhl, G. S. and Odenkirk, J. E. 1979: Assessment of spectator aggression at intercollegiate basketball contests. *Review of Sport and Leisure*, 4, 40–52.

Lorenz, K. 1966: *On Aggression*. New York: Harcourt Brace Jovanovich.

Mann, L. 1974: On being a sore loser: how fans react to their team's failure. *Australian Journal of Psychology*, 26, 37–47.

—— 1979: Sports crowds viewed from the perspective of collective behavior, In J. H. Goldstein (ed.), *Sports, Games and Play*, Hillsdale, NJ: Lawrence Erlbaum Associates.

Mark, M. M., Bryant, F. B. and Lehman, D. R. 1983: Perceived injustice and sports violence. In J. H. Goldstein (ed.), *Sports Violence*, New York: Springer.

Marsh, P., Rosser, E. and Harré, R. 1978: *The Rules of Disorder*. London: Routledge and Kegan Paul.

Mummendey, A. and H. D. 1983: Aggressive behavior of soccer players as social interaction. In J. H. Goldstein (ed.), *Sports Violence*, New York: Springer.

Nosanchuk, T. A. 1981: The way of the warrior: the effects of traditional martial arts training on aggressiveness. *Human Relations*, 34, 435–44.

Phillips, D. P. and Hensley, J. E. 1984: When violence is rewarded or punished: the impact of mass media stories on homicide. *Journal of Communication*, 34, 101–16.

Proctor, R. C. and Eckard, W. M. 1976: "Toot-toot" or spectator sports: psychological and therapeutic implications. *American Journal of Sports Medicine*, 4, 78–83.

Russell, G. W. 1981: Spectator moods at an aggressive sports event. *Journal of Sport Psychology*, 3, 217–27.

Smith, M. D. 1974: Significant others' influence on the assaultive behavior of young hockey players. *International Review of Sport Sociology*, 3–4, 217–27.

—— 1983: What is sports violence? A sociolegal perspective. In J. H. Goldstein (ed.), *Sports Violence*, New York: Springer.

Storr, A. 1968: *Human Aggression*. New York: Atheneum.

Taylor, I. R. 1971: Soccer consciousness and soccer hooliganism. In S. Cohen (ed.), *Images of Deviance*, Harmondsworth: Penguin.

Williams, J., Dunning, E. and Murphy, P. 1984: *Hooligans Abroad*. London: Routledge and Kegan Paul.

Yeager, R. C. 1979: *Seasons of Shame*. New York: McGraw-Hill.

Zillmann, D., Bryant, J. and Sapolsky, B. S. 1979: The enjoyment of watching sport contests. In J. H. Goldstein (ed.), *Sports, Games, and Play*. Hillsdale, NJ: Lawrence Erlbaum Associates.

Zimbardo, P. G. 1969: The human choice: individuation, reason and order versus deindividuation, impulse and chaos. In W. Arnold and D. Levine (eds), *Nebraska Symposium on Motivation*, Lincoln, Nebr.: University of Nebraska Press.

Contributors

William Baccaglini is Assistant Director for the Comprehensive Planning/Program Development Unit with the New York State Division for Youth and a doctoral candidate in Sociology at the State University of New York at Albany. His current research focuses on the impact of the media on fear of crime in and across American cities. He is also studying the relationship between attitudes and behavior utilizing a general network analysis approach.

Leonard Berkowitz is the Vilas Research Professor in Psychology at the University of Wisconsin, Madison. He has researched and published extensively in the area of experimental analysis of aggressive behavior, focusing particularly upon variables relevant to a learning theory perspective. He is editor of *Advances in Experimental Social Psychology*.

Anne Campbell is an Assistant Professor at Rutgers University. Her research interests within the area of aggression include sex and social class differences, situational factors, the consistency of individual differences and the sequential structure of aggressive episodes. She has also completed a two year participant observation study of female involvement in New York street gangs reported in her book, *The Girls in the Gang* (1984).

Ann Teresa Cordilia has done extensive research on the relationship between alcohol and crime and on the prison experiences of alcoholic inmates. She is the author of *The Making of an Inmate: prison as a way of life* (1983). She received her doctorate from the University of Chicago and teaches Sociology at the University of Massachusetts, Boston.

Richard B. Felson is Associate Professor of Sociology at the State University of New York at Albany. He received his Ph.D. from Indiana University. Most of his work is published in Social Psychology journals and is concerned with either the self-concept or interpersonal aggression. He has written, for example, about aggression between siblings, homicide and assault, and the role of impression management and social control in aggressive interactions.

Joseph P. Forgas gained his D.Phil. from Oxford University and is now at the University of New South Wales, Australia. His research interests center on collective social representations and he has pioneered the use of multi-dimensional scaling as a means of mapping cognitions about social interactions from romantic involvements to bar-room brawls. He recently edited *Social Cognition: perspectives on everyday understandings.*

James J. Fyfe is an Associate Professor at the American University, School of Justice, Washington, DC, and a senior fellow of the Police Foundation. He was a New York City police officer for sixteen years, and left that agency as a lieutenant. Fyfe holds a Ph.D. from the School of Criminal Justice, State University of New York at Albany, and has written and lectured extensively on police matters. He currently directs a police–citizen violence reduction experiment in Dade County, Florida.

John J. Gibbs obtained his Ph.D. from the State University of New York at Albany. He is currently Associate Dean for Research and Associate Professor at the School of Criminal Justice, Rutgers University. His primary research interest is in the area of jail stress.

George Gmelch is Associate Professor of Anthropology at Union College in Schenectady, New York. He did his under-graduate degree at Stanford and his Ph.D. at the University of California, Santa Barbara and has undertaken considerable ethnographic field research in Ireland, England, Alaska and Barbados. He has written and edited four books and numerous articles concerning Ireland, particularly Irish travellers, urban Anthropology, and return migration.

Jeffrey H. Goldstein is Professor of Psychology at Temple University, Philadelphia. His research is on aggression, particularly violence in the family and in sports; the psychology of humor, and on the social construction of science. His books include *Aggression and Crimes of Violence*, *Sports Violence*, *Handbook of Humor Research* (with P. E. McGhee), and *Reporting Science: the case of aggression.*

Robert Johnson holds a Ph.D. in Criminal Justice from the State University of New York at Albany. His books include *Culture and Crisis in Confinement* (1976), *Condemned to Die: life under sentence of death* (1981), *The Pains of Imprisonment* (1982; edited with Hans Toch), and *Hard Time: understanding and reforming the prison* (forthcoming). Johnson is currently Professor of Justice at the American University in Washington, DC.

Peter Marsh obtained his D.Phil. from Oxford University, where he was also Co-Director of the Contemporary Violence Research Unit. He has published a number of books and articles on various aspects of aggression and is best known for his work on football supporters' behavior. He is co-editor (with

Anne Campbell) of *Aggression and Violence*. His latest book, written with Peter Collett, is *Driving Passion: the psychology of the car*.

Renée Paton obtained her Ph.D. from the City University of New York in 1972. She worked as a clinical psychologist in the United States, England and Israel specializing in childhood and adolescent problems. Since 1977 she has been a Senior Lecturer at Oxford Polytechnic teaching Social and Abnormal Psychology.

Lawrence Pervin has received his doctorate from Harvard University and has been a Professor of Psychology at Rutgers University since 1971. He is the author of two personality texts, *Personality: theory and research* (4th edn) and *Current Controversies and Issues in Personality* (2nd edn), and serves as a member of the editorial board of *Psychological Review*, the *Journal of Personality and Social Psychology*, and the *European Journal of Personality*. He has been an active contributor to the personality and person–situation controversy literature, most recently in the form of a review article for the *Annual Review of Psychology* (1985). His 1965 *Psychological Bulletin* article on individual–environment interaction has been noted as a Citation Classic.

Robert J. Powers is a Psychologist at the Veterans Administration Medical Center, East Orange, New Jersey, and a Clinical Assistant Professor of Psychiatry at the New Jersey Medical School, Newark, New Jersey. He received his Ph.D. at the University of Maryland and is the author of a number of essays and articles on family aggression, anxiety and stress, and substance abuse.

Hans Toch obtained his Ph.D. in Psychology at Princeton University. He is Distinguished Professor at the State University of New York, Albany, where he is associated with the School of Criminal Justice.

Index